Foreign Language: Lessons from the Past, Innovations for the Future

Celebrating Fifty Years of Foreign Language Teaching in Uganda

Edith R. Natukunda Togboa & Enoch D. Sebuyungo
(Main Authors)

Copyright © 2016 Nsemia Inc. Publishers
All rights reserved.

This publication may not be reproduced, in whole or in part, by any means including photocopying or any information storage or retrieval system, without the specific and prior written permission of the publisher.

This book is sold subject to the condition that it shall not, by way of trade or otherwise, be re-sold, hired out, or otherwise circulated without the author's or publisher's prior consent in any form of binding or cover other than that in which it is published and without a similar condition including this condition being imposed on the subsequent purchaser.

First Edition: August 2016
Published by Nsemia Inc. Publishers (www.nsemia.com)

Main Authors: Edith R. Natukunda-Togboa and
Enoch D. Sebuyungo
Cover Concept Illustration: Kemunto Matunda
Cover Design: Danielle Pitt
Layout Design: Cyrus Kioko
Production Consultant: Matunda Nyanchama

Note for Librarians:
A cataloguing record for this book is available from
Library and Archives Canada.

ISBN: 978-1-926906-48-5 Paperback

TABLE OF CONTENTS

List Of Figures - vii

List Of Tables - ix

Foreword - xiii

Preface - xv

About the Co-Authors - xvii

PART ONE
CONTENT IN A FOREIGN LANGUAGE CLASS

Chapter One 3

How Teaching Foreign Students Can Lead to Questioning one's Cultural Identity: The Case of Teaching Gender in French - Edith Natukunda-Togboa and Joel Bertrand

CHAPTER TWO 19

A Lexical and Morphological Analysis Of Students' Written Work in Higher Institutions Of Learning: The Case Of French Beginners at Makerere - Enoch D. Sebuyungo

Chapter Three 43

Factors Determining the Value of a Text In Foreign Language Teaching - Harriet K. Namukwaya

Chapter Four 61

Integrating Internet-Based Materials in Foreign Language Teaching at the Tertiary Level: The Case of Arabic Language Teaching at Makerere University in Uganda - Ebraheem Ssali

PART TWO
FOREIGN LANGUAGES: PEDAGOGY

Chapter Five 77

Literacy Constraints on Fluency in Foreign Languages at University Level in Uganda - Titus Ogavu

Chapter Six 89
French Language Education in Uganda: Understanding the Causes of Limited Numbers of Learners Choosing to Study Advanced French at Kyambogo University - Victoria Bakurumpagi

Chapter Seven 111
Analyzing Pedagogical Valences of Inter-cultural Communication in the Teaching of French as a Foreign Language: The Case of Secondary Schools in Kenya - Crispus Mwakundia

PART THREE
TRANSLATION AND INTERPRETATION

Chapter Eight 131
Nomenclature and Authenticity of Translated Plays from English to Lusoga - Cornelius Wambi Gulere

Chapter Nine 149
Animal Farm across Cultures: Challenges of Translating Aspects of Culture - Isaac Ssettuba

Chapter Ten 163
Translation and Conflict: A Comparative Analysis of Conflict Discourse in the Translation of George Orwell's Animal Farm - Margaret Nanfuka Mbalule

Chapter Eleven 179
Analyzing Inter-cultural Communication through Translation: A Case Study of the Arabic Language - Idris Mohamed Osman

Chapter Twelve 197
Translation and Interpretation of Foreign Languages - An Endangered Profession: The Case of French - Edith Kalanzi

PART FOUR
THE FUNCTIONALITY OF FOREIGN LANGUAGES

Chapter Thirteen   211

The Acquisition of Inter-cultural Competencies amongst University Students: A Case Study of Makerere University - Samuel Wandera

Chapter Fourteen   229

Thai Young Adults' Interest in the German Language and Culture - Yap Lian Chee Sandra

Chapter Fifteen   249

The French Flair In Ugandan Branding: A Successful "Affaire" Or Failed Affair? - Edith Natukunda-Togboa

Chapter Sixteen   263

Analyzing the Relevance of the Curriculum of Language for Specific Purposes: A Case Study of French for Tourism in Makerere University - Sarah Nanyanzi Kawungezi

Chapter Seventeen   277

Foreign Languages and International Business with a Special Focus on French in Uganda - Julius Singoma Kagamba

Index - 291

LIST OF FIGURES

Figure 2.9.1: Corpus analysis	**25**
Figure 2.12.1: Orthographical anglicisms having a French equivalent with a very similar spelling	**30**
Figure 2.12.2: Oral similarity of the equivalents in English and French causing spelling errors	**30**
Figure 2.12.3: Orthographic anglicism: words with an equivalent in French that has a different spelling	**31**
Figure 2.14.1: Gaps due to 'false friends'	**36**
Table 2.18.1: Summary of Study Findings	**40**
Figure 5.2.1: A View of the Reading Situation	**81**
Figure 7.2.1: The Classical teaching example	**114**
Figure 7.2.2: Simulated Communication Situations	**115**
Figure 7.12.1: Cultural aspects in Parlons Français	**122**
Figure 7.12.2: Cultural aspects in Entre Copains	**123**
Figure 8.2.1: Nomenclature in the play: Omugole	**135**
Figure 8.3.1: Nomenclature in the play: Nantameigwa	**137**
Figure 8.6.1: Summary of Nomenclature in Kyabazinga Mukama	**141**
Figure 10.5.1: Comparing the notion of conflict	**169**
Figure 10.5.2: Reaction to pigs "taking care" of the milk	**170**
Figure 10.5.3: Layers of Conflict in Animal Farm	**173**
Figure 10.5.4: Text of disgruntlement	**174**
Figure 10.5.5: Translation of disgruntlement	**174**
Figure 12.4.1: Example of Machine Translation	**203**
Figure 13.2.1: Distance between Learner & Target Language Cultures	**213**
Figure 13.3.1: Stages of Inter-cultural Learning	**217**
Figure 13.3.2: Deardorff's Pyramid Model of Inter-cultural Competence	**218**

Figure 13.5.1 : Inventory of Teaching approaches used for French Beginners **224**

Figure 14.6.1 Govt. Public Relations Dept. 20/02/2012 **232**

Figure 14.6.2 News Paper; 24/06/1897 **233**

Figure 14.8.1 German Music in Bangkok **236**

Figure 14.8.2 German Open Air Cinema **236**

Figure 15.7.1: Summary of Brand Names and Commentary **255**

LIST OF TABLES

Table 2.1.1: Lexical and Morphological Gaps	20
Table 2.18.1: Summary of Study Findings	40
Table 6.2.1: Number of French students the graduating class since August 2008	92 92
Table 6.16.1: Causes of the low numbers of French learners at Kyambogo University	102
Table 6.16.2: Suggestions made by the students on strategies to reverse the trend	103
Table 6.16.3: Reasons given by lecturers and executive members of APFO for the low numbers of learners of French	104
Table 13.4.1: Inter-cultural Content in the Grammar Text books	220
Table 13.4.2: Inter-cultural Content in the Civilization Text books	221
Table 13.4.3: Inter-cultural Content in the Literature books	222
Table 14.7.1: Image of Germany among German language learners in Thailand	234
Table 14.10.1: Demographic Profile of participants	238
Table 14.13.1: Number of Languages Spoken	239
Table 14.13.2: Foreign Languages Spoken	239
Table 14.14.1: Languages of Interest	240
Table 14.15.1: General Idea of Germany	240
Table 14.16.1: Initial Source of Germany Related Information	242
Table 14.17.1: Visual Recognition of German words	243
Table 14.18.1: Pronunciation of German words	244

Foreword

This publication is celebrating 50 years of Foreign Language Teaching in Uganda, and it is important to mention that, it is through the implementation of several respects that we got to get to 50 years and still going on. The first respect is a more than 20-years-old link between Makerere and Poitiers. The starting point was a 1993 visit to the Department of French at Makerere by Prof. Hélène Chuquet for an MA Seminar on Linguistics and Translation. A durable relationship was then established, and in 2007 came a request from Poitier to supervise a PhD in Linguistics, which the author of these lines was more than glad to accept. Thanks to the support of both the Ugandan and French institutions involved and to the determination of Dr. Enoch Sebuyungo, the above mentioned PhD project was successfully completed

Today, collective work coordinated by Dr. Edith R. Natukunda-Togboa, Head of the Department of European and Oriental Languages at Makerere University, has led to the completion of this comprehensive Jubilee Book Project, sup-ported by a wide range of international organizations.

It is well-known that teaching duties and administrative responsibilities leave little time to pursue academic research, but it is important not to lose sight of the latter. One of the merits of this volume is that it associates theoretically oriented articles and bibliographies and more applied studies reporting empirical experience. The fields covered are first and foremost foreign language teaching (grammar, typology of errors, texts and the Internet as material), translation problems (from literary to machine translation), language across cultures, and their use in in economic life.

Throughout the four parts of the volume, French takes pride of place, a reflection of a long-standing tradition in Uganda, even though English comes first and continues to gain ground. Two articles specifically examine the attitude towards French in Uganda and in neighbouring Kenya. Other languages considered in the various contributions include Luganda, Lusoga, Arabic, German, and occasionally a few others.

It is to be hoped that the tradition of teaching and speaking French will continue in Uganda, and the only realistic response to the de facto predominance of English worldwide is the deliberate promotion of multilingualism, an inbuilt heritage in both Europe and Africa. In an age dominated by confrontation, may the defense of linguistic diversity help to put cultural differences into a distinct perspective.

Michel Paillard,
Former Professor of English Linguistics,
University of Poitiers, France.

Preface

Makerere University has been teaching foreign languages since 1963. French was taught first, as part of the History Honours Degree. Someone must have made an association between the history of the French Revolution, Universal Human Rights and language use. The next language to be taught was German and later Arabic, Russian, Chinese and Spanish were introduced. In August 2014 (20th -22nd) the Department of European and Oriental Languages, under the School of Languages, Literature and Communication organized the first Foreign Languages Conference at Makerere University which attracted many esteemed scholars wishing to present papers relating to foreign languages. These papers have come to constitute the content of the Jubilee Book Project published under the title; ***Foreign Languages: Lessons from the Past and Innovations for the Future.***

I take this opportunity to thank our key stakeholders who supported us during the organization of the conference, which led to the processing of this book. Due to space constraints, I will not be able to name persons individually but the organizations and departments which assisted us include : The Centre for Language and Communication Services, Britannia Allied Industries Ltd, Alliance Française de Kampala, Goethe Zentrum Kampala, The School of Languages, Literature and Communication, The Management of Makerere University, The French Embassy in Uganda, The Royal Saudi Arabian Embassy in Uganda, and The Ministry of Foreign Affairs of the Government of Uganda.

This book is divided into four parts. It has been specifically fractioned categorically to delve into the topics that challenge both teachers and students as we teach and learn foreign languages. It also deals with issues surrounding the application of these languages as we try to be more persuasive and effective communicators.

The first part elaborates the main aspects involved when teaching grammar, syntax and morphology. It brings out issues of identity and linguistic concerns; such as cultural questions that arise from the teaching of gender in French and lessons from the analysis of student errors in the same language. In two other articles, textual and internet-sourced materials are assessed in order to compliment them with the different methods of teaching used in class and also serve effectively for all different levels of proficiency.

The second part discusses the use of iconic examples. It explains the intricacies of nomenclature and authenticity in translation, from foreign to local languages, semiotic equivalence across cultures, the threats to the art and profession posed by machine translation. The important aspect of harnessing the power of language is to craft compelling and engaging discourse-wise translations and examining skills in Inter-cultural communication.

The key debate on literacy and its facilitation of learning foreign languages opens the third part of the book, which focuses on foreign language pedagogy. This part also traces the history of foreign language education in Uganda and its current institutional challenges and the pedagogical values of Inter-cultural communication. Indeed, the authors discuss the difficulties encountered in the teaching environment of foreign languages based on empirical data and propose effective strategies to cause pedagogical change. This may sound like a repeated message, but as the target audience reads this publication, they may question the way they teach these foreign languages for the first time.

The last part takes us through the functionality of foreign languages; making a link between language learning, acquisition of Inter-cultural competences and language choice among young learners getting influenced by cultural competition. This part also demonstrates the role played by foreign languages in local branding, the relevance of a curriculum for specific purposes and the importance of such languages in international business.

For most readers, I believe, the most important lesson in this book is to see how the different authors transform the abstract character of foreign language teaching into the concrete experience of daily communication.

Consequently, we pay more attention to the way teaching messages are framed and the environment that helps us to remember them better. Lastly, throughout all the articles, the advice on how to spot innovations for the future seems just as important as understanding how to, translate, teach and communicate in foreign languages better. *Foreign Languages: Lessons from the Past and Innovations for the future* is extremely instructive and impact-oriented due to the fact that it has been written by language practitioners who are citing examples from what they preach and teach.

Edith R. Natukunda –Togboa (Ph.D.),
Principal Author, Senior Lecturer,
Head of Dept. of European & Oriental Languages,
Makerere University.

About the Authors

As part of the celebration of the fifty years of teaching foreign languages, the Department of European and Oriental Languages at Makerere University, in the School of Languages Literature and Communication, under the College of Humanities and Social Sciences, organized an international conference where all the contributors to this book participated. Therefore, it is from the bigger number of papers, which were presented as papers at the Foreign Languages Conference from 20th to 22nd on August, 2014 that a few were selected, reviewed and reconstructed into chapters of this book, which we familiarly refer to as the Jubilee Book Project.

It is in honour of the collective effort that I have the pleasure to present the list of the seventeen co-authors according to the order of their chapters:

1. **Natukunda-Togboa Edith R. and Bertrand Joel**: How Teaching Foreign Students can lead to questioning one's Cultural Identity: The Case of teaching Gender in French
2. **Sebuyungo Enoch D.**: A Lexical and Morphological Analysis of Students' Written Work in Higher Institutions of Learning: The case of French Beginners at Makerere University.
3. **Namukwaya Harriet K.**: Factors Determining the Value of a Text in Foreign Language Teaching.
4. **Ssali Ebraheem:** Integrating Internet-based Materials in Foreign Language Teaching at the Tertiary Level: The case of Arabic Language teaching at Makerere University in Uganda.
5. **Ogavu Titus**: Literacy Constraints on Fluency in Foreign Languages at University Level in Uganda.
6. **Bakurumpagi Victoria:** French Language Education in Uganda: Understanding the causes of limited numbers of learners choosing to study Advanced French at Kyambogo University.
7. **Mwakundia Crispus:** Analyzing Pedagogical Valences of Inter-cultural Communication in the Teaching of French as a Foreign Language: The case of secondary schools in Kenya.
8. **Gulere Wambi Cornelius:** Nomenclature and Authenticity of Translated Plays from English to Lusoga.

9. **Ssettuba Isaac:** *Animal Farm* across Cultures: Challenges of Translating Aspects of Culture.

10. **Nanfuka Mbalule Margaret:** Translation and Conflict: A Comparative Analysis of Conflict Discourse in the translation of George Orwell's *Animal Farm*.

11. **Osman Mohamed Idris:** Analyzing Inter-cultural Communication through Translation: A Case study of the Arabic Language.

12. **Kalanzi Edith:** Translation and Interpretation of Foreign Languages: An Endangered Profession? The case of French

13. **Wandera Samuel:** The Acquisition of Inter-cultural Competences Amongst University Students: A case Study of Makerere University.

14. **Yap Lian Chee Sandra:** Thai Young Adults' Interest in the German Language and Culture.

15. **Natukunda-Togboa Edith:** The French Flair in Uganda Branding: A successful "affaire" or failed affair?

16. **Nanyanzi Kawungezi Sarah:** Analyzing the Relevance of the Curriculum of Language for Specific Purposes: A Case Study of French for Tourism in Makerere University.

17. **Singoma Kagamba Julius:** Foreign Languages and International Business with a Special Focus on French in Uganda.

PART ONE

CONTENT IN A FOREIGN LANGUAGE CLASS

CHAPTER ONE
HOW TEACHING FOREIGN STUDENTS CAN LEAD TO QUESTIONING ONE'S CULTURAL IDENTITY: THE CASE OF TEACHING GENDER IN FRENCH

Edith Natukunda-Togboa and Joel Bertrand[1]

Abstract

Teaching French to foreign students can be a pleasurable but at the same time, an intriguing task. It is pleasurable because as a native speaker of the language you are interested in sharing your knowledge with a captive audience of eager learners of the language. If teaching French to such an audience was not for the grandiose purposes found in French textbooks, that target unsuspecting audiences abroad, then, at least in my case, I would be looking forward to having interlocutors to chat with in French. That may be the reason as to why I never saw these questions of "why feminine? Why masculine?" When I was invited to participate in the conference celebrating the fiftieth anniversary of teaching Foreign Languages at Makerere University, after the many years of teaching French, its social study and literature, a lot of memories came to my mind, including the 8 academic years I spent teaching French as a foreign language to students, who were quite often, beginners. Then I remembered a problem that I met regularly and which puzzled me quite often and to which this article tries to find an answer; how can I explain the teaching of gender in French in the context of French as a foreign language? This article retraces the classic notions of teaching gender and the challenges they pose in a French language class for foreign students. Subsequently, it proposes alter-native strategies for dealing with the issue within a wider context of societal shifts, and language change.

Key words: *French as a foreign language, native speaker, foreign students, gender, masculine, feminine, epicene nouns.*

---

[1] Joel Bertrand, who hails from Aíx en Provence, Southern France, is a retired public servant of the French Government who has worked in several posts abroad in several capacities including those of lecturer and cultural attaché in Uganda. He now works as an independent development consultant. This chapter was adapted by Dr. Edith Natukunda-Togboa basing on his presentation at the Jubilee Conference organized by Makerere University in August 2014. Dr. Edith Natukunda-Togboa is a senior lecturer and Head of Department of European and Oriental Languages, Makerere University.

Foreign Languages: Lessons

1.1 Introduction: Why is this word "masculine" or "feminine"?

When you are teaching French to Beginners who are evidently non-native speakers of the language, there are a few challenges that you encounter as teacher of French as a foreign language, which are peculiar to this level of learners. These are real beginners of the language as much as you the teacher may be a real beginner in teaching French to foreign students. If luck has it and you have some experience in teaching the language outside the Francophone space, you could bring in the basic vocabulary, and ask your students to start repeating after you:

Le bureau, *la* table, *le* stylo, *la* salle, *le* livre, *la* porte, *la* chaise

Most likely the lesson is being conducted with the help of those pictures or better still images, projected on the wall of your class with the listeners fully attentive to "Monsieur le Professeur" preaching the gospel from France.

Usually, or always, on the second or third repetition of nouns with their article, a student will ask in a shaky voice showing that s/he is lost:

WHY?? Why **LE** here, and **LA** there??

Then, in a very masterly tone, you come to the front of the class, right in the middle of the line of projection and you tell them slowly that:

*We use **LE** when nouns are masculine and **LA** when nouns are feminine.*

But it does not solve the problem at all; because the students are more perturbed. Immediately comes another question:

WHY? What is masculine about STYLO; the phallic shape? Then what about LIVRE? What is feminine about TABLE, the long legs? Is there anything in between? What about BUREAU? Why is it not like CLASSE?

At first, full of calculated patience, I would attempt explanations to get to the end of the lesson peacefully. Unfortunately, most times these do not work. I try to skirt the problem telling a story here and there to calm the situation. Then as a last resort I have to show authority. After all, who is the teacher here? Finally, with a stern voice, eyes wide open I say:

It is like that, repeat the grammatical rule, and learn it, use it, full stop.

However, when all is said and done, when the books are folded and put away and you have withdrawn to the security of your office or the staff room, it still makes you think. You ask yourself questions you never considered before:

"These guys were right. My final answer was a cowardly defense."

This is because for a native French speaker, gender is so obvious. A book is masculine, a chair is feminine. You are taught that from Primary 1 or even before at home by your mother. When you were a toddler, uttering your first words, you were corrected:

"*No, we say "une table", not "un table".*

And you did, and the lesson sunk in, at that tender age. You integrated your rule on gender into your early acquisition of the language.

But for foreign students, like the Ugandan class, for whom French was the third or fourth language, gender could be a discouraging mystery. They want to understand, they have an idea about the masculine and feminine in real life. Especially since they are young adults, they have just gone through the socialization stages of learning their femininity and masculinity. Therefore they will try to make the connection, and failing to get a physical connection or the social construction equivalence that they have about gender in their societal structure, they will feel frustrated.

I know this from my experience in class because I was confronted by many of my students while discussing with them outside the classroom environment.[2] Some confided in me that this is the issue that makes many students hate learning French and often drop it. So, having regained my senses after my pedagogical failure, I would ask myself, what should be done?

1.2 The Gender Of Nouns In The French Language

Let's go back to some basics of French. In the French language, all nouns have a **grammatical gender**, that is, they are masculine or feminine for the purposes of grammar only. This has no direct link with the physical gender as we know it in our daily life or the social construction of gender that we get socialized into in our respective societies. The grammatical gender in French is actually linked to an elaborate noun class system of the language. Anglophone linguists like Robin Keller (2013: 2) have rightly commented that:

> "Grammatical gender is a feature of the French language that is especially foreign to native English speakers. For English native speakers, the distinction of these basic parts in a foreign language is not a natural skill. Whereas in English gender is semantic and not grammatically marked, gender in French is a formal component of its grammar.

---

2 The French class in Uganda, at Makerere University took place in the 1970s; those politically landmarked years of President Field Marshal Idi Amin Dada VC, MC, Conqueror of the British Empire.

The problem lies with the fact that only 10.5% of nouns in French have semantically based gender (Ayoun: 119). For the English native speaker, which only rules gender semantically, the French grammatical gender system is seemingly completely arbitrary".

If we can smile and forgive the lack of good will in some linguists' comments, we can calmly go on to observe that in French, luckily, there are just **2 genders, called "Masculine" and "Feminine".** We don't have the **NEUTER** or "smaller" genders[3] as do other languages (which are much more complex!). In France, one has to choose distinctively on which side the noun is located: there is no clumsy middle way.

The gender of the noun is very important, because it affects the determinants (article, demonstrative, possessive, plural etc.); as well as pronouns and adjectives, which unlike in English, agree with the noun. Gender can also affect the verb sometimes when it is used with an auxiliary.

> **Le** stylo est vert. **Il** est posé sur la table. The pen is green. It is placed on the table.
> **La** règle est vert**e**. **Elle** est posé**e** sur la table. The ruler is green. It is placed on the table.

The "Masculine" and "Feminine" in French refer (at least metaphorically) to a reality in nature: the sexual differentiation among individuals of the same species. But a bright student can pin you down:

> What about nouns referring to abstracts with no gender connotation – no sexual differentiation? Are there any rules?
> Is there any way to understand or explain the distribution into gender?

With this bright student, I would advise the teacher to take a stand of modesty: *"Let's consider some examples".*

1.3 Gender rules for Names of animals

There is a "masculine" and "feminine" version for each animal, although sometimes, the noun changes for the male and female. It applies to a few familiar animals: pets, farm animals, and game. Obviously, this differentiation goes back far into the past, to the Middle Ages, and referred to the daily life of that time. A lot of these noun class/gender distinctions go back to before the historical record began. This was probably a distinction

---

3 Some Bantu Languages have up to 16 noun classes, Thsibula; a Bantu language of the Congo has a noun class that means that the noun in question is small. (http://whatthefrench.com/)

between animate (usually this is a class including humans and other animals capable of movement) and inanimate nouns (plants and other things) (http://what-thefrench.com/). It is said that even English used to have grammatical gender, but it was given up sometime between the 12th and 15th century. Anyhow, in French, for the part, which is non-arbitrary, like the distinction of some animals there is a pattern associated with gender:

    Un chien, une chienne (dog M-F)
    Un chat, une chatte (cat M-F)
    Un taureau ou un bœuf, une vache (cow M-F)
    Un cheval, une jument (horse M-F)
    Un coq, une poule, (hen M-F)
    Un lapin, une lapine (rabbit M-F)
    Un cerf, une biche (deer M-F)
    Un sanglier, une laie (boar M-F)
    Un loup, une louve (Fox M-F)
    Un lion, une lionne (lion M-F)

Some language teachers have explained that what probably began as a logically motivated distinction underwent changes that removed the original meaning of the gender distinction. By this view, **grammatical gender, in French and related languages, is essentially like** human vestigial parts **such as the appendix: it used to serve a purpose, but no longer does;** the organism (language) keeps it but the body no longer uses it (http://what-thefrench.com/).

However, for all other species, more than 98%, there is only one word, either masculine or feminine – randomly -, and you have to add "male" or "female" to stress the difference:

    Un pigeon, **une** souris, **une** girafe, **un** aigle, **un** hippopotame, **une** antilope

LE perroquet,	le marabout	**LA** cigogne	la pintade
LE pigeon,	le paon	**LA** colombe,	la grue couronnée
LE capitaine,	le tilapia	**LA** carpe	la morue
LE ver de terre,	le batracien	**LA** limace,	la grenouille
LE scorpion,	le hanneton	**LA** fourmi	la cigale,

1.4 Gender rules for Names of countries

One notes that even countries are either Masculine or Feminine according to their classification.

LE Canada	**LA** France	**LE** Kenya	**LA** Tanzanie
LE Maroc	**LA** Tunisie	**LE** Pakistan	**LA** Birmanie
LE Honduras	**LA** Guyane	**LE** Soudan	**LA** Guinée

Interestingly, depending on which version you choose to use, the same country can be both feminine and masculine: For instance you can refer to the United Kingdom as:

LA Grande Bretagne or **LE** Royaume Uni

Apparently, there is a pattern in the differentiation. When the name of the country (in French) ends with –e, the country is feminine, if not; it is masculine (with the exception at least of Mexico LE Mexique *These exceptions, you sternly tell the students that they have to learn them to pass their exams (sic!)*

On an interesting cultural note, is Uganda more masculine than France? Is there any connotated sign of virility or senility? The pun is intended! There are indeed a few more interesting or funny cases. The same reality can have 2 names, which are nouns of a different gender. I will just mention 2 cases of such homonym. These are the two we can refer to:

Un cartable, *une* serviette (school bag).

Un tube, *une* durite (hose)

At this point you look at the bright student who pinned you down with that difficult question and you task him to: *"Find some other similar examples and bring them up for sharing in the next lesson!"*

Our classroom dynamics are notwithstanding, more of the gender controversies can be found in the military field. Most nouns, as expected in the military institution, which has been for a long time male dominated[4], are masculine:

Un capitaine, *un* sergent, *un* officier, *un* soldat, *un* artilleur, *un* sapeur,

Nonetheless, in the same masculine-prone army, you also find:

Une sentinelle (sentry), *une* estafette (courier), *une* ordonnance (orderly, batman)

---

4 Although women have been involved in the French army since the 1800s, they have been serving as support staff near the front, their recruitment increased in the 1930s in the Health section of the army during the World War and more recently, in 1972 their status evolved to sharing the same ranks as those of men with equal pay.

One wonders, why is there this peculiar reverse of genders? Though not heroic, those positions have never been a preserve for women or gays or trans-gender persons in the army.

1.5 Gender Classification Of Sexual Organs In French

Since gender deals with biological differences in the languages class, we have to deal with their gender in French. Probably to humour us, our ancestors generated so many names for them in French. Interestingly enough, the nouns for the male organs can be either masculine or feminine:

Un v..., *une* b..., *un* b..., *la* v..., *le* z..., *la* p..., etc.[5]

The same ambivalence applies to the female organs:

Un v..., *une* c..., *une* m..., *la* p..., *le* c..., le *m*..., *la* p..., etc.[6]

Where you would have expected an alignment with biological distinction, in the grammatical gender, you find none. There is nothing like any explanation to be given, nothing like a guide line to help the learner. Whereas we may thank God that knowing whether a word is masculine or feminine will not hinder communication in most circumstances, these subtle distinctions are indispensable to becoming fluent in French as the second language.

1.6 The Reality Of The Language
1.6.1 Noun Classes in the French Language

In a typically dramatic Cartesian move, let us abandon our beliefs, criticize them, and look at the language itself, without any prejudice or reference to the traditional categories. In French, there are **2 classes of nouns**. The only characteristic, which actually differentiates them is that each class uses a different set of words, or paradigm (determinants -articles, interrogative or possessive clauses as well as pronouns -personal, possessive, etc.) They "agree" with the preceding according to the appropriate gender.

---

5 It is our request that for decency's sake, the reader fills in the male organs as s/he reads. The non-French speaking reader is invited to check the translation of the English version in any advanced French –English dictionary, which will provide the set of variants.

---

6 It is our request that for decency's sake, the reader fills in the sexual organs as s/he reads. The non-French speaking reader is invited to check the translation of the English version in any advanced French –English dictionary which will provide the set of variants.

One class will use *le, un, mon, ce, il, celui-ci,* or « agree » as *beau, vert, écrit,* etc.

The other will use *la, une, ma, cette, elle, celle-ci,* or « agree » as *belle, verte, écrite,* etc.

The other way around, the issue to note is that a noun belongs to this or that class according to whether it fits with *le, un, mon, etc.* paradigm, or *la, une, ma, etc.* paradigm.

Note should be taken that I use the term of **noun classes** like the term which is used to describe Bantu languages, where there are **more**.[7] In Kiswahili for instance, you can find the **m-/wa- class** (mtu, watu – mzee, wazee), the **ki-/vi class** (kitabu/vitabu), the **ji-/ma-** class (jicho/macho), and several other classes, where each influences agreements:

Mzee **w**angu **m**zuri	**Wa**zee **w**angu **wa**zuri	(my elder(s) is/are fine)
Kitabu **ch**angu **ki**zuri	**Vi**tabu **vy**angu **vi**zuri	(my book(s) is/are nice)
Jicho **l**angu uzuri	Macho yangu mazuri	(my eye(s) is/are good)

In spite of the fact that we have a prefix in Kiswahili and a detached determinant in French, the systems are quite similar. Thus, analyzing the category of **noun classes to** describe the French language also looks relevant. In French, gender will also impose the "agreement" with the adjectives or the verbal participles.

1.7 Which nouns belong to which class?

If we go back to the initiation of gender in the French language, can we say that its distribution is or was done 100% randomly? The honest answer is: no

It so happens that most nouns with a male gender connotation belong to one class (a.k.a "masculine"), together with so many other nouns without any gender connotation at all. Nouns with a female gender connotation belong to the other class (a.k.a "feminine").It applies in about 99% of cases, but not always, as we mentioned earlier.

In both noun classes, those with a gender connotation are a small minority. Yet, the whole class of nouns is usually traditionally named, in French grammar, after that small portion of nouns. In fact, it is a kind of metonymy, which is not acknowledged. Ideologically, it is taken for granted.

---

7   In Luganda (a Bantu language of Central Uganda), there are twenty one.

1.8 Naming the noun classes

Does the classification of noun classes, as critiqued above, imply that we abandon the use of the words "masculine" and "feminine" since they are confusing and inadequate in describing the reality they refer to? What do we replace them with? Let us discard them as A and B, or 1 and 2, etc. as they imply a hierarchy, an order, a superiority of one over the other. In one of my blog entries previously[8] I proposed to name one noun class with hash (#) and the other a star (*).

Why did I propose something so radical? First of all those signs, though not in the alphabet, are now found in each and every handset keyboard. They would thus be so accessible for the foreign language learners who constantly swear by Google. Secondly, they would not be associated with any hierarchy between the two noun classes. Thirdly, in French, when we say **UN dièse** (#) and **UNE étoile** (*), each of these two nouns can easily symbolize the class they belong to.

Anyway, this is just a proposal, with a little pinch of salt to break down language barriers. We would then be able to talk about noun classes by symbols and NO LONGER about "masculine" and "feminine". This could make things easier when teaching foreigners. Especially, when it corresponds to a reality students are used to in their own vernacular languages; they will not get confused if you refer them to what they know. They will no longer ask the "WHY?" question: They just have to know, which class a noun belongs to and that's all.

But in France, proposing to drop the Masculine and Feminine from Grammar cannot even be suggested. Those are sacred components of the language. I don't know who would dare utter such a change, as this idea is merely a linguistic abomination.

1.9 Why such a resistance?

For centuries these categories (Masculine/Feminine) have been and are still imposed on French speakers. As native speakers, we suckle them from the mother's breast. They are self-imposed. Since we are not conscious of the conditioning, they become a form of alienation. We take it as a matter of fact. A kind of accepted servitude, as La Boetie (1997) would say: whether "nouns are either masculine or feminine is as obvious as the sun is bright and the night is dark." At school, we learn that rule: "*le masculine l'emporte sur le feminin*" the masculine prevails over the feminine, and indeed, in French, you have:

---

8   http://ettasoeurellebatlebeurredotcom.wordpress.com

Paul est beau. Jeanne est belle.

Jeanne, Sophie, Marie, Dorothée, Agnès, ... (+ 50 girls), sont **belles)**.

Jeanne, Sophie, **Paul**, Marie, Dorothée, Agnès... (+ 50 girls), sont **beaux)**.

However numerous the feminine nouns may be, the agreement will be with he masculine, even if there is only one noun of this gender in the list. That is what the language says about the reality of life. The feminine may be many, but the societal rule has decided that the masculine will prevail.

Those categories (M/F) imply and spread certain ideas about gender differences and their respective roles not so much in the language, as in the society. On the other hand, if we accept my suggestion of using some symbol, saying # prevails over * would be meaningless. But the *"masculine prevails over the feminine"* tells a lot about the prevailing ideology of the source society of that language.

Language indeed does not exist in a vacuum; it is the language of a society. It is informed by the values and uses of that society: its social, ideological, religious and economic values. It embodies the "unconscious mind" of the society. As a native speaker, when one takes some distance and reflects, one thinks through the values one is unconsciously imposed upon by the language.

A language is a "vision of the world". So what one sees in the case of gender in French is evidently the "world" or the "truth" that is projected through the particular lenses of the French. As the French philosopher Louis Althusser (1972), puts it: "Ce que je pense n'est que l'effet de ce que j'impense."(What I think is the effect of what is unthought of). Therefore, teaching a language is also teaching those values enshrined in the language itself.

Teaching a language to native speakers is a way of socializing them into the society, by transmitting those values. It is part of community or citizen building, a type of inner bonding. In contrast however, I have come to learn that teaching a foreign language is a way of helping the learner to discover a different world, or a world seen from a different perspective. To discover some values, which are not hers or his – and that she or he is invited to share, or at least feel and be sensitive to, if she or he wants to be fluent in that language.

The point I am making here is that a class of grammar, as much as that of literature or philosophy, participates as well in transmitting identity values. Many people may think that grammar is just ideologically neutral, but this is not true, as the evidence submitted above demonstrates.

From this perspective of teaching French to foreign students, I observe that grammar is not a scientific discourse about a language. It does not objectively describe an object called a language, as an entomologist would describe an insect. Grammar enunciates a way the language should be looked at – not necessarily as it is. It is an interpretation of the language. It is the way a society looks at its own language, as it ex-presses its explicit or implicit values. Teaching gender in the French is taking an ideological stance. As you try to convey that aspect of grammar, you are taking up a mirror displaying, not the image of a language, but the image that a society has of itself. You are, in today's language, taking a kind of "selfie".

Inevitably then, the teaching of gender contributes to strengthening this image, to transmitting values and representations. For the native speakers, it is meant to reinforce the strengthening of social cohesion and the transmission of some classical knowledge. It serves as a kind of inner bondage.

However, such aspects of teaching a foreign language can give the teacher the opportunity to break the illusion, to take a self-distancing view. The teacher of a foreign language does not have to be locked in the ideological circle. He can have a look at the language from the outside. He does not have to adhere to the image the native speakers have of the language he teaches. I would even add that in order to be objective to his class, he must not.

Sigmund Freud, in his psychoanalytic work, showed that an outsider is necessary to allow one to dilute one's fantasies in order to cope positively with the reality. This is the meaning of constructive psychoanalysis. The same idea can be applied to the teacher of a foreign language. If he has a critical eye, if s/he remains an outsider, looking from the outside, s/he will be in a position to point to the discrepancies between a language and the idea the native speakers have of their own language. S/He can use this to help the latter out of some illusions and help the foreign learners to make some sense of seemingly arbitrary aspects like gender in French.

When you teach a foreign language, from the standpoint of a Ugandan teacher, you are certainly conscious of the fact that the language does not belong to you. You have to teach it as it is; as the fluent speakers speak it. However, when teaching your students, you don't have to submissively adopt the image the native speakers have of their own language. It may be deceitful and may cause confusion to the learners, especially, the Beginners. Allow yourself to have original approaches. You should dare to use the similarities you have noted with the languages that your students speak without hesitation; if it helps them. Be critical with the grammar and methods coming from the native speakers, they are meant for their own use in their own context and therefore need to be adapted to suit other contexts.

1.10 Gender and the changes in French

Life is characterized by change and movement. Societies change a lot, more and more and especially these days, in so many areas. Among other major changes we have seen in France and the Western world at large over the last 50 years is the gender equality issue. One has to qualify though that the gender debate has advanced more quickly at the social level, rather than the linguistic one in France. The French language is conservative, although it is indeed affected by the changes; it changes more slowly than the society. Given this scenario, one wonders: how has the French language adjusted to the progress of gender equality? Does this have an impact on how we teach gender in French?

Like any other language, French changes according to what the native speakers do with it. Some new words appear while others are no longer used at all. All sorts of influences play their part. The French language has also prescribers, those with some authority to propose changes. Stephane Mallarmé (http://www.philagora.net/mallarme/) assigned this task to the poets: "*Donner un sens plus pur aux mots de la tribu*" (give a clearer meaning to the tribe's words). In addition, France is probably the only country in the world where the language is political and ruled by the law. The language agency, *l'Academie Française* and the National Assembly debate language changes as national issues.

Within this context, how are the societal evolutions (gender equality) being translated into language change, and how does that impact the teaching of gender in French grammar? Let us take an example to demonstrate our argument.

The names of jobs and positions in French are duly classified by grammatical gender. Women have now had gradual access to most jobs, which have always been a preserve of men. Most of them have "masculine names", without any feminine equivalent, which is very much resented by women in these positions. This is the case of:

> Un ingénieur, un professeur, un soudeur, un charpentier, un bijoutier, un pasteur, un maçon, un auteur, un écrivain

At the same time there are many cases, in French, where names of jobs have a feminine equivalent:

Un infirmier	Une infirmière	Un danseur	Une danseuse
Un instituteur	Une institutrice	Un marchand	Une marchande
Un postier	Une postière	Un paysan	Une paysanne
Une sage-femme (midwife) does not have a masculine form.			

Note must be taken though of the fact that in many cases, the corresponding feminine form does not refer to a woman in charge; but rather to « the wife of »:

| Le boulanger | la boulangère | Le général | la générale |
| L'ambassadeur | l'ambassadrice | Le maire | la mairesse |

Some have got a very different meaning that is always derogatory:

| **Un entraîneur** Trainer | **une entraîneuse** (one who leads you on) | **Un professionnel** A professional | **une professionnelle** |
| **Un rapporteur** A reporter | **une rapporteuse** One who reports on others | **Un maître** A master | **une maîtresse** A mistress or Concubine |

There have been attempts to adapt to the use of a feminine agreement. *Madame le Maire, Madame le Ministre.* According to some feminist activists, that was not enough. Another approach, which I think leads to grammatical nonsense, was attempted by adding a final –e to the masculine term. Probably this stems from the teaching we had in Primary school that you can turn an adjective into the feminine version by adding a final–e. In the case of gendering nouns this is a big simplification, as the reality is much more complex. But it produces a fantasy somewhere at the back of some minds: that the final "e" is feminine. Today therefore, there is a trend (somehow officiated) to add a final –e to nouns of professions or positions when one refers to a woman:

Une écrivaine, une auteure, une procureure, une professeure

The trend seems however to work only with prestigious jobs. For the low calibre jobs like: "une fraiseure, une facteure, une soudeure",[9] there are no feminized equivalents to be seen. As a consequence, many writers and journalists use these forms, to sound women lib friendly, or gender correct.

Personally, it hurts my ears just like a false note in a sweet and familiar piece of music and hurts my feelings for French as a language teacher. The addition of this final –e is pure nonsensical fetishism as it is not in tandem with language change but is rather being affixed superficially. Considering the history and uses governing the life of the French language, the final –e is very common with masculine nouns, while many feminine nouns do not have it. The rules to turn masculine adjectives and nouns into feminine are much more complex than a simple addition of –e (-eur / -euse, -teur / -trice, etc.).

---

9   Respectively translated into English as : milling machine operator, post man and blacksmith

instituteur	institutrice	directeur	directrice
Coiffeur	coiffeuse	chanteur	Chanteuse
Romancier	Romancière	poète	Poétesse

In fact, *un prieur / une prieure* **(prior),** which is not a very modern or exciting example, is the only existing case in French of a final –eur becoming –eure when the position is occupied by a woman.

The trend I presented above then reveals some unconscious ideas about what is pertaining in the society. The final –e then becomes an emblem, or a kind of flag telling the world that this position has been conquered. It is ostentatious but it does not help in integrating the ordinary speaker's perception of gender changes. On the other hand though, this trend shows us that grammar is also a ground where fantasies can grow and flourish. This view may be perceived as short-sighted and perhaps does not help much in the fight for gender equality, but it reflects a genuine and documented perspective of a language teacher who for a long time has kept his ear to the ground. Anyway, the debate is still raging on. We need to keep researching on the next developments.

1.11 An alternative method: Using epicene nouns

Some nouns and names are both masculine and feminine – or the masculine noun and the feminine noun are exactly similar: *un enfant, une enfant* whether boy or girl. Some first or Christian names are used for both boys and girls: *Claude, Dominique, Camille.*

This form of classifying nouns has a name in grammar: they are referred to as "epicene nouns", which the English dictionary defines as: "denoting a noun that may refer to a male or a female, such as teacher as opposed to businessman or shepherd".

In the mass media, it is getting to be used more and more frequently: *la ministre, la deputé.* The noun, originally masculine, is treated as feminine (using the determinants, agreements, etc. that correspond to feminine nouns) when it refers to a woman. In the Language class on gender, one can then have:

Ce grand écrivain est un excellent romancier.

Cette grand**e** écrivain est **une** excellent**e** roman**cière**.

This approach breaks a very strong French grammar rule: it introduces an agreement according to the meaning, to the referent, and no longer according to the grammatical gender or the signifier. So, how about considering all nouns as epicene, and use them as masculine or feminine according to the person they refer to? It would certainly go a much longer way into abolishing gender inequality than the cosmetic or mythical final –e. It is also an approach that is rooted in actual language reality since it borrows from existing practice in French: the personal pronouns of 1st and 2nd person (*je, tu* and also *nous, vous*) are epicene. They are either masculine or feminine according to who speaks or is spoken to. So, this approach to teaching gender within the context of social change, as they say in Latin, *nihilnovi sub sole*, is not something that is extraordinary.

1.12 Conclusion

When you are teaching French to Beginners who are evidently non-native speakers of the language, there are a few challenges that you encounter as teacher of French teaching a foreign language, which are peculiar to this level of learners. To foreign students for whom French is the third or fourth language, gender could be a discouraging mystery. They have an idea about the masculine and feminine in real life and they want to understand this concept. After the initial skirmishes of trying to avoid the questions, the genuine teacher of French as a foreign language has to go back to the basics of grammar and explain the historical origins of the grammatical gender, the linguistic presentation of both the feminine and masculine noun classes and their respective rules, which govern their use and agreements. However, in this article I also observe that Language indeed does not exist in a vacuum, so gender carries with it values of the French society and is informed by the values and language users of that society. When teaching gender to foreign learners therefore, we can:

- Avoid submissively adopting the image the native speakers have of their own language and allow ourselves to have original approaches; using the similarities you have noted with the languages that your students speak.
- Be critical with the grammar and methods coming from the native speakers, which are meant for their own use in their own context and therefore need to be adapted to suit other contexts.
- Propose alternative approaches to teaching gender, which take into consideration the history and uses governing the life of the French language - like the approach of treating them as epicene nouns.
- Encourage students to read about recent research on gender in French because social changes continue and the debate is still raging on.

References

Althusser Louis (Ed.), (1972) : «L'impensé de J.-J. Rousseau», in *Cahiers pour l'Analyse*, N°. 8 Éditions du Seuil s/d Paris.

Keller Robin F. (2013): "La Barbe: Feminine Beards and Other Mysteries of French Grammatical Gender", Senior Honours Projects, University of Rhode Island.

http://whatthefrench.com/ask-a-linguist-why-does-french-have-grammatical-gender Accessed 10/01/2015

"What the French? Why does French have a grammatical Gender" Accessed 11/01/2015.

La Boetie, Etienne de (1997) : *Discours de la Servitude Volontaire*, (first published in 1574) – Edition Mille et Une Nuits, Paris.

Mallarmé Stéphane : "L'art Poétique", in *Le Tombeau d'Edgar Poe*

http://ettasoeurellebatlebeurredotcom.wordpress.com Accessed 11/01/2015.

http://whatthefrench.com Accessed 10/01/2015

http://www.philagora.net/mallarme/mallart1.php. Accessed 11/01/2015

CHAPTER TWO
A LEXICAL AND MORPHOLOGICAL ANALYSIS OF STUDENTS' WRITTEN WORK IN HIGHER INSTITUTIONS OF LEARNING: THE CASE OF FRENCH BEGINNERS AT MAKERERE UNIVERSITY

Enoch D. Sebuyungo[1]

Abstract

French is one of the foreign languages that are taught in some Ugandan secondary and tertiary institutions. The importance of teaching French to Ugandans is that, it gives them an added advantage as far as communicating regionally with Francophone neighbouring countries and also at international fora. This study examines the teaching and learning of French at Makerere University with a focus on French for Beginners Programme. Graduates who have studied French need to use it effectively in their work places. Adequate oral and written communication is therefore of paramount importance. Are these graduates able to use written language effectively? How can they be aided to improve their proficiency? Such are the questions that underpin this study. The methodology involved a corpus analysis of 33 students' written work. These were final year French Beginner students. Anchored in the Error Analysis Inter-language theoretical framework, the investigation focused on lexical and morphological gaps amongst the learners to determine the possible causes and propose strategies to improve French language mastery. These gaps were examined according to interlingual and intra-lingual factors. These were further sub-divided into 4 categories: first language interference (mother tongue), second language interference (English), intra-lingual interference (French) and multiple interferences (a combination of some or all of the 4 categories). The interplay of these factors on foreign language learning is crucial and this investigation points out how these should be taken into account in the teaching-learning process, to improve foreign language mastery in a Ugandan context.

Key words: *French language learning, lexical and morphological gaps, error analysis, interlingual, intra-lingual.*

---

1   **Dr. Enoch Sebuyungo** is a Lecturer, Department of European & Oriental Languages, Makerere University. He obtained a Ph.D. in Linguistics from the Université de Poitiers (France) in 2010. He teaches French and Linguistics at the Makerere University School of Languages. His research interests include Foreign Language Pedagogy and Translation Studies. In these, he explores the interaction between indigenous languages and international languages like English & French.

2.1 Introduction

Learning a foreign language is often beset with challenges and they include pronunciation, prosody and grammar to mention but a few. A number of studies on this subject emphasize that language learning and acquisition are influenced by factors like; individual teacher differences, teaching methods, learning exercises and activities, learning materials (textbooks, audio-visuals etc.), learning strategies, learner attitude, motivation, intelligence, perseverance, personality, age, socio-linguistics context, learner socialization as well as mother tongue interference. One such study by Narayanan et al. (2008) identifies other factors like anxiety and gender as being responsible for individual differences in learning a second language.

Other studies have demonstrated the correlation between first language learning by a child and second language learning by an adult. This begs the question of the factors that come into play when it comes to third language learning by an adult. Certainly, in such a scenario, errors are bound to occur; these are part of the natural language learning process of a child. As J. Dubois (1994: 12) states "during language acquisition, the child makes several attempts to generalize, to transfer, his learning by trial and error demonstrates ability to make hypotheses, to anticipate, to risk and to reject." According to Richards (1974), the study of errors is important because it provides data on the nature and importance of learning obstacles faced by learners in their discovery of the target language grammar. Such studies also throw more light on how learners construct their own linguistic system, which neither belongs to their mother tongue nor to the target language. This involves making a number of generalizations from a limited number of data acquired from the target language.

As a lecturer of French, I have always been intrigued by the lexical and morphological gaps in students' written work. These appear to stem largely from translations from English. While trying to express themselves in French, many learners tend to transfer English structures and lexical items. For instance, they write sentences like:

Table 2.1.1: Lexical and Morphological Gaps

Student's sentence	Corrected Version	Translation
C'est moi qui va au bureau	C'est moi qui vais au bureau	I am the one who is going to the office
J'avais un bon jour	J'ai passé une bonne journée	I had a nice day

Je finirai par juin	Je finirai d'ici le mois de juin	I will have finished by the end of the month
Il n'achète pas rien	Il n'achète rien	He is buying nothing
Elle est pharmaciste	Elle est pharmacienne	She is a pharmacist

Source: *Study Findings 2002*

The analysis of these errors could take several dimensions but this paper will limit itself to discussing the morphological and lexical aspects. Morphological errors relate to the internal word structure whereas lexical errors are linked to vocabulary. These errors are infact gaps or deviations from the norm. According to Dubois (1994:163), a norm is 'general usage of language that is common to all speakers'. A gap is 'any speech act which appears to transgress one of these usage rules; the gap is hence a decision of the speaker'.This means that the speaker has the capacity to correctly use language rules but can choose to manipulate the language in his or her way for stylistic reasons. Therefore, learners' errors in the example indicated, like lack of grammatical agreement according to gender and number or poor conjugation of verbs are simply gaps which project a lacuna that needs to be closed up. A child who is learning his/her mother tongue fills these gaps while speaking vernacular and participating in the life of the community that uses this language. It is in this context that we prefer to use the term 'morphological and lexical gaps' and not 'errors'.[2] These gaps demonstrate a creative and constructive process in the mind of the learner.

The main objectives of this article therefore are to identify the written errors, classify them and propose educational strategies that can be adapted to the difficulties encountered by the foreign language learners. As Corder (1973:263) points out, the objective of research on such linguistic gaps should be to construct syllabi and appropriate didactic materials. Indeed, an analysis of language errors and learning strategies will help to improve effective language teaching and learning for Ugandan students of French. This view is corroborated by Ladefoged (1971:3) when he cites The International Conference on Second Language Problems, a semi-official Anglo-Franco-American group which meets annually to review developments in the teaching of languages of wider communication: "the basic linguistic information necessary for mounting a truly effective programme of English or French instruction is simply not available in most

---

2   Even though from time to time we will use the term 'errors' this will not be with a negative perception but rather from the perspective of learning strategies.

African countries". It is thus interesting to examine this problem from the perspective of learning a foreign language (French) in a multilingual African country whose official language is English, after more than 20 years of teaching the French Beginners programme in Makerere University.

2.2 The French Beginners programme at Makerere University

This programme was borne from the fact that a number of students at Makerere did not get the opportunity to study French in secondary school and yet are interested in learning the language. The Beginners' programme (FRB) was hence established in 1989 to enable such interested learners pursue courses in French and German alongside other subjects in the B.A. Arts and B.A. Social Sciences programmes. The FRB programme registers about 40 students per year. The courses cover 8 hours per week or 120 hours per semester which totals to 240 hours per year. The content revolves around grammar and cultural studies.

In the first year, students are introduced to the basic notions of French grammar, French Civilization and the Francophone world. A variety of teaching materials are used like *Bienvenue en France Tome 1, Reflets 1* (textbook and audio visuals), *Panorama 1* (textbook). At the end of the first year, the learners are supposed to be capable of describing and narrating events in the present, near future and past tense. In the second year, students broaden their grammatical knowledge and communication skills and acquire new cultural knowledge regarding France and the Francophone world. Teaching materials include *Bienvenue en France Tome 2, Reflets 1et 2, Panorama 1et 2 –* (textbooks and audio-visuals) in addition to case studies from the francophone world done with the aid of various authentic documents written in simplified French. At the end of this year, a learner is thus deemed capable of listening, reading and commenting on authentic texts using simple French. The third and final year comprises 2 broad categories: grammatical knowledge applied through communication activities, which put emphasis on language use in professional situations like writing official letters, curriculum vitae, filling in administrative forms and introduction to the translation of texts from French to English; and exposure to extracts from French and Francophone literature. Through these texts in simplified French, learners are able to reflect on aspects of Civilization, make analyses and comparisons as well as give brief presentations on various given themes. Some of the texts include: *Maigret tend un piège* (Simenon 1973), *Joal* (Senghor), *Les Blancsseulement* (Oyono) and *Recommencer à zero* (Mariama Ba). Linguistic competencies are thus taught in a progressive manner form the first to the third year.

2.3 Background to the Study

This study was based on 4 research questions: Are morphological and lexical gaps due to mother tongue interference? Can morphological and lexical gaps be attributed to translations from English? Can morphological and lexical gaps be attributed to some grammatical inconsistencies within French itself? Are morphological and lexical gaps caused by a combination of factors: English translations, French grammar irregularities etc?

2.4 Mother tongue interference

This factor is premised on the basis that the first languages serve as springboards for learning other languages. A case in point is that of a 3rd year French beginner (FRB) respondent who asked his lecturer at the beginning of a class: *"Excusez-moi Monsieur, est-ceque nous sommes tombés?" (Excuse me sir, did we fall?'* The lecturer did not understand what he meant. Seeing the lecturer's confusion, the student clarified his question by saying: *"Est-ce que nous sommes tombés le test?" ('Did we fall the test?')*. There was laughter in the classroom. One bright student corrected his colleague by reformulating the question: *"Est-ce que nous avons échoué le test?" ('Did we fail the test?')*[3] The erroneous expression *'tomber le test'* was a direct translation from Luganda, the student's mother tongue (*"Twagudde ebigezo?"*). This lends credence to the hypothesis that learners transfer expressions from their mother tongue, while trying to express themselves not only in a second language but also in a foreign language.

2.5 Influence of English

Errors in French by Ugandan learners are largely attributed to the transfer of English lexicon and expressions. This is corroborated by Chen (1996:4):

> "English plays a big role in the school life of our learners. Since they learned it when they were very young, it conditions their intellectual mechanisms of perspective analysis. When they meet a particular fact in French, they are unable to assimilate it immediately. They try to understand but when they fail, they resort to English rather than their mother tongue. Automatically, the verbal habits acquired in English work against the efforts made and their understanding of the French verbal chain; more so, if they are good in English."

---

3   The correct expression in French is actually Est- nous avons échoué au test?

Our corpus has numerous examples, which illustrate that learners formulate sentences whose structure is identical to that in English: *"Mon père est soixante quatre ans.* (d 8 1 iii)" My father is sixty four years (old). Learners tend to think that French and English are almost identical probably due to their geographical proximity, their historical role (colonial languages) and their cultural status (international languages representing modern culture).

2.6 The influence of French

Some errors may be attributed to the French linguistic system as explained by Doneux; they are faced with a series of operations taking place within the context of the language being learned, (Jean-Léonce Doneux, 1991:68). In other words, the system of the language being learned appears to be regular and many rules seem predictable for verb conjugation or word formation. However, owing to the occasional arbitrary grammatical patterns, some seemingly correct constructions are erroneous. Generally, every language system has its limits and no language possesses totally consistent grammatical rules.

2.7 Methodological Issues

Data was collected through the use of compositions written by the learners. According to (Corder, 1973:269) the best way of analyzing learner errors is through their written work, where they are expressing themselves spontaneously. 13 written assignments on various topics were given to the learners over a six-month period. These compositions were written during the learners' free time and returned to the teacher for correction. The scripts were returned to the learners after correction and photocopies kept by the researcher for analysis.

2.8 Corpus Selection and Description

The 3rd year FRB students were selected to provide the corpus on the basis of 3 criteria:

1. Their knowledge to manipulate elements of the French language. They are at the stage of learning where it is assumed that they have already acquired sufficient vocabulary.
2. Their number is much more significant than the 'advanced' group (those that studied French at 'O' and 'A' Level). In this respect, they are likely to provide a much larger range of morphological and
3. Lexical gaps and therefore a more adequate basis for research in this area.
4. This is a group whose numbers are on the increase especially as young people endeavour to study courses at the university that enable them to compete on the job market and get employment in international bodies.

The selected third year French Beginner students were asked to write 13 different assignments over a period of 6 months. This written work can be categorized into 3 groups: narrative, imaginative, argumentative and descriptive compositions based on the literary study of Georges Simenon's *Maigret tend unpiège*. The second category comprised of general compositions expressing opinions on certain issues or recounting personal experiences. The third category included official letter writing. 5 compositions were done at home while 8 were written during tests and examinations (without the use of a dictionary). The written corpus was produced by 33 Ugandans speaking different indigenous languages: Luganda (17 respondents), Lusoga (1), Lugbara (1), Runyoro (5), Lugisu (2), Ateso (1), Runyankore (1), Kinyarwanda (1), Rutooro (2), Acholi (1) and Lukonjo (1).

2.9 Corpus Analysis

Morphological and lexical gaps were identified and classified according to the four research questions:

Figure 2.9.1: Corpus analysis

Mother-tongue interference.	This consisted of identifying gaps attributed to translations from local Ugandan languages.
Influence of the target language (French).	The identified gaps are due to regularities or irregularities of the French language systems.
Influence of English.	These gaps stem from direct translations, word for word from English. They borrow and transpose English sentence structures.
Influence due to a combination of factors.	These gaps can be traced to several causes. Sometimes it is a combination of the above or even a learning problem.

According to (Corder, 1973:263), some learner errors are caused by the teaching methods, materials or programmes especially when they are not adapted to the learners' needs. The gaps or errors were coded using 4 criteria: the student or learner, the composition (assignment) given, the error number and the error type.

A case in point is that of a learner who, in a composition entitled "*Mes vacances de Noël*" ('My Christmas Holidays'), wrote the following sentence: "*j'étais très content de voir venir le nouveau millennium.*" (I was very happy to see the new millennium). The word '*millennium*' was used instead of '*millénaire*'. Such a gap is categorized in the following manner: **A 3 6 IV**.

A: The arbitrary letter given to each learner in the study. Since the alphabet letters are only 26 and there were 33 subjects of the study, the capital letters **A - Z** and the small letters **a – e** were used to code all the learners.

3: This refers to the third topic or assignment (composition) given. Each of the 6 compositions is identified by a number.

6: This refers to the 6th error made by the learner in his/her written assignment. Each error is underlined and numbered for easy identification.

IV: This is the error type and in this case it is attributed to a combination of factors. That is to say, this gap is due to the influence of English (borrowing) but also due to the irregularity of the French word formation rules. In French, the two words exist but '*millennium*' in French does not carry the sense of 'millennium' in English. In French, this term restricts itself to the religious notion of 'the one thousand years reign'.

2.10 Mother Tongue Interference

According to the data collected, mother tongue interference accounts for 3.4% of the morphological and lexical gaps in the learners' written work. Furthermore, this error type was committed by 6 out of 33 learners or 18%. In the first instance, some verbs were translated directly from the mother tongue (Luganda in this case). For example: *"voir le football"* (O 9 5i) ('see football') instead of *"regarder le match de football."* ('Watch the football match'). This is the only case of a direct verb translation from Luganda.

Secondly, there were preposition errors due to mother tongue interference, notably involving the prepositions '*en*' and '*sur*'. They included sentences like "*J'ai décidé d'aller <u>en</u> hôpital*" (O 9 7 i) instead of "*d'aller <u>à</u> l'hôpital*". All these cases indicate direct transfer of preposition use from the mother tongue to French:

    e.   *Mbaddeemirundimingikumbaga.*
    f.   J'ai été   fois plusieurs sur (des)fêtes.
    g.   (I have been) (times several) (on) (weddings).

Thirdly, we noted that some adjectives are transposed directly into French from the learners' mother tongue. For example, in the sentence «*Je suis bon, je ne suis pas malade.*» (O 9 8 i), the adjective '*bon*' is a direct translation from Luganda meaning 'in good health'.

    a.   *Ndi bulungi sirimulwadde*
    b.   (I am) (in a good state) (I am not) (sick).

By writing "*je suis bon*", the learner makes an approximation in French of the original meaning in Luganda. Overall, the study shows that mother tongue interference is insignificant as a cause of written work errors of Ugandan learners. This is corroborated by other studies like that of Storch and Aldosari (2010) where it was found that Saudi Arabian learners of English as a Foreign Language make reference to their mother tongue (Arabic) to a limited extent in their compositions.

2.11 The Influence of French

This error category accounts for 9.2% of learner errors and 57.6 % of the subjects of the study (19 out of 33).These errors can be subdivided into 3 categories: word invention, confusing pronunciation with spelling and grammatical rules. In terms of word invention, in order to form new words out of existing ones, French employs 3 processes (Chevalier 1964:49): <u>derivation</u> (suffixation and prefixation) for example *feuille-feuillage, honneur-déshonneur,* <u>compounding</u> (union of independent elements) for example, *station-service, avant-coureur* and <u>the formation of technical words</u> (particularly from Greek origin) for example *pithécanthrope*. Learners create new words by drawing from other French examples. They try to manipulate French grammatical rules to form new lexical units. For instance, words like *"villageurs", "filme"* (O 9 3 ii, d 9 3 ii). The verb *'diriger'* is nominalized to create *"dirigement"*(Q 10 1 ii). Thus, by basing on word formation rules in French, learners construct new words, which are nonetheless in some cases, incorrect.

The confusion between pronunciation and orthography is especially common with consonants. Here are some examples from our study:

a. »*Tous ce qui s'est passé.*» (P 2 2 ii, g 2 2 ii)
b. »*Tousce qu'elle peut faire.*» (M 8 4 ii)
c. »*A cause de tous ça.*» (F 13 7 ii)

In this case, the grapheme<s> is used by the learner instead of<t>. This is explained by the fact that<t> is not pronounced in French before a consonant and [s] belongs to the following word. The learner writes what s/he hears. These two letters are often substituted to create the following:

"*Tout les persons*"   (b 9 2 ii),"*Tous le monde*"   (Z 8 3 ii, E 8 3 ii) The grapheme is thus substituted for the phoneme.

In the category of the confusion between pronunciation and orthography: vowels, we have examples like "*un droit*" (Q 4 1 ii) instead of '*endroit*', "*commancé*" (h 8 2 ii, b 9 1 ii), which is probably confused with other words like '*commander*'. Other examples include: "*rancontrons*" (V 12 1 ii), "*pansé*" (Q 8 4 ii), "*contante*" (e 8 2 ii) and "*attendu*"(N 9 15 ii). This substitution of open vowels by nasalized vowels is probably explained by the fact that Bantu languages do not have the nasal vowel /ā/. The majority of Bantu speakers do not thus distinguish between 'j '*attends*' et *'j'entends'*. It is in this context that phonetic errors are translated into written ones as well. The same applies to the other vowels like /a/ et /Ẽ/: "*deux fois par moins*" (W 13 3 ii). In some cases, the silent final consonant is omitted in writing: «*Chaque paroisse est représentée au moin par un conseiller* (W 13 4 ii).

At the level of grammatical rules, this causes errors especially the exceptions to some grammar norms. A case in point is the use of the indefinite article *'des'* in French, which is deployed immediately before plural nouns, for example, *'des choses'*. However, when plural nouns are used with the quantity adverb, *'beau-coup'*, they are preceded by the article *'de'* rather than *'des'*. This is the cause of certain lexical difficulties amongst learners as the following example demonstrates:

«*J'ai vu beaucoup des amis.*» (Q 8 2 ii)

An **example** with the comparative adverb canals cited above: «*Le suspect était interrogé pendant plus que 12 heures.*» (M 2 1 ii, J 2 1 ii, O 2 1 ii). This illustrates that learners make generalizations and false hypotheses from a limited amount of data that has been acquired in the target language. Under this aspect we can also mention the case of irregular verbs. While using the past tense and using past participles of verbs like *'j'ailu'*, *'j'ai vu'*, *'j'aimis'* etc. learners tend to generalize this formation for other verbs and come up with erroneous expressions like : "*j'aipru le train et je suis passé la journée à Paris*" (f 11 1 ii). The past participle of the verb *'prendre'* is confused with other similar ending regular verbs like *'rendre'* and *'vendre'* or irregular ones like *'croire'* and *'boire'*.

Gender-related errors were also frequent. Distinguishing between masculine and feminine nouns as well as their respective agreements with related adjectives, and past participles is a challenge for the Anglophone learner as the following examples illustrate:

    a. «*Les avantages socials.*» (F 13 9 ii)
    b. «*cet habitation est très dangereuse.*» (F 13 8 ii)
    c. «*Ma grand-mère est venu.*»(M 8 3 ii)

Example (b) is particularly interesting because this error is probably influenced by other similar nouns [beginning with the vowel 'h'] such as 'cet hôtel', 'cet hôpital', lexical items, which are very common in the beginners' vocabulary. In addition, the sentences (b) and (c) once again highlight the influence of pronunciation on orthography. The pairs "cette/cet" and "venue/venu" are markedly different in writing though perfectly identical in \pronunciation.

Another case of lexical difficulties is linked to the use of complement pronouns designating persons. These are subject to elaborate rules in

French, which do not exist in English, the second language of the learners and through which they often communicate while learning French. This example will help to elucidate this fact:

    a. *Je **lui** téléphone.*
    b. *Je **l'**appelle.*
    c. *e **le** convoque.*

The three complement pronouns here all refer to the same person yet manifest in 3 different allomorphs. In English and Luganda, this is the same morpheme 'him' with no allomorphs. This probably explains the following errors:

    a. On ne peut pas lui (arrêter).»(f 4 2 ii)
    b. «*Je lui admire.*»   (d 8 2 ii, f 8 1 ii)
    c. «*La police lui a interrogé pendant six heures.*»(W 2 1 ii, B 2 1 ii)
    d. »*Il les dit.*»(O 6 2 ii)

To summarize this section, we note that learners make hypotheses drawing from the grammar of the target language to create words and formulate structures. Sometimes these formations do not correspond to the rules of the target language. Such constructions also indicate the stage of learning at which learners have reached as prescribed by their curriculum and shows the kind of challenges they face.

2.12 The Influence of English

This category accounts for 67.4% of the errors and represents 97% of the subjects of this study [32 out of 33]. These errors are basically anglicisms and can be classified as follows: borrowing, literal translations and '*les faux amis*' or 'false friends'.

In the study, we noted 75 occurrences of borrowing. They can be can be categorized into 2 groups: orthographical anglicisms, which have a French equivalent with a very similar spelling and those with a completely different French equivalent.

Figure 2.12.1: Orthographical anglicisms having a French equivalent with a very similar spelling.

Musicians (O 8 2 iii)	Packet (b 8 4 iii)
Independent (K 5 1 iii)	Pork (h 8 8 iii)
Example: (b 9 4 iii, e 1 2 iii,	Dances (h 8 3 iii)
L 8 1 iii, M 1 2 iii,	Dancé (O 8 3 iii, c 8 2 iii)
R 1 2 iii)	Space (c 8 3 iii)
Vest (N 3 1 iii, N 3 2 iii)	Tissue (W 3 2 iii , h 3 1 iii)
Post (f 10 4 iii, b 10 1 iii)	Brief (c 3 1 iii)
Tourist (P 1 12 iii)	Authorité (K 13 1 iii)
Problem (a 8 1 iii)	Scholarizer (M 8 2 iii)
System (L 9 5 iii)	Restorer (K 13 5 iii)
Symbol (Z 8 1 iii)	Parliament (V 12 3 iii)
Evoké (P 1 3 iii)	Dinner (N 9 6 iii)
Provoker (P 1 1 iii, H 6 2 iii, P 4 3 iii)	Address (W 3 3 iii)

All these are borrowed from English but are also related to the pronunciation of their French equivalents. In lexical items like (*vest, post, tourist, problem, system and symbol*) the last letter 'e' in French was omitted. This is probably due to the fact that the pronunciation of the English word is identical to its French equivalent. There is therefore some confusion between the oral and the written form.

Figure 2.12.2: Oral similarity of the equivalents in English and French causing spelling errors

Appartment (V 13 5 iii)	Chocolate (Z 11 2 iii)
Resemblance (V 8 4 iii)	Affairs de government (Z 8 10 iii)
Object (f 10 1 iii, B 10 1 iii)	
Response (B 10 2)	Exceptionalle (G 8 3 iii)
Destruirait (T 1 1 iii)	Naturalement (Z 8 1 iii)
Les persons (b 9 3 iii, T 8 3 iii)	Sanitation (F 13 2 iii)
Advantage (f 3 1 iii)	Théathre (L 9 4 iii)
Advantageaux (f 3 1 iii)	Trapper (G 3 1 iii)
Adjuster (G 13 1 iii)	L'individuel (V 13 1 iii)
Responsible pour (b 8 2 iii, O 6 1 iii)	Un conflict (K 5 2 iii)
Establishé (c 3 2 iii)	Confuser (N 1 1 iii)
Comments (N 8 1 iii)	Protecter (U 3 2 iii)
	Arresté (L 6 1 iii)

These examples are not linked to pronunciation but they demonstrate that learners transfer English words into French due to French equivalents with the same spelling. Learners can export English words into French then try to modify them to adapt to the target language: *'establishé'*. The last six examples also point to the irregular word formation system in French, which produces *'individuellement'*, *'conflictuelle'*, *'confusion'*, *'protection'*, *'arrestation'*, *'interrogateur'*, *'collaborateur'*. The learners simply remove the underlined derivational suffixes to create verbs: *'confuser'* from *'confusion'*, *'protecter'* from *'protection'* and *'arrester'* from *'arrestation'*. The learner thus makes an over generalization of the rule governing the verbal noun formation.

Figure 2.12.3: Orthographic anglicism: words with an equivalent in French that has a different spelling.

Word with English spelling	French equivalent
(H 10 3 iii) transcription	relevé de notes
(B 10 3 iii) degree	diplôme (de licence)
(N 9 13 iii , N 9 4 iii) relatives	parents
(h 9 2 iii , g 9 3 iii , P 9 1 iii) service	le culte
(K 2 1 iii , c 2 1 iii) managé	géré
(C 6 3 iii) expecté	attendu
(b 9 5 iii) advisé	conseillé
(P 1 6 iii) case	cas
(C 6 2 iii) trap	piège
(N 9 10 iii) task	tâche
(N 9 2 iii) discharger	renvoyer (un malade)
(b 8 3 iii) vegetables	légumes
(e 8 4 iii) reporté	signalé
(b 3 5 iii) obtainer	obtenir
(P 1 9 iii) advocate	plaider en faveur de
(Z 13 1 iii) courts	tribunaux
(d 9 2 iii) caroles	cantiques (de noël)

Sometimes, words in English and French have similar spellings and this creates morphological and lexical gaps for the learners.

2.13 Literal Translations

Concerning this case, sentences were translated word for word from English. English words are simply replaced by their French equivalents resulting in unnatural sentences or expressions. For example: "...*jesuis 35 ans*" (O 10 1 iii). Although this is the domain of syntax, we are limiting ourselves here to an analysis of certain lexicon in these sentences. Learners tended to construct their thinking in English and simply substitute English words with French equivalents: "*Sur le dimanche, nous allons à l'église*" (J 12 4 iii) "*On Sunday, we go to church*" which is translated as "*le dimanche, nous allons à l'église*".

Learners in the study also encountered lexical challenges in the use of French prepositions. Although prepositions play the same grammatical role in English and French, they are not always syntactically equivalent. The following examples from the study illustrate this fact:

-»Je travaillais avec l'Air Alliance pour 10ans. (f 10 3 iii)....*for 10 years*.

The sentence is grammatically correct in French but it is semantically different from the English original. The respondent in this case is speaking about the duration of work with Alliance Air. She or he should have used the preposition '*pendant'*, which is employed to express 'the duration of an action and not '*pour'*, which expresses 'a planned duration' (Grégoire et al 1995:76). English, as opposed to French uses the same preposition 'for' to express both the duration of an action and a planned duration.

Other examples show that translating the English word '*for*' to French can sometimes have a tautological effect:

    a. «La police cherche pour les marchands...» (A 3 1 iii)
    b. » Après, Maigret est allé chercher pour l'assassin.» (g 3 1 iii)
    c. « Tout le monde a eu les moyens de payer pour la pièce.» (c 9 1 iii)
    d. « *Après église* nous allons pour déjeuner avec mon amie.»(J 12 6 iii)

Similarly, the English preposition '*on*' does not necessarily translate as its French equivalent '*sur*'. The same applies to the English preposition '*in*', which does not always necessarily translate as '*dans*' or '*en*':

    e. »Sur le Noël on s'est levé à 6h 30 du matin.»(X 9 1 iii)
       On Christmas...
    f. »...nous avon attendu un annoncé sur la radio...»(N 9 17 iii)... *on radio*.
    g. »...beacoup de femmes en le monde...»(Z 8 7 iii) ...*in the world*.
    h. »Elle est morte le 22 *Décembre* ici à Kampala en hôpital de Mulago.» (O 9 1 iii) ...*in Mulago hospital*.

A Lexical and Morphological Analysis of Students' Written Work

i. »...ma soeur et moi *ont décidé* pour jouer <u>dans</u> la pluie.» (A 8 2 iii)...*in the rain.*
j. «<u>Dans</u> réponse de votre (annonce)... (Y 10 1 iii)
   In reply...
k. »...il divise les policiers <u>dans</u> groupes...»(H 6 1 iii) ...*in groups...*
l. »Maigret utilise cet idée <u>dans</u> la façon suivante... (M 6 1 iii)...*in the following way...*
m. "Nous avons arrivé à Entebbe à 11:00 <u>dans</u> temp pour le service.
n. ...*in time for the service.*

The strong influence of English in the learners' writing is highlighted by the words in italics. In sentence (d) we note the use of the capital letter for the month. Sentence (e) portrays the phenomenon of *'have decided'* in English where the 1st and 3rd person of the plural are conjugated in the same manner for all verbs. (C'est moi qui *est* le premier.)

Some verbs have different semantic fields and this can pose lexical difficulties:

a. »Quand il était <u>apporté</u> à la Police Judiciaire l'homme cachait son visage derrière son chapeau. (G 2 1 iii)
b. »...notre père a eu un task de <u>apporter</u> notres relatives qui étaient dans la ville...» (N 9 11 iii)
c. »...pour <u>prendre</u> son fils pour les études...»(b 8 1 iii).
d. »...il a essayé de me <u>prendre</u> dans les bon écoles.» (M 8 5 iii)
e. »...le mouvement de Résistance Nationale <u>méné</u> par Yoweri Museveni Kaguta, le président actuel.
f. »Mon père <u>est</u> soixante-quatre ans.» (d **8 1 III)**
g. »Elle était 25 ans.» (c **3 2 III)**
h. »J'<u>étais</u> faim.» (d 11 1 iii)
i. »Le couple qui <u>avait</u> marié...»(T 8 2 iii)

The verbs *'apporter'* and *'prendre'* are to a large extent the French equivalents of *'bring'* and *'take'* in English. However, in this case, French possesses a wider lexical field than English:

English -French

Bring:
a) An object -**Apporter** un objet.
b) A person -**Amener** une personne.

Take:
a) An object - **Prendre** un objet.
b) A person - **Emmener** une personne.

Similarly, the verb *'être'* expresses among other things age, hunger and thirst. Conversely, however, these aspects are expressed by the verb *'avoir'* in French.

Other examples show the behaviour of articles and possessive adjectives. The possessive adjective in English does not agree with gender and number as it does in French; the transfer of the learners' knowledge of English grammar into French caused errors like:

a. «La police vont aller avec le bouton <u>à les</u> tailleurs.»(G 3 3 iii) b) - «Maigret ne dit rien <u>à les</u> journalistes et il ne répond pas à leurs questions.»(M 1 1 iii)

b. »...des vacances de deux semaines - de 19 décembre 1999 <u>à le 2eme</u> janvier 2000»(K 9 1 iii).

c. »En <u>28e</u>decembre...»(C 8 1 iii).

d. «Veuillez agréer, Messieurs, <u>mon</u> salutations distinguées.» (A 10 2 iii)

e. »Je suis allé en France pour passer <u>mon</u> vacances.» (E 11 1 iii)

f. «Sa vetements (étaient) déchirés.» (U 3 1 iii)

g. «Avec <u>son</u> mesures secretes...» (e 1 1 iii)

Other similar errors collected from our corpus include ; «<u>leur</u> agents»(G 6 2 ii), «Elle aime beaucoup <u>notre</u> enfants»(G 8 1 ii) et «<u>notres</u> (parents)»(N 9 12 ii).

Learners also tend to rely heavily on bilingual dictionaries, which present English and French equivalents without a communication context. Their transfer of lexical items results in rather inappropriate diction in French:

a. »Elle travaille plus <u>en ordre</u> d'obtenir de l'argent.» (G 8 2 iii)

b. «L'argent qu'elle gagne comme un salaire n'est pas <u>assez.</u>» (F 12 1 iii)

c. »Il reste toujours dans son bureau et donne ses ordres seulement au téléphone, donc <u>ce</u> montre qu'il était très *secrètif* dans son investigations.» (L 1 2 iii) d)-»Ils croient qu'on les met là pour remplacer leurs collègues en vacances, <u>cet</u> est nécessaire parce que quelqu'un peut parler trop dans les affaires difficiles comme celles-ci.» (M 1 4 iii)

The translation of *'this'* in English by *'ce'* in French is often inappropriate depending on the context. This lack of equivalence between demonstrative pronouns in English and French is highlighted by (Vinay and Darbelnet, 1968) who affirm that in English the demonstrative pronouns can stand alone whereas in French they need some reinforcement. (Vi-nay et Darbelnet 1968: 133)

Many other examples of 'gaps' stem from transferring English word structures into French:
- a. »Une femme...était attaquée mais elle n'est pas <u>blessuré.</u>» (X 6 1 iii)
- b. »Les pièges que Maigret emploie (étaient) <u>provocatives.</u>» (P 1 3 iii)
- c. »Il tue des femmes parceque sa mère est très <u>authoritative.</u>» (f 5 1 iii)
- d. »L'amour est <u>unconditionnel,</u>» (A 8 1 iii)
- e. »Nous sommes allés à l'église pour la cérémonie <u>chritien.</u>» (h 8 4 iii)
- f. »Les <u>chritiens</u> celebrent un jour quand Christ est né.» (h 9 1 iii)

2.14 The 'faux amis'

These refer to words in English and French, which have a similar form but have a partially or totally different meaning (Chuquet/Paillard, 1989:224). The learners meet these words with a familiar spelling and jump to the conclusion that their meaning corresponds to the English word. Their hypothesis is justified by several examples like: 'hôtel' (*hotel*), 'pharmacie' (*pharmacy*), 'hôpital'(*hospital*), 'aéroport'(*airport*), 'pilote' (*pilot*), 'journaliste' (*journalist*), 'téléphoner'(*to telephone*) , 'danser' (*to dance*), 'invitation' (*invitation*) etc. However, many 'false friends' abound, which do not correspond to this pattern like 'actuel', 'sensible' et 'blesser', which do not correspond to the English words of similar spelling: '*actual*', '*sensible*', '*bless*'. The study findings yielded the following examples:

Figure 2.14.1: Gaps due to 'false friends'

	The 'faux ami'	**The appropriate word**
(G 10 1 iii)	Officier	Administrateur
(M 2 2 iii, J 2 2 iii, O 2 2 iii)	Interrogation	Interrogatoire
(W 13 2 iii, h 8 9 iii)	Chance	Occasion
(N 10 3 iii, C 10 2 iii)	Attaché	cijoint
(g 9 2 iii)	Peuples	Gens
(F 10 1 iii)	Député	Adjoint
(a 10 1 iii, b 4 1 iii)	Place	Endroit, lieu
(D 10 1 iii)	Application	Demande
(J 10 1 iii)	Appliquer	Faire unedemande
(G 3 2 iii)	Tracer	Retrouver

	The 'faux ami'	The appropriate word
(M 9 2 iii)	Charges	Frais
(G 13 2 iii)	Affaire (d'amour)	Liaison
(F 13 1 iii)	Arrangée	Rangée
(F 13 5 iii)	Caractère	Comportement

2.15 The Influence of Combination of Factors

This category accounts for 20% of the gaps observed and it was evident among 67 % of the respondents (22 out of 33). In this case, it was to make a clear distinction between the influence of English and that of several factors. For instance, *'protecter'* is an example of a loanword from English but it can also be attributed to learning difficulties or the inconsistency of word formation rules in French. If the French nouns 'invention' and *'détection'* are derived from the verbs *'inventer'* and *'détecter'*, it would follow that the French noun 'protection' is also derived from the verb *'protecter'*. It is such deductions from the grammatical rules in French that sometimes cause learners to come up with a mixed grill of gaps. This mixed grill of factors can be classified into 3 groups: gaps due to the influence of English and French, translation, using a bilingual dictionary and gaps whose cause is difficult to determine.

2.15.1 Gaps due to the influence of English and French

Some words are borrowed from English with the mistaken assumption that they are French words because other French words have similar forms. For instance, *"millennium'* bears a strong resemblance to other French words like 'album' and 'forum'. Sometimes there is the mistaken assumption that since a verb of the same form exists in both English and French; the nominal form is also identical. In the study we note the following:

   a. «Le Noël dernier qui était aussi le noël dernier *dans* le millennium était bon pour notre famille.» (g 9 1 iv)
   b. «Ça n'était pas ma concerne.» (M 9 1 iv)
   c. «Ils ont bu des bières, des sodas, de l'alchool.» (N 9 9 iv)
   d. »Mais les organiseurs ont appelé la police immédiatement pour *controler* la situation.» (c 9 2 iv)
   e. «....qu'est-ce qu'il va faire pendant son retraitement» (V 12 2 iv)

Sometimes there is a mixture of English spelling and French structure, while imitating French word formation in the same grammatical category. The learners, as can be seen from the above examples, have a tendency to over-generalize certain grammatical rules. Here we note the over-generalization of the rule governing the formation of substantives by suffixation of *'-ment'*.

We also observe a mixture of French spelling and literal translation of the English structure of a word:*"J'admire Charlotte parcequ'elle est très intelligente, très jeune et très amicalement." (K 8 1 iv)*

'Amicalement' is used to designate 'friendly' in English. The English suffix '*-ly*' is normally translated by the French suffix '*-ment*' for a considerable number of adverbs.

Another source of confusion is the mixture of different semantic fields of the verbs 'savoir' and 'connaitre' as well as *'avoir'* and 'être':

f. «*C'est-à-dire qu'il est intelligent parcequ'il connait à se cacher même s'il y a beaucoup de police.*» *(S 7 1 iv)*

g. »*Il y était un disco pour la nuit et nous dansions.*» *(g 8 2 iv)*

The prepositions 'to' and 'from' are not exactly equivalent on the syntactic plane in English and French. This therefore becomes a trap for many learners who simply transpose English structures into French:

h. »*Il allait encore essayer à tuer une autre femme.*» *(O 1 1 iv)*
   ... try to...

i. «*Il a échappé de la police.*» *(Q 4 2 iv)*
   ...escape from...

In English, '*what*' is both an interrogative particle ('*que*' or '*qu'est-ce que*') and a conjunction ('*ce que*'). In French, the two roles use different lexical items, thus creating a source of errors:

j. »*Il a l'intention de tuer et il sait bien qu'il fai.t*» *(M 7 1 iv)*

k. »*Quand on demande à Jim qu'est-ce qu'ilva faire pendant son retraitement, il dit qu'il va devenir un représentant du parliament.*» *(V 12 4 iv)*

l. «*Il les dit qu'est-ce qu'ils sont faire.*» *(O 6 3 iv)*

2.16 Translation by means of a bilingual dictionary

Learners sometimes make poor lexical choices because of relying heavily on translations proposed by bilingual dictionaries. These reference materials offer some grammatical notes on conjugations and tenses that are handy for learners. They are also the beginners' favourite tool for learning new words along with their pronunciatlons. However, this type of dictionary hardly presents these lexicon in a communication context or situations in which they can be used. Neither the idiomatic nor the syntactic uses of the words are portrayed. These include dictionaries such as:*'Collins Pocket French Dictionary, French-English, English-French, Harper Collins Publishers 1995'* or the '*French- English, English- French Dictionary', Geddes &Grosset 1998.*

This last one comprises not only a limited number of words but also contains inadequate explanations and descriptions. The lack of context for these lexical items makes these words often ambiguous. For instance, a learner who wanted to say: *'I have a French lecture at 8'*, and not knowing the equivalent, consults the dictionary, which gives the word *'conférence'*. The student therefore writes *'J'ai une conférence de français à 8h.'* instead of the correct *'J'ai un cours de français à 8h'*. This is not to say that there is no positive learning from such dictionaries. The fact is that these dictionaries tend to give the false impression that a language is composed of individual words without a communication context. This probably explains the presence of some bizarre constructions in the learners' written work:

    a. «L'expression <u>moyen</u> que l'assassin ne tue pas quelqu'un.» (H 4 1 iv)

        The expression <u>means</u> that... (L'expression....veut dire).

The learner looks up *'means'* in the bilingual dictionary (Geddes & Grosset) and finds it designated as: *'npl*moyens*mpl:-vt vi* signifier'. Apparently, some learners are not capable of comprehending the technical abbreviations and ends up making a wrong choice. Sometimes they do not even know how to use dictionaries since they sometimes fail to interpret dictionary meanings; 'npl' (plural substantive), 'vt' (transitive verb).

    b. «A la maison, je <u>dépense</u> de temps avec ma famille.» (d 9 1 iv)

        At home, I <u>spend</u> time with my family.

According to Geddes &Grosset (1998:219), the verb *'spend'* is presented as: **Spend** *vt* dépenser; passer. The two equivalent verbs are presented without a context. The second option is the appropriate one for the learners' situation but she or he does not know because of lacking guidance from the dictionary and is simply reduced to guesswork. The same applies to the example below where no illustrative sentences are given by the dictionary to aid the learner choose the correct word:

    a. «Elle est <u>bref</u> avec petite bouche, elle est brune...» (J 12 2 iv)

    b. *She is <u>short</u>, has a small mouth and is brown...*Geddes &Grosset (1998:214): **short** *adj.* court, bref.

    c. «Le Commissaire a lui <u>demandé</u> beaucoup de questions mais il a refusé de répondre.» (D 2 2 iv, H 2 2 iv, f 2 2 iv)

        The Police Commissioner <u>asked</u> him many questions but he refused to answer.

Geddes & Grosset (1998:122): **ask** *vt*demander. The other possibilities of *'ask'* in French such as 'poser' (une question) do not feature in the dictionary and the learner is left with no option but to use the verb 'demander'.

d. »Elle a visité beaucoup de places pour <u>mélanger</u> avec les pauvres de monde. "(Z 8 5 iv)

She visited many places in order to <u>mix</u> with the poor of the world.

For the verb "mélanger" Geddes & Grosset (1998:187) provides: **mix** *vt*mélanger. The other possible options of the translation of '*mix*' like 'se mêler' are absent. There is therefore a limited representation of lexical equivalents. The same scenario applies to:

e. »Cette maison est trop grande donc elle a décidé de louer quelques <u>salles</u> pour gagner de l'argent.» (F 8 2 iv)
f. *This house is too big so she decided to rent some <u>rooms</u> in order to earn some money.*
g. »Toute le matin, je suis resté dans <u>mon salle</u> ici à Makerere.»
h. *All morning, I remained in my <u>room</u> here in Makerere.*

(Geddes &Grosset, 1998:209) indicates: **room as** *n* pièce, salle *f*; espace *m*. Such decontextualized words in bilingual dictionaries result in poor lexical choices, on the learners' part. . The appropriate word in this case, which is '*chambre*', does not even appear in this dictionary. The presentations of English and French lexical equivalents by this type of dictionaries are not an appropriate reflection of the actual usage of words in daily communication.

2.17 Ambiguous Gaps

Very often some categories of gaps or errors are quite complex and it is difficult to establish their direct cause. Some are due to interferences but could also be linked to learning difficulties; poor comprehension by the learner, learner attitude, learner's state of mind (whether tired, hungry, bored, sick), mistaking one sound for another or lack of vocabulary…etc. Such examples include:

a. «Elle aime ses enfants <u>très bien.</u>» (F 8 1 iv)
b. «Ce criminel tue des femmes parcequ'il<u>veux</u> montrer qu'il est fort.» (G 5 1 iv)
c. «Elle a eu vingt ans et <u>lui</u> famille n'était pas riche.» (f 8 3 iv)
d. «Elle a donné d'argent pour <u>lui</u>soeurs et frères.» (f 8 4 iv)
e. «Cher mon ami Paul, c'est <u>celui</u>, votre ami, Robert qui voudrait <u>lui</u> dire mon expérience que j'avais fait en ville de Paris. Quand j'<u>est</u> arrivée dans cette ville se trouve en France, je m'<u>a</u> trouvé j'étais <u>confusé.</u>» (W 11 1-4 iv)

Interestingly, this last case was written during an examination. These errors can be associated with panic, anxiety, stress, tension, which easily hinders clear language expression. We hence note that sometimes these gaps may not necessarily be errors but mistakes. Mistakes are made even by native speakers and stem from performance. Errors, on the other hand, stem from competence. At times, it is difficult to draw a clear dividing line between an error and a mistake.

2.18 Conclusion and Recommendations

The summary of the study findings indicates that most gaps stem from the influence of English. This comprises 'false friends', literal translations and poor lexical choices influences by bilingual dictionaries to a considerable extent. This confirms our second assumption that English affects written expression of Ugandan learners of French. It is actually the most important factor causing lexical and morphological gaps among the learners in this study.

Table 2.18.1: Summary of Study Findings

	No. of gaps	No. of respondents
Mother tongue interference	9 (3.4%)	6 (18%)
Influence of French	35 (9.2%)	19 (57, 6%)
Influence of English	215 (67.4%)	32 (97%)
Combination of factors	62 (20%)	22 (67%)

The second most important factor is the combination of different factors. This is especially due to the influence of both English and French. For instance, certain lexical units exist in both languages but possess different semantic fields. This type of error also stems from inadequate learning where certain grammatical rules or morphological elements have not been properly mastered. According to the results, the influence of the target language (French) is quite minimal as a cause of errors. The third research assumption is therefore not significant.

Mother tongue interference was observed to be a very rare cause of gaps in the learners' written work. Apparently, learners were rarely translating from their mother tongues into French. This is probably explained by the rather unique foreign language setting in Uganda where English is the medium of instruction. This is also supported by the fact that there is a proliferation of English to French bilingual dictionaries. Per-haps there is also the feeling that the two European languages are very similar given their often similar historical, economic and cultural characteristics.

The gaps highlighted in this study indicate the extent to which learners have mastered different grammatical rules and where emphasis needs to be laid in teaching and curriculum organization. Foreign language learning should favour more contextual communication and learners ought to be sensitized to the proper use of bilingual dictionaries. Junior monolingual dictionaries adapted to the learners' level should be encouraged, because these enable learners to construct their thinking in the foreign language. Dictionaries like *'le Dictionnaire Hachette Junior', Hachette Livre 1998'* present useful illustrations alongside simple sentences, which place lexical items in wider communication contexts.

It could be said that learners tend to use the same strategies to learn French as they did while learning English (second language). Could there be a correlation between learning English and learning French? What is the nature of errors in the con-text of learning English in Uganda? These answers would help one understand better the linguistic learning strategies of Ugandan learners. It would also be interesting to know the morphological and lexical gaps at an equal level of studying other foreign languages like German and Arabic. The similarities and differences would inform foreign language teaching and learning strategies in Uganda.

References

Ander S., Yildirim O. (2010).Lexical Errors in Elementary Level EFL Learners' compositions. *Procedia Social and Behavioural Sciences 2 (2010) 4352-4358.*

Carl J. (1998). *Errors in Language Learning and Use. Exploring Error Analysis.* London: Taylor & Francis.

Chen H. (1996).*Vers une prise en compte de l'influence de l'anglais dans l'enseignement du français en Chine*, Mémoire de DEA, Université de Rouen.

Chuquet H., Paillard M. (1989).*Approche Linguistique des Problèmes de Traduction.* Paris : Ophrys.

Corder S.P. (1973). *Introducing Applied Linguistics.* Middlesex: Penguin Books Ltd.

Corder S.P. (1980). La sollicitation de données d'interlangue. In Perdue C., Porquier R. *Langages: Apprentissage et Connaissance d'une langue étrangère* (pp. 29-38). Paris : Larousse.

Doneux J.L. (1976) «La Composante Linguistique dans l'apprentissage» in Gardin B. (Ed.)1976 Langue Française: L'apprentissage du français par les travailleurs immigrés, no.29 Fév.1976, Swets & Zeitlinger BV, Lisse.

Dubois J. et al. (1994).*Dictionnaire de Linguistique et des Sciences du Langage.* Paris : Larousse.

Dulcie E., Myles F. (1996).*Teaching Grammar: Perspective in Higher Education.* London: AFLS-CILT.

Dumont P., Maurer B. (1995).*Sociolinguistique du Français en Afrique Francophone,* Paris : Edicef., 210p.

Grégoire M., Thievenaz O. (1995).*Grammaire Progressive du Français (Niveau Intermédiaire)*, Paris : Clé International

Kirgoz Y. (2010). An Analysis of written errors of Turkish Adult Learner's of English. *Procedia Social and Behavioural Sciences 2 (2010) 4352-4358.*

Ladefoged P. (1971).*Language in Uganda,* Oxford University Press, Nairobi, 168p.

Lafage S. (1993). French in Africa. In Sanders C.*French Today - Language in its social context*, (pp. 215-238). Cambridge: Cambridge University Press.

Narayanan R., Rajasekaran N., Iyyappan S. (2008). Some Factors affecting English learning at a tertiary level. *Inte-rnational Journal of Language Studies, Vol. 2, Issue 4, 485-512.*

Richards J.C. (1974).*Error Analysis - Perspectives on Second Language Acquisition.* Essex : Longman.

Savli F. (2009). Interférences lexicales entre deux langues étrangères: anglais et français. *Synergies Turquie, 179-184.*

Storch N., Aldosari A. (2010). Learners' use of first language (Arabic) in pair work in an EFL Class. *Language Teaching Research 14:* 355-375, Sage Publications.

CHAPTER THREE
FACTORS DETERMINING THE VALUE OF A TEXT IN FOREIGN LANGUAGE TEACHING
Harriet K. Namukwaya[1]
Abstract

One of the main objectives within the area of Foreign Language Teaching (FLT) is for the language learner to develop communicative competence through, among other me-ans, working with different text types in the language class. There are as many text types as there are methods of working with them. The value of or the value attached to a text may be determined by a number of factors: What does the teacher want to achieve with the help of the text? What do the language learners know and expect from the text being used? What do the language learners know and expect from the topics, which dominate the academic, social-cultural and political context within which the teacher and the learner operate? Additionally, text value may also be determined by the teaching in class, the texts selected for particular purposes (e.g. University examinations, among others), and the way information and knowledge is managed and disseminated in a given learning situation. The purpose of this paper is to demonstrate that different factors determine the value of texts in a foreign language class. The paper bases the discussion on the assumption that the value attached to a particular text is, first, dependent on the way texts are used to teach specific language skills. This paper discusses, in particular, how different text types are used in the French classes at the university level to enhance various language skills.

Key words: *Text, text value, foreign language teaching, language skills*

3.1 Introduction

Foreign language teaching in a country where there is no community of practice and limited reading, teaching and research materials for the target foreign language poses a challenge not only to the teachers of the

---

1   Harriet K. Namukwaya has been teaching in French Studies at Makerere University. She is currently pursuing her Ph. D. in Modern Languages and Cultural studies, at the University of Calgary, Alberta, Canada. She has researched and published on error analysis and text analysis in French as well as Inter-cultural competences.

foreign language, but also to the students. A community of practice (CoP) is a concept put forward by Lave and Wenger (1991). A CoP is defined as a group of people who share a concern or passion for something they do and learn to do it better as they interact regularly. A CoP is formed by people who engage in a process of collective learning in a shared domain of human endeavours. For Lave and Wenger (1991), knowledge, learner and learning are socially situated. Lave says that knowledge is not just stored in an individual's mind but it is understood relatively as located in the evolving relationships between people and the settings in which they conduct their activities. This means that learning a language requires one to engage actively in social interactions or engage in joint activity, in a CoP For instance, we could consider the French club or the French classes to be CoP but unfortunately not all students offering French have the same purpose or attach the same value to French; in other words, not every student of French shares practices of the community (French Club).What makes the situation more difficult for French language students is the fact that, French is not spoken elsewhere apart from one or two hours of lecture.

Additionally, basing our teaching on only the limited learning or teaching resources that were prescribed ten or five years ago or recycling of notes by teachers year in year out, in this era of globalization does not only provide students with limited knowledge but also deprives them of new learning and teaching methods. That is why in most cases, language teachers resort to online resources or authentic documents which contain good teaching material but whose language may not be appropriate to the students' language level. Creativity in language teaching or innovative language teaching is commendable but unpreparedness on the part of the teacher, may negatively affect language learning as the latter has been observed in foreign language classes. The current study on the factors, which determine the value attached to a particular text used in a foreign language class, specifically French as a foreign language (FFL). It highlights the criteria used in the selection of texts used in a language class. It also demonstrates the different factors that determine text value and last but not least it suggests possible tasks that can be done with the texts selected for a particular language lesson.

Before going into details of the factors that determine text value in a foreign language class, it is important to first of all, explain what a text is, text types and sources as well as to talk about the tasks that can be done with a particular text. This will give us a clear view of how valuable texts can be in a foreign language class.

3.2 Definition of a Text

Bloome and Egan-Robert (1993) cited in Wade and Moje (2000, p. 610), define a text as "organized networks of meaning that people generate or use to make meaning either for themselves or for others." Crystal (1985) defines a text as a pre-theoretical term used in linguistics and phonetics, to refer to a stretch or a piece of language recorded for the purpose of analysis and description. What is important to note is that, texts may also refer to a collection of written and spoken material (transcribed) e.g. conversations, monologues, rituals, and adverts among other materials.

In the past years, the study of text has become a defining feature of a branch of linguistics referred to as "text linguistics" and text here has a central theoretical status. Crystal (1991; 350) posits that texts are seen as language units, which have a definable communicative function, characterized by such principles as cohesion, coherence and "informativeness", which may be used to provide a formal definition of what constitutes the identifying "textuality" or "texture". On the basis of these principles, texts are classified into text forms, such as road signs, news reports, poems, conversations among others.

Crystal (1991), notes that some linguists, from the opposite viewpoint, have defined "text" as an "abstract notion" and "discourse" as its realization. Apart from these theoretical distinctions, there is also a tendency to think about texts as monologues; usually written and often very short (e.g. *No through road, No parking*). In contrast, discourses are often thought of as dialogues, usually spoken and of a greater length. He also notes that, some linguists make a distinction between the notions of text, viewed as a "physical product" (surface structure) and, viewed as a dynamic process of expression and interpretation (deep structure). Halliday (1976) uses the term "cohesion" to refer to those surface structure features, which link different parts of sentences or large units of discourse together.

3.3 Types of Texts

There are various types and sources of texts. A value is attached to the various types of texts depending on the user of such texts. It should be noted that texts are classified into two major text types; informational texts and literary texts. Informational texts simply refer to texts and contexts that have a function of communicating information about the natural social world, typically from one presumed to be more knowledgeable on a subject to one presumed to be less knowledgeable. Such texts have a durable factual content, for instance, a newspaper article on presidential elections in Uganda, gay rights, child sacrifice, and landslides in the eastern part of Uganda among others. Literary texts are defined as texts that deal with or have to do with literature, e.g. novels, poems, fables, plays, fairy-tales and short stories.

Informational and literary texts are further classified into narrative, descriptive, argumentative, prescriptive, and conversational (dialogue) texts. We should note that different texts have different value(s) in different language classes depending on the user, especially the teacher in the context of a language class. It is also worth noting that texts are further categorized into genres. According to Biber (1988: 70,170) & EAGLES (1996), "genre" is based on external, non-linguistic criteria while "text type" is based on the internal, linguistic characteristics of texts themselves. In this view, a genre is defined as a category assigned on the basis of external criteria such as intended audience, purpose and activity type, that is, it refers to a conventional, culturally recognized grouping of texts based on the properties other than lexical or grammatical (co)-occurrence features, which are, instead, the internal or linguistic criteria forming the basis of text type categories. Biber (1988: 170) posits that genre categories are assigned on the basis of use (speaker's purpose and topic) rather than on the basis of form. The table below presents Partridge's examples of genres and text types based on Hammond et al. (1992)

Genre	Text type
Recipe, Health brochure	Procedure
Personal letter	Anecdote
Advertisement, Police report	Description
Student essay, Formal letter	Exposition
Student assignment, News item	Recount
Biology text	Report
Film review	Review

3.4 Sources of Texts

The texts that the foreign language teacher uses are usually obtained from different sources: text books, novels, songs, newspapers, television, radio, the Internet, recorded texts, magazines, telephone short mes-sages, sermons among others. We should take note of the fact that different kinds of text may be used in different ways, in different classes and for different purposes. Uses of text depend on differences in the pedagogical approach and purpose; the subject content, pedagogical knowledge base of the teachers, teachers' and learners' beliefs and attitudes about knowledge and their cultural, social and linguistic backgrounds or dispositions.

3.4.1 Features of texts

Texts are not simply understood as every day tools for language teachers; they are rather an embodiment of the aims, values and methods of a particular teaching or learning situation. Therefore, the selection of teaching materials probably represents the single most important decision that the language teacher has to make before any work with any form of text may be undertaken in class.

As outlined above, texts embody or should embody aims, values and creativity in the process of teaching a language. Nunan (1991; 209) states that in the process of selecting a text, it is important ideally to match the text with the goals and objectives of the language lesson, and the needs of the learner in order to ensure that the text is consistent with one's beliefs, attitude about the nature of language and learning as well as learner's attitudes, preferences and beliefs.

Different views of what counts as text lead to different views of what constitutes "learning" with texts in a language class. These different views, consequently, expand or limit the opportunities learners may have to learn in classrooms.

3.5 Criteria of Text Choice

There are various criteria used in choosing, which text to use in a foreign language class and these are determined by the language level of the learners and what the teacher wants to tackle in a particular lecture or lesson.

3.6 Language level of the learners

Texts that match the language level of the learners are good and appropriate to use in a foreign language class. The teacher selecting the text should know the language level or the category of the learners she or he is selecting the text for. Texts that have vocabulary that the learners cannot easily understand are considered hard and therefore are not read. Hard vocabulary hinders comprehension of the content in the text because the learner has to keep on checking every new word in the dictionary. This is not only frustrating but also time consuming. In brief, texts should be first appropriate to the language level of the learners to facilitate comprehension and make reading enjoyable. In fact, Nga (2003) cited in Thom (2008; 121) suggests that the difficulty of a text in terms of lexis, grammar, and style must relate to students' language level.

3.7 Text length

Sheer length of text may be an important factor of learners or readers. Texts that are overly long may seem overwhelming to the struggling language learners of French as a foreign language, or any other foreign language in an environment where there are many other languages. The text length may add to the simplicity or difficulty of the text. Long texts or complex ones are perceived to be hard or difficult to understand. Such texts diminish learners' will to learn, and as a result affects their general performance and comprehension of the language. For example, if a teacher has a one hour lecture or lesson for beginners, she or he may not wish to be spending the bigger part of that time reconstructing a text, if she or he wishes the class to have opportunities to practice the language they are learning.

3.8 Learners' own experience

Texts that relate to the learners' own experience notably leisure, new technologies, the Internet, smart phones, IPhone, IPad, IPod, television, school, sports among others can be or are good to use in a language class. Such texts give learners what to talk about and in fact encourage learners to talk more or communicate in the language they are learning. Many learners will be happy to talk about the concrete matters, which affect their daily lives more than abstract ideas.

3.9 Texts that relate to important topics from the world around the learners

Since the teachers have a wider duty to educate the learners rather than simply teach them a language, texts on worthy issues such as HIV/AIDS, cross generation sex, the environment, poverty, intolerance among others are recommendable to use in a language class. The learners' proficiency in the French language may be limited; despite that fact, they also need the challenges and stimulation of addressing themes and topics, which have adult appeal and which encourage them to draw on their personal opinions and experiences (Lazar,19-94). Such texts not only teach language to the learners but also how to be critical and analytical in their thinking. With such texts, learners learn how to filter information out of the texts and apply it to their life situations.

3.10 Target language culture

Texts that convey information about the target language culture are also good to consider when selecting teaching or learning materials for language learners. Such texts are also useful in teaching learners about the way of life, traditions, values and customs of the speakers of the language they are in the process of learning. This teaches them to be appreciative, tolerant and aware of cultural differences. In fact, Tseng (20-02) posits that culture effects changes in individual perception and is vital in expanding an individual's perspective of the world. Shanahan (1997:168) also states that cultural content provides exposure to living language that a foreign language learner lacks. It is important to note that texts dealing with the target language culture should not be esoteric. In other words, they should not be understood or enjoyed by only a few learners with a special knowledge or interest in the target language culture. Texts should basically interest every learner; this enables them to appreciate other people's culture and even compare theirs with that one they are learning about. This does not only teach them how to compare and contrast but also how to speak or communicate in the language they are learning as well as communicate effectively with people from different cultures.

3.11 Nature of text

Texts for language teaching need not to be completely authentic. An authentic text simply refers to a piece of language that is not originally meant for class work or language teaching but which a teacher may and can use as a tool for teaching the language. Here, the teacher adapts the source text to suit the language learners being taught. Authentic texts expose language learners to real language situations and to language use in the *communit y* Guariento & Morley 2001: 347). In fact, (1988:467) cited in Kilickaya (2004) defines an authentic text as appropriate and quality in terms of goals, objectives, learner needs and interest and natural in terms of real life and meaningful communication. The selected text should therefore not be too hard or too easy in terms of vocabulary or text language. Texts that are too hard will be off-putting and most learners will have so much difficulty deciphering meaning that they will not be able to go on to other tasks that can be done using the text, such as discussion, comprehension exercises among others. On the contrary, texts that are too easy may well be a good source for other activities but will do little to improve the reading skills and even the vocabulary on the part of the learners.

3.12 Goals and objectives of the lesson

Among the objectives, we have the basic pragmatic, linguistic and socio-linguistic objectives and each lesson should at least have these principal objectives. The teacher, the language level and needs of the learners usually determine these objectives. If it is a group, learning a language for specific purposes, such as French for Tourism, the text to select should match with the goal or outcome the teacher wants to achieve at the end of the lesson as well as the academic needs or objectives of the group, i.e. a text that tackles aspects of tourism. It should be noted that such a text not only teaches the learners aspects of tourism but also, the text acquires a high value since it is in line with the objectives and needs of the learners.

3.13 Concept of Text Value

Within the framework of this article, "text value" refers to the way a text may and can be put to maximum use, i.e. using a text to exhaust all the opportunities and possibilities a text can offer in a foreign language class. In other words, "text value" refers to the uses and functions a particular text makes possible in a language class. "Text value" is primarily, dependent on the user of the text as well as the methodology to get or use the information from a particular text. A text may contain valuable information, but that alone does not make it valuable to the user of that text in a given situation. In brief, "text value" refers to the usefulness and usability of a text depending on the condition and purpose for which the text is used and is usable.

3.14 Factors Determining Text Value in a Foreign Language Class

3.14.1 Learner's Interest and Background

Texts that respond to the learner's interests and expectations are considered to be of high value to that particular learner. Familiarity with the topic or theme in the text and vocabulary also helps a great deal in making the learner make sense of the text content she or he may be encountered with. In addition, texts that match the learner's interests and expectations are likely to be motivating thus increasing the value of that text and the chances of a successful and satisfying reading experience for the language learner. For instance, a text on hotels in France was used in a 'French for Tourism' class. Despite the students' limited proficiency in French, they actively participated in the lecture simply because it tackled a topic well known to them of their interest.

3.14.2 Text language and Theme

The language used in the text qualifies the text in two extremes; i.e. in terms of difficulty or simplicity. The perception and reception of a given text, largely depends on the individual language competence and proficiency of a learner before encountering any text. A text usually demands prior or supplementary knowledge of the theme in it and its content, and if a learner does not have any prior knowledge, she or he may not attach any value to that text. On the contrary, a learner who has some knowledge about the topic and theme in the text will most likely attach more value to such a text. For instance, a text on politics will be more valuable to a learner who is interested in political issues or political science, be-cause this enables him or her to relate to what is being read in the text, since she or he is already familiar with the subject at hand. This also enables learners to make a connection or compare the political issues in the text with those of his or her country or what one has already covered in his or her political science class.

Similarly, when the language of the text matches the learner's language level then the text acquires value, because the text language helps the learner to understand the content of the text. Whenever there is a mismatch between the text language and the learner's language level, the text would be considered difficult to comprehend and therefore will be of no value to the learner. The explanation for this is simply because the language in the text is not easy to understand and therefore difficult in the interpretation of the meaning of the text. This brings us to another factor that determines text value in a language class.

3.14.3 Content of the Text

Content refers to the ideas that are contained in a piece of writing or text. Content also refers to the topic or theme being discussed in a particular text. Texts that contain culturally and socially relevant material such as issues related to family, work, youth, health, sports, relationships or love often reflect the deepest emotions of the learners and the latter are, to a large extent, familiar with such issues or topics. Language learners usually have the personal desire to be able to read texts successfully. In other words, the content of such texts is relevant to the learner when it tackles day-to-day issues, which consequently enables the learners to relate to what they learn with what goes on around them. The major advantage of such texts is the fact that they become a reflection of the learners' interests since they contain topics or themes that have a bearing on the learners' day-to-day life. In essence, such texts contain topics and themes about what the learners know. The learners, at this stage, already have complete comprehension, conceptual control and high interest in the text content. This does not only increase the learners' motivation but also automatically adds value to the text being used or studied. For example, a text titled "*Ma famille*" was used in a Beginners class. Such a text had the language appropriate to the language level of the group and addressed a topic familiar to the students so they were able to talk about their family members, their ages, professions, hobbies among other things. Such a text did not only introduce something new to the students but it also enabled them to put into use the grammatical aspects that they had already learned in class.

3.14.4 Usability and relevance of the text content

Usability refers to how functional the content of the text is and how applicable or usable the content of such a text is or may be in the day to day life of the language learners. In the Ugandan context in particular, a text whose content conforms to the mainstream curriculum, therefore contains material or information that is usable for examination purposes. At the end of the academic year or semester, it would be considered to be more valuable and easier to read than all other texts, which may have little to do with the examinations. In this particular case of "learning (French) for examination purposes", the value attached to texts is specifically relegated by an examination-oriented curriculum.

Additionally, the function(s) the text serves or may serve to the foreign language learners, contribute to the value attached to it. The purpose for which a particular text is or may be used defines or determines its value to the user. The purpose could be academic, medical (prescription of drugs), for literacy skills, or even leisure e.g. tips on how to earn quick money. For instance, if a text is for academic purposes, like the case of prescribed texts, are ranked high in value. This is simply because they are used to teach analytical and thinking skills as well as content. These constitute an important requirement in the final examinations at the end of semester. Learners and teachers may indeed attach value to such texts; this value could only have been added at the education level, because such texts are part of the mainstream curriculum. What determines the values of such texts is the likelihood that a text of that kind will be examined at the end of semester or academic year. If there were no such examinations, such texts would certainly not be read intensively since they would have another purpose attached to them.

3.15 Possible Tasks on the basis of a given text

The kinds of tasks that are possible on the basis of a given text determine the value of the text. It is important to note that various tasks can be assigned to a particular text. There are tasks that test the learners' comprehension of the content of the text, reproduction skills. These are texts, which enhance the learners' listening, oral and writing skills; texts that teach analytical, thinking and translation skills. These skills not only make the text valuable to the teacher but also to the learners, because at the end of the lesson or lecture the teacher would have achieved his or her objectives for the language lesson. Similarly, the learners would have acquired the skills the teacher would have wanted them to acquire in a particular lesson or lecture. It should be noted that, the satisfaction derived from a given text causes the user to attach greater or lesser value to it. A text or texts to which great value is attached enhance(s) the learners' motivation, consequently language learning and acquisition and performance of the language learner.

Factors Determining the Value of a Text in Foreign Language Teaching

Various activities can be done using texts in a foreign language class. These are based on the learning objectives and outcomes the teacher would want the students to achieve at the end of a particular lesson. The tasks may range from oral or written comprehension to production of more text as illustrated below.

3.15.1 Vocabulary brainstorming and learning

This could be done before the text is read or better, at a later stage. The teacher can do a vocabulary brainstorm around the class, but with the provision that words must relate to the topic area covered by the text. With very able groups, the teacher could allow learners to intervene if they think the word is not relevant or correct. Learners should not, of course, repeat a word they have already heard. This enables them to improve on their vocabulary and learn new vocabulary in a relaxing way. For instance, in an intermediate French class, the following stanza of the poem *"Les vacances au bord de la mer"* by Michel Jonasz (1974) may be used to study vocabulary related to family (*père, mère* etc...) or activities that can be done by the seashore.

> On allait au bord de la mer
> Avec mon père, ma sœur, ma mère
> On regardait les autres gens
> Comme ils dépensaient leur argent.
> Nous, il fallait faire attention.
> Quand on avait payé le prix d'une location,
> Il ne nous restait pas grand-chose.

3.15.2 Reading

The teacher could read the text aloud or play a recording of the text. This allows students to hear correct pronunciation and encourages them to read slowly and carefully since they have to go at the pace of the reader. It is a good "settling in" activity, but the teacher has to make sure that the learners are actually following the text and listening. The teacher could encourage this by assigning an exercise. For instance, she or he could tell the students that after the reading or listening to the recorded text, someone will be picked randomly to say what the text is generally about. Alternatively, the teacher could ask someone about a particular fact in the text or to read the text aloud for the rest of the class. This makes the learners more attentive and even encourages them to learn how to pronounce words the way their teacher or reader does.

The teacher can get learners to read aloud. Learners generally are happy to do this if the text is not too difficult. It is also a good opportunity for the teacher to monitor and correct the learners' accent and intonation. It is worth noting that learners who read aloud are then to talk ably about what they have read. The process of reading aloud concentrates a learner's mind on both form and meaning of what one is reading, but learners should not be made to read chunks, which are too long.

Reading aloud allows the teacher to work on stress and intonation. In French, for example, the teacher and the learners can practice the rising intonation at the end of words, groups of words and can also work on the slight final syllable stress, which corresponds to the rising intonation. The purpose of such an activity is to teach and enable learners how to speak the language they are learning, and to pronounce correctly the sounds or words of the target language. Another purpose for this activity is to help the learner to be able to make a distinction between different phonemes or sounds as the following excerpt from "*Les vacances au bord de la mer.*" Michel Jonasz (1974) illustrates:

> Et on regardait les bat<u>eau</u>x,
> Le matin on se réveillait t<u>ô</u>t.
> Sur la <u>p</u>lage pendant des h<u>eu</u>res
> On prenait de belles coul<u>eu</u>rs.

From the excerpt above, we note that several phonemes can be taught but the focus in this example is on two phonemes: /o/ and /œ/ and the graphemes that represent the two phonemes. The "Eau" in *bateaux*, "ô" in *tôt* represent the sound /o/ and "eu" in *heures* and *couleurs* represent the sound /œ/. From my own teaching experience, it is more interesting and motivating to the students to learn any aspect of the French language in a given context; the use of text in this case, than introducing it out of context.

Reading also helps learners to develop their skills of reading quickly for gist or specific details. For example, in a text with facts and figures, the teacher may get students to quickly pick out where figures are mentioned, and then get them to note the significance of the figure. This also teaches students to interpret and infer specific information from the text being studied.

3.15.3 Comprehension exercises

The teacher could ask questions in the target language to the learners that test general or detailed comprehension of the text. This is the most traditional activity of all, but one which should not be underrated. Good questioning technique (oral and written) allows the teacher to test grammar points, vocabulary, comprehension and speaking skills of the students. A good Q/A (question/answer) technique will involve the full range of questioning styles including yes/no questions, true/false/not mentioned questions, either/or questions and open-ended questions. The teacher can ask questions orally and get students to write down the answers or respond orally to the questions. Questions can be designed to allow students of all abilities to take part. Asking questions affords many opportunities for listening practice and can be finely tuned to each group. In short, question-answer remains an indispensable tool for the language teacher. This can be illustrated by the following excerpt from "*Les vacances au bord de la mer*"

>On allait au bord de la mer
>Avec mon père, ma sœur, ma mère
>On regardait les autres gens
>Comme ils dépensaient leur argent.
>Nous, il fallait faire attention.
>Quand on avait payé le prix d'une location,
>Il ne nous restait pas grand-chose.
>Alors on regardait les bateaux.
>On suçait des glaces à l'eau.
>Les palaces, les restaurants,
>On ne faisait que passer devant

The following questions could be asked to students: *Where is the scene taking place? Who are the people in the text? What are they doing? Etc.* Such questions test the students' general understanding of the text. The teacher can also ask learners to define words or phrases from the text, for instance; *Il ne nous restait pas grand-chose, on suçait des glaces à l'eau.* This is an extension of question-answer work. Learners, either orally or in writing, have to give the meaning of a word or phrase in the target language.

Additionally, learners could be asked to make up questions in the target language. This enables learners to practice their question structures. However, to be able to do this well, the learners have to carefully decipher meaning. They can then use the questions with a partner for oral practice. This allows for creativity, learning and acquisition of the language.

3.15.4 Making a summary

After having studied the text well in class, the teacher can get the learners to summarize the main points to the whole group or, perhaps better, to a partner. This could be done both orally and in writing. In the latter, the learners have to show good comprehension of the content of the text. This also enables them to get a chance to use written language creatively, mainly through the use of paraphrase.

3.16 Grammar

A text could be used to teach various grammatical aspects such as logical, spatial connectors, tenses, voices, parts of speech and even changing the point of view. For instance, if the text is in the form of a first person narrative, it can be a useful grammatical task to get learners to change the text into the third person. This enables the learners to learn and practice the conjugation of verbs, pronouns and other grammatical aspects in an implicit way. The following text illustrates this fact better:

> Et on regardait les bateaux,
> Le matin on se réveillait tôt.
> Sur la plage pendant des heures
> On prenait de belles couleurs.
> On allait au bord de la mer
> Avec mon père, ma sœur, ma mère.
> Et quand les vagues étaient tranquilles,
> On passait la journée aux îles,
> Sauf quand on pouvait déjà plus.

From the two stanzas of the poem « *Les vacances au bord de la mer* », several grammatical aspects can be taught to beginners or intermediate students. We can teach the imperfect tense (*regardait, se réveillait* etc.), adjectives (*belles, tran-quilles*), possessive adjectives (*mon, ma*), articles (*des, le, la, les*) among other grammatical aspects. The use of texts help to contextualize the language aspects a teacher would want to tackle in a language class. In other words, texts enable language learners to see how grammatical aspects are used in a given context and how they can be applied to real life situations.

3.17 Translation

Translation from the target language into another language could also be one of the activities that can be done when working with texts. This could be from French into English or even in the learner's mother tongue. This is a high level skill, but a good "real-life" practical skill and one which demands detailed comprehension of the text. On the negative side, it is partly a test of the learner's skill with English and, of course, it is not allowing a learner to use the target language as re-quired. It is important to note that it is a very good task, but one which should not be over-used at the expense of tasks done fully in the target language.

In addition, the teacher can ask the learners to re-translate into the target language. After a text has been fully exploited and well-studied, the teacher can make up a text or sentences, for instance, in English, which the learners have to translate into the target language. This is good for recycling vocabulary and language structures. However, this may have the negative effect of encouraging learners to work from English or their mothertongue when they are speaking or writing in the target language.

3.17.1 Contextual Support

Texts may also contain contextual features. These features are not necessarily part of the essential body of the text that may make a text more or less valuable to the learners. These features include clearly stated headings that properly delineate appropriate levels of the text to the learners: pictures, figures, illustrations, tabular information that support the content of the text, the pre-reading of questions, overviews and text organizers that enable the learners to have an insight into the organization of the text. These contextual features make the text more appropriate for the learners to use and to understand the content. These features may add to or diminish the learners' success and satisfaction with a text and therefore boost the learners' motivation and interest in reading particular texts. This means that the value attached to texts also depends on the contextual features that enable learners to clearly follow and understand the content of such texts.

3.17.2 The underlying structure of the text

This simply refers to the type of the text being used and the writing style of the author. The text type and the author's writing style may add or reduce the value of the text. In this, we refer to the type of phrases used, the tense, the use of images or figures of speech, the rhymes and rhythm in the text, which are usually perceived as difficult to understand. These aspects of style may influence the way the language learner perceives and receives the content of the text. Learners tend to like texts that have detectable rhyme and rhythm patterns such as songs. These patterns make the texts highly predictable and interesting. In addition, the melody of songs adds to another layer of contextual support that increases the ability to memorize the texts. This not only enables learners to acquire the language and make the lesson enjoyable but also to attach a value to such texts.

Additionally, the length of text contributes to the value attached to it. Learners tend not to attach any value to long texts for they perceive them as hard to comprehend and time consuming even when the texts may contain valuable information.

3.18 Conclusion

Texts play a major role in foreign language teaching; they are the basis for a language lesson par excellence. Texts are not only a source of reading, structures, and vocabulary, but also a starting point for grammar practice, listening work, pronounciation and intonation practice as illustrated in section 3.1.5 above. Texts exploit the visual dimension and are our prime source of cultural information. Successful language learning requires language users to know the culture underlying the language in order to negotiate meaning as well as to get the meaning across. Good texts can be the basis of a multi-skill lesson conducted in the target language. Based on my personal experience as a French language teacher, the use of texts in teaching has given students valuable opportunities to exploit all aspects of the French language (linguistic, cultural, oral and written expression) as well as to use and develop skills such as deduction of meaning, analytical, critical thinking and presenting ideas in a coherent way. In addition, the use of texts enables the students to develop reading proficiency and improve upon their writing skills. Text value is therefore derived from the multi-functionality of the text, and this is dependent on the perspective from which the text is read, categorized and used by its user. In other words, the way one perceives, receives and uses the text adds or reduces its value.

References

Biber, D. (1988). *Variation across Speech and Writing.* Cambridge, UK: Cambridge University Press.

Crystal, D. (1985).*A dictionary of Linguistics and Phonetics*, 2nd Edition. Oxford: Basil Blackwell Ltd

Crystal, D. (1991). *A Dictionary of Linguistics and Phonetics*, 3nd Edition. Oxford: Blackwell Expert Advisory Group on Language Engineering Standards.(1996, June). *Preliminary Recommendations on Text Typology.* EAGLES Document EAG-TCWG-TTYP/P.

Guariento W. & Morley J. (2001). *Text and task authenticity in the EFL classroom.* ELT Journal 55(4), 347-353

Halliday, M.A.K., & McIntosh, A., &Stevens, P. (1964). *The Linguistic Sciences and Language Teaching.* Longman.

Hammond, J., Burns, A., Joyce, H., Brosnan, D., & Gerot, L. (1992). *English for social purposes: A handbook for teachers of adult literacy.* Sydney: National Centre for English Language Teaching and Research, Macquarie University.

Janasz M. (1974) *Les Vacances au Bord de la Mer* les compositeurs ver 2.wps   ekladata.com/piBWP8VhIX3WB05lPSdEtvUcuCo.pdf.   Accessed 4/01/ 2015

Kilickaya F. (2004-July). *Authentic Materials and Cultural Content in EFL Classrooms*. The Internet TESL Journal, 10 (7) Lave, J., & Wenger, E. (1991). *Situated learning: Legitimate Peripheral participation*. Cambridge, UK: Cambridge University Press.

Lazar, G. (1994). *Using Literature in Lower Level*. ELT Journal, 48

Nunan, D. (1991). *Language Teaching Methodology*. London: Prentice Hall International Schmidt. Clint (Spring 2010)"Live Mocha and the power of Social Language Learning" IH Journal of Education and Development http:// seed camp .com/pages/mini-seed camp; 10

Shanahan, D. (1997). Articulating the relationship between language, literature and culture: Toward a new agenda for foreign language teaching and research, in *The Modern Language Journal*, 81(2), 164-174

Thom, N. T. T. (2008). *Using literary texts in language Teaching*. VNU Journal of Science, Foreign Languages, 24, 120-126

Tseng, Y. (2002). *A Lesson in Culture*. ELT Journal, 56(1), 11-21

Wade, E.S. & Moje, E. B.(2000).*The role of Text in Class-room Learning*. The Handbook of Reading Research, Vol III.

CHAPTER FOUR
INTEGRATING INTERNET-BASED MATERIALS IN FOREIGN LANGUAGE TEACHING AT THE TERTIARY LEVEL: THE CASE OF ARABIC LANGUAGE TEACHING AT MAKERERE UNIVERSITY IN UGANDA

Ebraheem Ssali[1]

Abstract

In this article, the writer defines the integration of Internet -based materials into the teaching of Arabic and explains the advantages of integrating Internet based materials in the whole process of foreign language teaching. He goes ahead to demonstrate his experience of using Internet based materials in the process of teaching Arabic at Makerere University in a bid to move from the traditional methods and embrace the new technological trends in pedagogy. This experience is premised on a fact, that Internet has become one of the most important and indispensable source of information in any academic field including the foreign language teaching at different levels of learning all over the world. It is also premised on the fact that there are very many sites with materials for different language which can be very resourceful in enriching and enhancing the process of foreign language learning and teaching at tertiary level. The article ends with some pointers towards improving the use of Internet–based materials to teach better Arabic in a non-Arabic speaking community.

Key words: *Internet based materials, teacher determined lesson, teacher facilitated lesson, learner determined lesson.*

4.1 Introduction

There is no doubt that Internet has become one of the most important and indispensable sources of information in any academic field, including the teaching of foreign languages at different levels of learning. From the

---

1 Ebraheem Ssali is a Ph.D. Candidate of Arabic Studies at the Islamic University in Uganda (I.U.I.U). He holds an M.A (Religious Studies) from Makerere University, B.A (Arabic and Islamic Studies) from World Islamic Call College, Tripoli, Dip in American Civilisation New York University U.S.A, Post Graduate Diploma in Education (I.U.I.U). He is the Co-ordinator of Arabic Language in the Department of European and Oriental languages (DEOL) in the School of Languages, Literature and Communications, College of Humanities and Social Sciences, Makerere University. He is also a translator and an interpreter of the same language.

0.1% Internet users in Uganda in 2000, to 10% in 2010 according to the 'Internet World Statistics,' indeed, there are thousands of Ugandans who refer to the Internet constantly to access the thousands of websites and the millions of documents with materials for teaching and learning different languages. These sites and links can be very resourceful in enriching and enhancing the process of imparting foreign language skills at the tertiary level. Being an English speaking country, Uganda's social environment offers very limited chances of accompanying the student of Arabic outside the formal class time. Yet our biggest proportion of students, are adult beginners at the tertiary level. In universities like the Islamic University in Uganda at Mbale, the beginners account for 60 % (I.UIU; 2014). In Makerere University, they account for 70 % (MAK; 2014). These students without doubt need learning sources to listen, hear, understand and practice the language besides what the teacher can provide. However, there is a very big challenge of how to choose the most effective Internet sources and select the best pedagogical approaches, that can yield the desired results basing on numerous researches carried out in this field.

In this article, I will endeavour to explore how I have been choosing the material used in Arabic teaching and how best these materials can be used in improving teaching and learning. I observe from the outset the fact that most Arabic language instructors and lecturers at the tertiary level, and the learners in these institutions, are still heavily relying on the traditional sources and methods. Despite the availability of such methods to the majority of tertiary institutions, whether rural or urban, they do not offer authentic sources, where we get the conversations or exercises presented by the Arabic native speaker (**Al-Muhadaatha**) like the material we find on the Internet.

In this article, I outline some of the best and most popular sites from the so many as ranked highest by some researchers that are available on the Internet. In the process of doing this, I will focus on defining the interment based materials for foreign language teaching in the context of the Arabic language teaching in Uganda. Then I will go ahead to outline the richest sources that I have used in respect of the most common usage in Makerere University and other Universities in the region. Lastly, I will make suggestions on how they can be effectively utilized in class according to my class experience in Arabic.

The integration of Internet based materials in foreign language teaching basically entails, as Dr. Jaroslaw Krajka (2010) points out, "the use of materials that can be acquired from the Internet as opposed to the usual and traditional sources of different languages' textbooks". In this case, the Internet becomes the main source of materials and the basis for language class work instead of the course book ... The same expert in foreign language teaching, also states that the Internet-based lesson may also make use of other means of communication made possible by the Web, namely email, chat, discussion groups or video conferencing (Krajkara, 2010).

4.2 Advantages of using Internet based materials in the arabic Language Class

In contexts where the source language is located far away from the community of the student, as is the case for Arabic here at Makerere, and in view of material scarcity, the Internet is gradually becoming a major point of reference of learning and teaching in all the areas of teaching this language and its rich culture. More so, this trend is of greater importance given the fact that at the tertiary level, the young adults that register with us come from varying cultural backgrounds and for the whole class of Beginners, it is their first contact with Arabic. Secondly, the time allocated to the subject in the programme of Bachelor of Arts in Arts and Bachelor of Arts in Social Sciences is very constrained[2]. Within that limited time frame. This kind of pedagogical approach certainly offers us a faster and effective means of ensuring that the desired results, as stated in the Arabic Beginner's curriculum, of getting the tertiary learner to acquire an acceptable working knowledge of Arabic, can be achieved within the prescribed three years. The integration of the Internet in the whole process becomes a means of extending contact with the adult learner so that he or she can access an unlimited amount of materials in different modes, shapes and styles at their own leisure. The content of Internet materials surpasses the teacher's traditional sources in terms of the abundance, speed, and variety. Commenting on such applications of the Internet in the education process, Bill Gates (1998), the CEO of the Microsoft Corporation, said that "... the information highway will help to raise educational standards for everyone in future generations, and will pave the way for the emergence of new methods of teaching, as it provides a much wider scope of learning and teaching materials. This will happen by learning using computer, which will be a starting point for continuous learning from the computer its self". Based on such views of the good teachers, we deemed it suitable to play not only the role of introducing students to how to find the information online, but also to prepare to be aware of when to teach, when to test, when to caution and when to raise attention, as we were learning these best practices along the way on the Internet.

---

2   Arabic is allocated four hours per course per week. The Beginners take two Core Courses of Arabic. The Advanced majoring in Arabic have eight hours per week of 2 Cores and 2 Electives.

Various education specialists have advanced various reasons as to why integrating Internet use in any education process is very crucial. Such educationalists are echoed by (Williams, 1995) who sums up the principal reasons for the use of the Internet in any learning and teaching process as follows:

With Internet, it is possible to access any information from any part of the world. In an Arabic learning situation like this one, the Internet enables our Ugandan students to pick texts, images and speech from all the corners of the Arab world, which avails them with an opportunity to appreciate the variety of dialects, styles and cultures of the Arabic speaking peoples.

The use of Internet plays a significant role in harnessing the collaborative and teamwork learning due to the volume of information available on the net. Because it is too much, it becomes very difficult for an individual student to search all the sites on the net at the same time. So this avails the teacher with an opportunity to use the team-work method with students. Each student can be assigned research work in a specific area whereby, they meet afterwards to discuss what has been discovered. For Beginners who are struggling with limited vocabulary, this can prove very productive.

The Internet helps to connect to the world at a very high speed with very minimum costs. With just one screen that is available for small number class use, one can connect to a cultural or media event as it unfolds in different time zones all over the world in real time.

The use of Internet can help to provide more than one method of teaching because it serves as a large library, where all the necessary and required materials are avail-able, in different learning formats whether easy or difficult. These online educational programmes and materials are available for different levels learners.

In the case of teaching Arabic in Makerere University, it has been interesting to view the differences of perspectives on cultural and media events as they were unfolding. Such was the case of teaching about Idd celebrations in different countries of the Arab World, in a paper of Introduction to Arab Culture and Civilization at beginners' level, which was viewed and commented upon as it actually takes place in different Arab countries Sudan, Yemen and Saud Arabia from videos recorded and downloaded on the net, in 2012. For the purposes of team work, the Internet based material was particularly helpful in enhancing the comprehension and speech skill of learners through groups. The Internet has also helped us to encourage the slower beginners to work with the faster ones outside the class premises. The faster ones help the slower learners to revise and understand what the lecturer has introduced in class using some other methods, which are most appropriate for that group of learners. For instance, the pronounciation of pharyngeal letters seem to be easier to master using pronunciation tool that is available at Memrise web site for non-native learners of Arabic rather than the usual method.

4.3 Experiences in Using Internet Sources for teaching Arabic

The following class sessions of trying out Internet based materials in Arabic teaching were mainly conducted during the following academic years 2011/2012/2103/2014). This was mainly with the students of Beginners level Arabic (ARB) throughout all its levels. In terms of numbers, ARB first year had 18 students, ARB second year 10 students, and ARB third year 6 students.

4.4 Busuu Sources at http://www.busuu.com/

This is a social network for learning languages and which is free of charge. All I had to do was register with my email ad-dress and I accessed a lot of material in **Arabic**. The pedagogical units work independently of one another and they are self-paced. It was comfortable to pick one unit, which we needed as a supplement for the course book Arabic for beginners (Book 2) for second year and Book 3 for third year. Busuu has more than 45 million users globally. With many of them sending in tips and comments on the use of the different units in different settings. This provides a very wide social network for sharing lessons in language learning through online for and the different applications. We accessed equally the free audio-visual teaching supports, which were most interesting from the learners' perspective for lectures on a typical Arabian Wedding **(Haflat Alzfaaf)**, and celebrating the new born **(Al- Aqeeqa)**.

This site was offering all levels of Arabic based on Common European Framework of Reference levels (A1, A2, B1 and B2). The study material for the Arabic language was broken down into around 150 units like it is in other Languages. These units had drills of multiple-choice questions, speaking assignments, and writing assignments. It is mainly the first two types, which were of interest to our classes in Arabic. The multimedia material, such as oral multiple-choice questions was useful for both student practice in class and self-applied tutorials after. In group work after class, students could correct one another's work. While one pronounced the answer the other checked on the available tutor correction. They also conversed with the lecturer via the chat-window but unfortunately this was mostly in English.

From the chats that I followed, I could observe that the plat-form encourages collaborative learning. Students were learning and practicing their listening, writing, reading and speaking with assistance from the community of native speakers. This was of great importance in our class because some students as I mentioned before were getting in contact with Arabic for the first time and some were not from the Moslem community. This is the category of students that enjoyed most the chats with the native speakers of Arabic. Given the fact that most students now have smart phones, they could download freely the applications for their phones. In a nutshell, I could say that the site offers a rich source of a well-rounded approach to language learning. There were also options for further reading, which I think can be made use of in the Advanced Arabic classes.

4.5 Livemocha at livemocha.com/pages/languages/learn-arabic/

The Livemocha package offers online language learning materials in 38 languages, including Arabic. It also provides a platform for speakers to interact with and help each other learn new languages. This was the more interesting application for our students in Arabic. With the 12 million registered members from 196 countries around the globe, there was always someone available to consult at any given time (Schmidt, 2010). As a teacher I would not have managed to be available all day and all night for the beginners unending questions. So the experience showed me that technology can offer a continuous service of consultation in foreign language learning. This is a very big bonus to our students because of the limited time allocated to language teaching as mentioned earlier. This site was free for use upon registering.

It is the concept of utilizing the power of social networking sites for language learning that distinguishes most of this site from the others that we tried in our classes. There was always an active virtual participation and exchange that allowed the students to learn practical skills, and improve the level and quality of Arabic language proficiency and fluency.

Unlike the Busuu method where units were broken down by content, Livemocha's lessons are broken down into target skills, with reading, writing, listening and speaking each studied separately. Each lesson presents new material, breaks it down for the learner, then reassemble the parts so the student can apply what they have learned. Because of its explanation of the process and the arrangement by skill this method attracted a lot of popularity in the third year Arabic class. Students found it very useful for practicing pronunciation and conversational skills in specific contexts- politics, business, sports ...etc.

4.6 Memrise at *www.memrise.com/courses/english/arabic/*

Memrise is an online learning tool whose courses were created by its community. Although we used its courses to learn Arabic, they can also be used for other academic and non-academic functions. Memrise uses flashcards that have been gathered form users enrich the speed of learning according to the learner. Memrise applications were available for download on both the App Store (iOS) and Google Play, which are quite accessible to students, on their phones.

This site uses mnemonic flashcards (mems) that use your pre-existing knowledge to help remember new vocabulary. For example, in learning the alphabets, they give you the letters to be learned accompanied by its sound in addition of a mem to help you remember those letters. A good example is the 1st letter of the Arabic Alphabets, which sounds as follows **(Alif)** this is accompanied with a **leaf** flash card, reason being that the reading of the above word rhymes with the sound of that letter. Another example is the letter **(Lam)**; with this they use a flash card of a lamb, which helps the learner to remember the letter. This is what is meant when they say that they use the pre-existing knowledge of a learner to make the learning of the new language more effective. The pictorial cards were very motivational for the real Beginners in the first year.

4.7 Approaches to Using Internet Based Material

As indicated in the introduction, one of the objectives of this article is to consider how best one can exploit these materials in order to achieve the best results. I will thus proceed to examine approaches I used in the Arabic language classes.

4.8 Teacher-Determined Lessons

In this approach, the teacher takes a centre stage and uses the computer as an online electronic workbook. I used this approach when I was introducing a new grammatical and cultural study objective. I would pre-screen the reading materials; select the text for use or cultural image from Internet-based resource. I would design the reading and comprehension activities and make them available through my Web page on the class laptop. After setting up everything, I would then invite the students to participate in the lecture.

The pedagogical advantage of this approach lies in using the text-specific approach for exploring authentic cultural documents whether textual or images. Pre-selecting and preparing the readings, enables the lecturer to present the contents and tasks according to the students' proficiency level. For the Second years for instance, I would ease the reading tasks by guiding the learners through the texts. I would provide definitions of some words not included in the online glossary.

The conversational tasks were later assigned as support to the reader's comprehension process. The method offered a good logical order progressing from textual, to linguistic and finally to cultural features.

Given the learners' background of very limited contact with Arabic and low proficiency levels, the reading is guided with instructions, to help manage the text and checks on comprehension. This approach had its pedagogical strength at the tertiary level of learning the foreign language. Our experience may have reflected what Cobb and Stevens (1996) cited in Brandl (2002) point out in their analysis of this approach:

"Second language readers may not have automated one or more of the component processes of reading in the second language, such as word decoding and recognition, resulting in working memory overload and diversion of attention away from the construction of a text model. Or, at a higher processing level, readers may not be familiar with semantic or discourse schemata, specific to the culture of the second language, so that they have no pre-activated scaffolding to help them summarize and organize the details of the incoming text, and quickly face overload." (p.122)

In our case, we avoided overload and diversion by preparing and ensuring that the text will be within reach of the learners' low proficiency of Arabic. We selected what we deemed "digestible" and provided supplementary information where necessary.

Furthermore, in particular at the beginning of second year level, the text-specific approach to reading allowed me to sup-port the vulnerable readers in decoding and recognition of vocabulary. For example, I would provide specific word glosses and give tips where necessary on word recognition training. There was no distraction of the readers rather, these additional gloss props-ensured more fluent reading of the selection and enhanced comprehension of the text.

This approach tended to lend itself well for the lower levels of beginners instruction. We noted however, that the second year students' responses to reading tasks were limited by the capacity of preset packages available for them. But this could be supplemented with some true/false or matching options prepared in advance on the teacher's screen. These would be photocopied for use in class. Open-ended responses that worked best were limited to one word answers. For the writing tasks, I relied on separate questions set for my intervention as instructor to assess the students' work.

4.9 Teacher-Facilitated Lessons

Using this approach, I would once again as an instructor, determine a particular topic and set of goals for the lesson in question. I would go ahead to pre-screen and select a set of sites to ensure its contents are appropriate for their pedagogical goals. Here as well, through a particular task design, I would facilitate the students' reading process and guide the learners to explore a variety of pre-selected resources, thus as Pennington (2015) suggests, I would be providing a clear goal to be accomplished by the students.

The tasks are designed in a way that "they are not so broad that students wander aimlessly through the material yet open enough to provide multiple paths, outcomes, and interpretations, which can form the basis for subsequent classroom interaction" (Furstenberg, 1997:24 cited in Brandl, 2002). In this way I, as the instructor, I would still have some control over the number and kinds of Internet sites that the students are going to access. Despite the restriction, the learner would still have some autonomy since in assigning the tasks, I would provide the learners with a choice in the sites so that they choose which one to accesses and explore. Such tasks would include task comparisons, gathering factual information, descriptions, and short summaries. The outcome of the student assignments is clearly defined, but a little open-ended. In this approach, my role can best be described as a guide and facilitator. The students were following my leads but they would get to explore the contents themselves after class, especially the cultural documents needing a bit of research.

This approach has the highest potential, especially with learners at intermediate level,- the third years who could at least gamble through the texts on their own. They no longer needed 100% of my presence for the exploration of the selected materials, and no longer required many close interventions from the instructor, to ensure that the comprehension process was on track. What was noticeable was that as the open-ended structure of this type of lesson design made the students' answers less predictable than in a text-specific approach. As an instructor I had to be prepared for diverse answers from students. Therefore, this required that the assessment criteria to be put in place in advance for students' evaluation. It was also necessary to estimate and control the students' time being spent on tasks. This was to ensure that they complete all the assigned pedagogical tasks.

4.10 Learner-Determined Lessons

This approach is entirely learner-centred. The learners deter-mine the topics, reading materials, and the way they go about them. They decide on the process and the product. They formulate the goals, identify Internet-based resources, and make a decision on how the outcomes should be evaluated. In this way, the students take on the roles of self-driven and autonomous learners, and take full charge and responsibility for their outcomes. The teacher only gets involved in the role of a facilitator, offering support and guidance throughout the process as much as necessary.

This approach, we noticed, could be very good for project-based learning, like the Research Project course in Arabic of third year Advanced, which will be our next target in 2015. Its benefits have been described by educationalists like Stoller (1997) as follows:

- Project work focuses on content learning rather than on specific language targets. Real-world subject matters and topics of interest to students can become central to projects.
- Project work is student-centered, though the teacher plays a major role in offering support and guidance throughout the process.
- Project work is cooperative rather than competitive. Students can work on their own, in small groups, or as a class to complete a project, sharing resources, ideas, and expertise along the way.
- Project work leads to the authentic integration of skills and processing of information from varied sources, mirroring real-life tasks.
- Project work culminates in an end product that can be shared with others, giving the project a real purpose and a real process towards the end point.
- Project work is potentially motivating, stimulating, empowering, and challenging. It usually results in building students' confidence, self-esteem, and autonomy as well as improving students' language skills, content learning, and cognitive abilities.

The major strength of this approach lies in its constructionist approach to learning. Just like Chun & Plass (2000; 160 cited in Brandl) observe: "Constructionist approaches to learning advocate, allowing learners not only to interact directly with information to be learned, but also to add their own information and construct their own relationships". Learning in this project approach is seen as a process in which the learner is cognitively involved in seeking answers, making generalizations about the foreign language, and testing the arguments they have generated. By taking a major role in planning and negotiating the course content, the students become active contributors to their language learning rather than being passive recipients of knowledge.

In the course of using Internet based resources, we noted that the use of the Internet for research purposes requires a variety of searching skills. It demands knowledge of different search engines and how they work. Furthermore, it assumes the user has some information-seeking skills. Now for some of our students who were not comfortable with computer usage, this demanded that they first have to learn how to search the Web. This was the case mostly for students who had come from the rural-based secondary schools. Luckily, web searching is a skill that they took on willingly, going as far as investing their own money in after class access of Internet cafés. As they got more comfortable with Web searching, they were completing their tasks with much more speed. This suggests the need to integrate information-seeking skills into the curriculum of teaching Arabic, as part of the technical competencies that we can attach to the research project.

The open-ended approach to exploring Internet-based resources requires language learners to have a relatively solid foundation in their language proficiency skills. This makes the project-based approach most appropriate for the Advanced Arabic learners in the Ugandan context. Our experience also showed us that the tasks on such Internet-based materials or readings for the research project are best assigned in stages on a long-term basis; in our case for an end of semester report. In the same way the teacher-facilitated approach took me, the instructor a lot of preparation time, the open-ended approach demands time from the students to nurture their product. This can make the assessment process subjective and time consuming. Therefore, it is recommended that assessment instruments are worked out in advance to indicate how each student, besides the student's product, will be evaluated.

4.11 Technological Considerations

With regards to the teacher centered approach, the development of reading lessons as demonstrated in this approach may be time consuming and tiresome. To create attractive and effective activities, skills and expertise in language pedagogy, instructional design and knowledge in programming are required. The latter may include experience with HTML editors or Internet-based authoring packages and use of graphic programmes. Such technological skills are recommended for inclusion in, in-service training of lecturers. Some usage of Internet-based resources may also require copyright clearance; this needs to be budgeted for in advance.

The development and preparation of the teacher-facilitated, Internet-based lessons as described in the second approach is fairly minimal. The pre-screening and selection process of the Internet sites may constitute the most time-consuming part, which makes knowledge about search engines and how they operate imperative. Usually, the Web sites run by associations of language communities are the best point of entry as far as technological skills are concerned. However, this approach of "guiding or facilitating" seems to be the most attractive approach for the intermediate foreign language classroom. Some experience with an HTML editing programme may be required if instructions and activities are to be provided online; but most word processors allow for the translation of a text file into an HTML document. In our case, these instructions on learning tasks were provided on a separate a photocopied worksheet that could be distributed for circulation [3]

One of the drawbacks of using authentic sites is that, the instructor needs to keep track of the functionality of the links. URL addresses constantly change and sites do disappear. Therefore, the teacher has to constantly search for alternative sites in case some sites are no longer accessible.

In the case of the open-ended or learner determined approach, the technological skills required to implement this approach are minimal. In order to provide guidance to the students on searching the Internet, the teacher has to be well versed with the knowledge about Web browsers, search engines and their effective use.

4.12 Concluding Remarks

The experience of integrating Internet-based materials in the teaching of Arabic may have had its few technological challenges, like limited access to the Internet after class. In general, it was an enjoyable and educative process for both the instructor and the learner. The benefits linked to integrating Internet resources in the teaching of foreign languages like Arabic, outweigh by far the constraints we encountered during our adventure. Competencies like expertise in language pedagogy, instructional design, and some programming, which are indispensable for the instructor's need to be included in the in-service teacher training. Minimal training of students in web searching would be very good for leveling the ground (in terms of computer skills) at the beginning. The instructor will trade off time usually spent on supervising the language class, to with a constant virtual check on what the students are doing. The use of Internet-based materials certainly changes the ways tasks are done, and therefore the assessment instruments need to be worked out in advance in order to indicate how each student will be evaluated.

---

[3] The Centre for Languages and Communication Services to which the Arabic section is affiliated provides photocopying and reproduction services free of charge.

References

Dr. Jaroslaw Krajka, "Introduction to Internet based Language teaching" http://www.latefl.org

Chun, D. M., & Plass, J. L. (2000). "Networked multimedia environments for second language acquisition", In M. Warshauer & R. Kern (Eds.), *Network-based language teaching: Concepts and practice* (pp. 151-170). New York: Cambridge University Press.

Cobb T. & Stevens V. (1996). "A principled consideration of Computers and reading in a second language", In M. C. Pennington (Ed.) *The Power of CALL* (pp. 115-136). Houston, TX: Athelstan.

Davis, J. (1989). "Facilitating effects of marginal glosses on Foreign language reading", In *Modern Language Journal*, 73, pp. 41-48.

Fidel, R., Davies, R. K., Douglass, M. H., Holder, J. K., Hopkins, C. J., Kushner, E. J., Miyagishima, B. K., &

Toney, C. D. (1999) "A visit to the information mall: Web Searching behaviour of high school students", In *Journal of the American Society for Information Science*, 50(1), pp. 24-37 Furstenberg, G. (1997). "Teaching with technology: What is at stake?" In *ADFL Bulletin*, 28(3), pp. 21-25. http:// www.ishraf.gotevot.edu.sa/qiraat/147.doc

"Busuu.Online S.L Private Company information - Business Week" investing.busunessweek.com, 18-12-2014 "Learn a new language with Busuu" www.lifehacker.com http:// en.wikipedia.org/wiki/Duolingo/ cite_note-DuoBlog http://eu.techcrunch.com/2010/11/17-europas-the finalist http:www.boston.com/business/technology, 18-01-2015

Holec, H. (1981). *Autonomy and foreign language learning*. Oxford, England: Pergamon Press for the Council of Europe.

Nahl D. & Harada V. H. (1996). Composing Boolean search Statements: Self-confidence, content analysis, search logic, and error. *School Library Media Quarterly*, 24, pp. 199-207.

Omaggio-Hadley, A. (2001). Teaching language in context (3rd edition). Boston: Heinle & Heinle. Stoller F. L., (1997). Project work. A means to promote language content in *Forum* 35(4), pp.1-10.

PART TWO
FOREIGN LANGUAGES: PEDAGOGY

CHAPTER FIVE
LITERACY CONSTRAINTS ON FLUENCY IN FOREIGN LANGUAGES AT UNIVERSITY LEVEL IN UGANDA

Titus Ogavu[1]

Abstract

In Uganda, French is taught as a foreign language since the main and official language used in the country is English. The pedagogy of French like any other language aims at transmitting the basic language skills (listening, speaking, reading and writing) to learners. Studies carried out on literacy flu-ency in French, in other universities indicated that several constraints are hindering learners' ability to read and write in French. For instance, the content of the teaching materials used can hardly turn students into good readers and writers particularly as expected in the institutions. This is due to the fact that reading and writing, which are the key elements for developing in literacy are not well emphasized in the French programmes. Consequently, students taking languages in institutions of higher learning have a low reading culture in the language. In order to boost their ability to read and write fluently for academic purposes such as research and translation, students need to acquire supplementary literacy skills in the process of learning French at the university level.

Key words: *foreign languages, literacy, fluency, constraints, teaching materials*

5.1 Introduction

A foreign language is a language, which is not indigenous to a country but is taught and learned in the country for distinct reasons like globalization, cultural insight et al.

Usually, it is taught and learned alongside the official or the

---

[1] Associate Professor **Titus OGAVU** was in the Department of Languages and Communication, Faculty of Arts and Social Sciences at Kyambogo University, Kampala, Uganda. He was a researcher and was teaching French as a foreign language, Francophone Literature and Research Methods. The author was a member of the Association of Teachers of French in Uganda, (APFO) International Reading Association (IRA), Reading Association of Uganda (RAU) and Chairman of the Reading Council of Central Uganda (RAU). This Chapter was his last research work and was published shortly after his death. May his soul rest in eternal peace.

indigenous languages of the country, which are the main local means of communication. Dictionary.com's 21st Century Lexicon (2003-2014) defines a foreign language as "*any language used in a country other than one's own; a language that is studied mostly for cultural insight*". Be as it may, for the purpose of the theme of this article, in Uganda's case, we shall consider all non-native languages taught and learned in Uganda and used by different communities in the country as foreign languages. The consideration excludes English, which is the official language in the country and serves as the medium of instruction. This also excludes Kiswahili, which is the regional language in the Great Lakes Region of Africa and holds an important political status in the East African Community in particular.[2]

Although several foreign languages are taught and learned in Uganda, literacy in the languages leaves a lot to be desired, as it is hampered by several constraints that limit fluency of their usage. Fluency is considered as the speed at which one can read, write, speak, and listen. In a bid to establish standards of measuring literacy, UNESCO (2005) published a working definition of literacy as; "the ability to identify, understand, interpret, create, communicate and compute, using printed and written materials associated with varying contexts". According to the same source, literacy evolves "along a continuum of learning, enabling individuals to achieve their goals, develop their knowledge and potential and participate fully in the community and wider society". The UNESCO yard-stick of literacy clearly illustrates that literacy is more than being able to read and write.

Furthermore, Powell as cited by UNESCO (1962) further re-fined the definition of functional literacy by asserting that "a person is literate when he has acquired the essential knowledge and skills which enable him to engage in all those activities in which literacy is required for effective functioning in his group and community, and whose attainment in reading, writing, and arithmetic make it possible for him to continue to use these skills towards his own and the community's development". We note the emphasis put on the use of functional literacy skills not only for individual growth, but also for the community's development.

---

[2] The Swahili language or Kiswahili is a Bantu language and the mother tongue of the Swahili people. It is spoken by various communities inhabiting the African Great Lakes region and other parts of Southeast Africa, including Tanzania, Kenya, Uganda, Rwanda, Burundi, Mozambique and the Democratic Republic of Congo. Around five million people speak Swahili as their mother tongue and it is used as a *lingua franca* in much of Southeast Africa.

In addition to recognizing the literacy skills that have been discussed above, Sensenbough (1990) goes on to emphasize the issue of permanency by asking what an individual has to do to be forever literate. The writer contends that modern culture involves many forms of language within which ways of thinking, working, negotiating and reading with experience are encoded. Being consistently literate in practicing foreign languages as stressed by Sensenbough is hardly demonstrated in Ugandan communities. Moreover, according to the National Curriculum Development Centre (NCDC) in the Curasse Project (2013), which is trying to reconceptualize the Lower Secondary curriculum, Life Education concepts are being focused upon at the individual, peer and community levels. Literacy is fundamental to all these three levels of learning and development as it unlocks access to the wider base of knowledge. The Curasse Project affirms that "language and literacy are of personal, social and economic importance. Our ability to use language lies at the centre of the development and expression of our emotions, our thinking, our learning and our sense of personal identity". If this has not been happening in the past in Uganda, our explanation is that, it is due to existing constraints.

From the foregoing discussion, it can be deduced that the primary sense of literacy still underlies the lifelong intellectual process, of gaining meaning from a critical interpretation of the written or printed text. The point to note here is that key to this lifelong process since the cognitive progression of skills that begins with the ability to understand spoken words, decode written ones and culminate in the deep understanding of any learning document. Reading development involves a range of complex language underpinnings including awareness of speech sounds (phonology), spelling patterns (orthography), word meaning (semantics), grammar (syntax) and patterns of word formation (morphology), all of which provide a necessary platform for reading fluency and comprehension. Once these skills are acquired the reader can attain full language literacy. At university level, we expect full literacy to be manifested through the abilities to approach printed material with critical analysis, inference and synthesis; to write with accuracy and coherence; and to use information and insights from text as the basis for informed decisions and creative thought.

Okech (2004) quotes Scribner and Cole (1981) who stated that literacy is "not simply knowing how to read and write a particular script but applying this knowledge for specific purposes in specific contexts of use". This relates well to the policy statement of the Uganda NCDC that alerts us to the fact that being literate increases opportunities for individuals in all aspects of life, including laying the foundation for lifelong learning and work, and contributing strongly to the development of all human capacities. The centre, in its "Languages Learning Area" policy 2013) further affirms that language learning contributes to the development of critical and creative thinking. It develops competence in listening and speaking, reading and writing. Learners acquire the personal, interpersonal and team-working skills, which are so important in life and in the world of work.[3] For the purpose of this article, we distinguish intellectual literacy learner, the one we have described above, from the basic literacy learner defined by Spiegel and Sunderland (2006) as "someone who is still learning to read a short simple text and struggles to write a simple sentence independently." Our assumption is that, it is the intellectual literacy learner who is better disposed to use the already imparted skills for foreign language learning.

5.2 Constraints to literacy fluency

In linguistics, as Professor Luisanna Fodde (2013/2014) puts it, "a constraint is defined as a restriction on the operation of a linguistic rule or the occurrence of a linguistic construction". Every text that the French learner is exposed to has its context of situation and a context of culture: a dimension of variation and a dimension of values. French as a foreign language has a wide range of situations in which it can be used and which are not easy to define to Anglophone students. But literacy fluency provides us situations with which we can associate texts. It also offers a wide variety of linguistic features that help us when grappling with the identities of a text. The cultural and situational constraints embedded in the language learning social context in Uganda are similar to those summarized in the figure below by Luisanna Fodde (2013/2014):

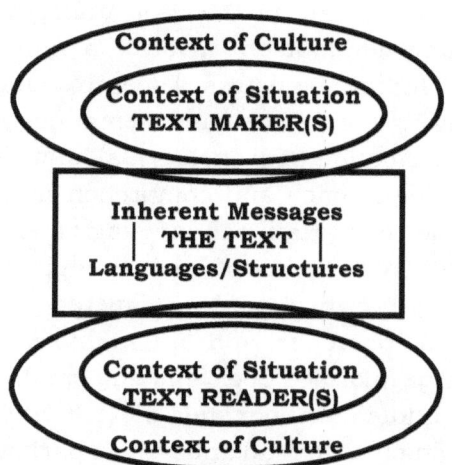

Figure 5.2.1: *A View of the Reading Situation*

Source : *Luisanna Fodde: Lecture Notes, Universta di Cagliari*

---

3 Languages Learning Area: Local Languages Syllabus, National Curriculum Development Centre, 2013

This article delves further into the cultural and situational factors that Fodde exposes as contributors to limitations to literacy fluency in learning a language. However, whereas Fodde's social context was that of Italian students learning English, this article applies the framework to the learning of French as a foreign language in universities in Uganda. At the university level in Uganda, literacy in French is severely hampered by a variety of constraints stretching from the political, through the social to the linguistic factors as will be discussed below.

5.3 Constraints to Literacy Fluency in French

Language policy

Christ, (1995:75) as cited by Wodak (2006) states that a language policy refers to the sum of those "top-down" and "bottom-up" political initiatives through which a particular language or languages is or are supported in their public validity, their functionality, and their dissemination. Wodak (2006); goes on to observe that "language policy and language ideologies both necessarily influence and define the prestige and value of languages in a linguistic market... via language policies. Certain languages, genres and discourses (and their users) acquire more or less prestige and "power". That is how, non-conducive language policies have come to constrain the promotion of language learning in Uganda.

The history of Uganda Education Language Policies falls into three distinct eras. First era is the colonial period (1894-1962), which includes the Post World War II Period (1944-1961). Second era is, the post-colonial period (1963-1988). Thirdly, the present policy based on the *Education for National Integration and Development,* Report of Education Policy Review Commission, (1989). Although Language policies in universities as well as in lower institutions of learning in Uganda are supposed to be based on "life education concepts", they do not explicitly promote literacy in foreign languages for functional motives particularly on the global scene.

In her foreword to the "Languages Learning Area Local Languages Syllabus" (2013), the Minister of Education and Sports, Uganda, Hon. Lt. Jessica Alupo, states that the study of languages contributes to the acquisition and development of literacy and communication skills. She further affirms that "response to the spoken word and written texts encourages critical thinking; interaction and production of language, e.g. in role plays, conversations and writing in different formats and for different purposes, fosters intelligibility, self-expression and creativity. Learners develop personal, interpersonal and team-working skills, which can be applied in everyday life and in the field of work". It is worth noting that the ministerial statement does not stress communication in foreign languages. This should be stressed in the language policy as a complementary necessity to boost local languages for international interaction. Unfortunately, the language policy in Uganda and the curriculum of educational institutions of learning in the country, do not stress the need for incorporating multilingualism and foreign languages in their programmes of literacy development.

For instance, in the circular N° 20/2008, titled *New Policy in the Delivery of Secondary Education*, issued by the Ministry of Education and addressed to the head teachers of secondary schools. It was declared that teaching and learning of languages had been grouped into language areas, namely, foreign languages (French, German, Arabic...) and local languages. In a paradoxical turn of events, the learners' choice from the latter cluster was made compulsory; rendering it practically almost impossible for students to pick foreign languages and use them fluently. However, due to some nationwide outcry and criticism of the policy, the circular was henceforth with-drawn, but the impact on practice could not be retracted. Some schools had already put a halt to the teaching of French and German[4] and they had to go through a lengthy re-negotiation with parents and the Ministry in order to reverse the decision they had taken. This implied that the ministry did not make thorough consultation with the stakeholders be-fore dispensing the said document. Even without being implemented, it can be noted that, the said policy had a negative impact on the teaching and learning foreign languages in the country because head teachers started to doubt the validity of teaching some languages. Logically, the reinforcement of teaching and learning of foreign languages in secondary schools greatly contributes to literacy fluency in the languages in universities. Ideologically, the language policies seem to be sending a different message.

5.4 Foreign Language Learning Environment and Literacy Accuracy

In forty or so public and private universities in Uganda, the majority of students who study French in 25% of the universities live in a background and an environment, that are mainly English speaking. This renders it hard for them to use the literacy skills acquired in that language to express socio-political and economical issues in their environment in French. This is partly due to fact that they lack the vocabulary and proficiency to think and articulate directly in French outside the learning centres. They cannot

---

4   The choice to teach foreign languages in Uganda continues to be optional. Some schools opted to put emphasis on Languages like Luganda which have a strong cultural backing, especially in the Central Region of Uganda.

practice what Hilliard (1981) recommends when he states that "daily usage of a language for communication at school and at home enhances learners' interest in communicating in a language". Unfortunately therefore, what is learned in class remains in class and cannot be reinforced by language constructs produced in discourses outside the learning institution.

5.5 Attitude and literacy in foreign language

The Education system in Uganda makes literacy in English mandatory at all levels of learning. In addition, the fact that English is the official language and medium of instruction and in the country has persistently kept the attitude of most Ugandans contented with mastering English only. They thus develop a lazy attitude towards communicating fluently in foreign languages. This is due to the fact that in Uganda, foreign languages such as French and German are hardly used by the communities. For instance, French is regarded as a language that needs to be promoted only in the French speaking countries like the Democratic Republic of Congo and Burundi. This defiance impacts on the public attitude towards the languages. For a long time in the 1960s and 70s, French was regarded as "the language of refugees" in Western Uganda, in reference to the influx of the 1959 and 1969 refugees from Rwanda and Burundi. As Mardsen (2014) puts it, learners who are in contact with language speakers shape their attitudes towards the language. Furthermore, much as communication in Kiswahili and French are being advocated for in the spirit of regional cooperation in the East African Community and the Great Lakes Region, the Ugandan language policy hardly enforces the need for promoting these languages in educational institutions and in the media. This has drawn back the integration of such languages in some university programmes that desire multilingualism in their course units since subjects, which are not backed by the national policy, can hardly benefit from Government funding and donor support mechanisms.

5.6 Content Not Adapted to the Local Situation

Dufficy (2000) observes that in language learning, there is need to distinguish between the content taught in class and its application in daily life. Some teaching materials used for teaching foreign languages lack components that can enhance spontaneous communication by the learners. Some of the older teaching materials based on contexts in France and the live voice or translation teaching methods, which still find their way into some university lecture rooms hardly motivate students to use the language frequently in their environment for its perfection. Literature sources in old French with eccentric diction and structures will certainly be learned by heart for exams, but never get used for application in daily life.

Studies carried out on the materials used for teaching and learning of French at both university and secondary level in Uganda revealed that they had inadequate local resources to access content (Ogavu, 2013). Consequently, the foreign content resources are not easily adaptable for day to day usage by the learners in their environment. This affects the literacy levels of French language users in the country as they show low interest in reading the materials used in class.

Ojijo (2012) recognizes the fact that the National Resistance Movement government in Uganda (1986-todate) has encouraged the Africanization of education. This relates to the efforts made embracing learning materials with glossaries that refer to African situations in their content. However, as Huyen et al (2003) put it, lack of French vocabulary that is systematically prepared for the Ugandan context hampers communication when learning that language. It is therefore important that, in order to develop literacy in French in Uganda, the teaching materials and the methods used will have to be prepared with goals of guiding the learners to accumulate lexicon for usage in their daily life situations (CEFR 2011). This will also substitute the status quo where by the current resources lead learners of French to cramming structures that they can hardly apply outside the class; thus hindering literacy fluency in the language.

Moreover, as language teaching and learning materials that are available and adapted to learners' situation impact positively on the learners' performance in literacy and their decision to continue reading and writing in the language or to drop it. Availability of instructional materials promotes lite-racy (Ellington 1981) since it fosters a good rapport between the teacher and the learner and a fertile ground for team work. If French language learning materials are adapted, contextualized and locally produced, instructional aides will increase in variety and literacy rate in the language will also rise in the learning institutions.

5.7 Variation of Teaching Materials in Universities

As much as programmes offered in the universities in Uganda are approved by the National Council for Higher Education, materials for teaching foreign languages, which ideally should be monitored by the National Curriculum Development Centre, are not harmonized. As universities with different objectives open up and engage in competing for teaching foreign language courses, they may be using varying or summarized content leading to low standards of the languages in question. The institutions engaged in French teaching need to forge partnerships and networks for promoting foreign languages. For instance, they can undertake inter-university joint ventures in the development of both didactic and supplementary teaching materials in foreign languages, which will greatly contribute to improved fluency in literacy levels amongst the learners of the language.

5.8 Incorporation of Foreign Languages into Science Courses

Currently, the Uganda government is aggressively encouraging teaching of science subjects and courses at the university level as a means of increasing the production capacity of the country. Unfortunately, this campaign has not included the promotion of language learning. Teaching programmes in universities in Uganda hardly promote foreign languages in the science based subjects. Literacy in scientific development globally has always privileged scholars who are well-versed in foreign languages, in addition to the attained. This is why outstanding scientist right from ancient Civilizations like in Greece, to modern times in Russia and Germany tended to take great interest in foreign languages.[5] Science students in Uganda are interested in foreign languages, as a means of enhancing their employability and increasing opportunities for further studies abroad among other things. Yet they do not have an option of taking an elective in languages anywhere along their educational continuum. The National Council for Higher Education will need to emphasize the importance of encouraging teaching of French as one of the key foreign languages in science courses in order to promote collaborative research and the exposure of literate Ugandans to science based job markets regionally and internationally.

5.9 Multilingualism and Literacy Blossoming

Educational policies in Uganda have tended to be insensitive to multilingualism and subsequently, university programmes in the country hardly promote it. Moreover, multilingual individuals in foreign languages in the past were not particularly sought after by the Government as the biggest employer in Uganda, although they are said to have a higher rate of rationality than the monolingual ones, since the former gain diverse knowledge from the various materials that they read. As Devi Hermasari (2013) has observed, multilingual employees bring a different perspective on situations and a different outlook to life. They are said to have greater tolerance of other people, cultures and behaviours. They tend to develop efficiency in communication, multi-tasking and analytical skills. Because of the versatility that they acquire when learning foreign languages, they are flexible and can take initiatives at work. As the work place demonstrates, knowledge of foreign languages supports improved productivity. Ugandan universities therefore, need to be aware of this and take measures to conform to the standards of other universities world-wide regarding multilingual literacy fluency.

---

5   Albert Einstein was fully bilingual-German and English.

5.10 Conclusion

The discussions above have elaborated how knowledge of foreign languages in universities enriches the students' lite-racy skills accuracy in reading and writing as well as their disposition to research. However, in Uganda, due to the various socio-political constraints, non-conducive language policies and the nature of the literacy imparted in the languages, students barely achieve the intellectual fluency to read, write and communicate in foreign languages. Besides English, which hold the status of 'official language' in Uganda, French is the next most important foreign language that faces such literacy fluency constraints. If universities in the country are to enhance literacy fluency in foreign languages, together with the other stakeholders, like the relevant government ministries, foreign embassies, multinational companies and concerned regional and international organizations, policies and mechanisms will have to be put in place to foster the development and usage of foreign languages.

References

Burlacu C.: «Importance des langues étrangères dans la vie»: http://christineburlacu.wordpress.com/2011/01/28/%E2%80%99 importance-des-langues-etrangeres-dans-la-vie Council of Europe. (2001).*Common European Framework of Reference for Languages: Learning Teaching, Assessment* (CEFR), Language Policy Unit, Strasbourg, www.coe.int/t/dg4/linguistic/.../**framework** en.pdf

Christ, H. (1995). *SprachenpolitischePerspektiven*. In K-R. Bausch, H. Christ & H.-J. Krumm (eds.), *Handbuch Fremdsprachenunterricht* (3rdedn). Tubingen: Niemeyer Dictionary.com's 21st Century Lexicon. (2003-2014). Dictionary.com, LLC http://dictionary.reference.com/browse/foreign+language

Dufficy, P. (2000, February 2000). Dialogue in a Multilingual Classroom. Paper presented at the Change and Choice in *The New Century: Is Education Y2K Compliant?* - Second Change in Education Research Group Symposium (CERG), Sydney.

Ellington, H. et al (1981), *Games and Stimulations in Science Education,* Kogan Page, London.

Fodde L. (2013/2014): «Lingua e Culture par la Mediazione Linguistica », Corso di Laurea in Economia esgestione Aziendale, Universita di Cagliari.

Hermasari D. (2011) Benefits of Bilingualism in the Workplace www.slideshare.net/.../**benefit**s-of-bilingualism-in-the-**workplace**

Hilliard, A. (1989). Teachers and Cultural styles in a Pluralistic society. *NEA Today.* Huyen and Nga (2003). In Language Learning Games: Why, When and How. Elizabeth Dalton Southern New Hampshire University, http://www.academia.edu/4998040/Language_Learning_Games_Why_When_and_How

Marsden, E. (2014). Perceptions, Attitudes, and Choosing to Study Foreign Languages in England: An Experimental Intervention http://www.researchgate.net/publication/268156460_Perceptions_Attitudes_and_Choosing_to_Study_Foreign_Languages_in_England_An_Experimental_Intervention Ministry of Education and Sports. (2008). *New policy reforms in the delivery of secondary education,* Circular No. 20/2008, 25th August 2008. Ministry of Education and Sports. (1992). *Government White Paper on Implementation of the Recommendation of the Report of the Education Policy Review Commissions* entitled "Education for National Integration and Development, Kampala. Ministry of Education and Sports. (1989). *Education for National Integration and Development,* Report of the Education Policy Review Commission, Kampala.

Muthwii M., Mweseli M., Nzomo J., Gathumbi A., Okumbe J., Maranga M., Opit E, Wagaba W, OkotBenge and Ogavu T., Research Case Studies on Language, Published as a Consolidated report titled: *Language Policy and Practices in Education in Kenya,* (Report compiled by Margaret Muthwii). Nairobi: Phoenix Publishers, 2002.

Nankindu P. (2014). *Language in education policy and Literacy acquisition in multilingual Uganda: A case study of Kampala urban district,* Thesis submitted in partial fulfilment of the requirements for the award of Doctor of Philosophy in applied linguistics in the Faculty of Arts, University of the Western Cape (Unpublished). National Curriculum Development Centre. (2013). *Languages Learning Area: Local Languages Syllabus,* Lower Secondary Curriculum, Assessment and Examination Reform Programme, NCDC/Cambridge, Education www.curasse.ncdc.go.ug Accessed on 25/01/2015. New Vision (September 29, 2005). *Museveni signs 3rd bill: From now on, Swahili is the official second language,* Kampala.

Ogavu T (2013). *Local Culture and Teaching Foreign Languages,* LAP LAMBERT Academic Publishing, ISBN 978-3-659-17730-9, Saarbrücken, Germany.

Ojijo P. (2012). Review of Education Policy in Uganda, http://fr.slideshare.net/ojijop?utm_campaign=profiletracking&utm_medium=site&utm_source=slideview

Okech A. (2004). *Adult Education in Uganda, Growth, Development, Prospects and Challenges*, Fountain Publishers, Kampala. Synergies Afrique des Grands Lacs, Numéro 2 - Année 2013, Revue du GERFLINT.

Wadok R. (2011). *Language Power & Identity*, University of Lancaster, UK, First Published online on 25 March 2011 http://www.academia.edu/1539836/Language_Power Identity

CHAPTER SIX
FRENCH LANGUAGE EDUCATION IN UGANDA: UNDERSTANDING THE CAUSES OF LIMITED NUMBERS OF LEARNERS CHOOSING TO STUDY ADVANCED FRENCH AT KYAMBOGO UNIVERSITY

Victoria Bakurumpagi[1]

Abstract

This article attempts to explain the causes of the current decline in the numbers of learners choosing to study French at Kyambogo University over the last five years despite the introduction of a local scholarship scheme initiated by the French Embassy in Kampala to support the teaching and the learning of French in three Ugandan universities in 2009. Using a qualitative approach, the author looks at issues of programme design, type of institutional support and the current language policy in Uganda, as possible causes of this phenomenon. She proposes that in order to change the trend, the university needs to support the redesigning of French studies by allowing a wider combination with subjects like Political Science, Business Studies and Sociology. This is an option which does not exist in the in the current programmes. The author proposes also that the University should solicit membership with Francophone organizations such as, the International Federation of Teachers of French and the Francophone University Agency just like Kenya and South Africa have done in order to popularize the learning of French. She contends that this opening will enable Kyambogo University to modernize the teaching of French by focusing on French for Specific purposes. She finally suggests that these reforms will have to be informed by a clear national language
policy in which a place is given to selected foreign languages that are deemed to be vital for regional and international cooperation.

Key words: *language policy, institutional support, teaching materials, teaching methods, French as a foreign language.*

---

1. Dr. Victoria Bakurumpagi worked as a teacher trainer under ITEK (Institute of Teacher Education Kyambogo since 1989 and was integrated as a lecturer in Kyambogo University since its inception in 2003. She is a Ph.D. holder from Limoges University, France and M.A. (French) from Makerere University and B.A.Ed. (French language and literature) from Burundi University. She is an active member of APFO (Association of teachers of French in Uganda) and an important resource person in the French teaching in Uganda.

6.1 Background to the study

Uganda is a multilingual country with English as the official language and vehicle of instruction. All languages, except English, are optional in secondary schools. Local and foreign languages are bundled together in one common trunk of subjects from which the learner has to choose. This means that when the learner chooses to study Luganda (a local language), or Kiswahili (a regional language in East Africa), French as a foreign language is foregone. When the student chooses to pursue German as an alternative, still, French gets dismissed automatically because there will be a clash on the teaching and examination timetables. However, French is not only disadvantaged by this generalized classification of subjects, it is also in competition with subjects such as Home Management, Religious Education, Fine Art, Technical Drawing, Accounts and Commerce. Given the fact that learners have prior contacts with most of the other subjects through the study of Social Sciences at Primary School, currently the ground offered for the selection of French is not leveled at all. In this competitive environment between subjects, when the learners get to the Advanced Level they have to further narrow down their combinations in accordance with the national principle of specialization. This means cutting down from the ten or nine subjects taken at the Ordinary Level to a combination of only three subjects whereas in the past, learners were allowed to combine 4 subjects. The consequences of this reform for French were very drastic. It shifted from being a service language that used to be selected by both scientists and artists to a foreign language that is targeted mainly by future foreign officers and language teachers. Visibly, the number of learners of French started drop-ping sharply from Senior 3.[2] According to the UNEB officer in charge of foreign languages as quoted by Nassaazi C. (2014: 2), about 2,500 students registered for O` level French Examinations in 2011. In 2012, they were 2,300. In 2013 they were only 2000 (Nassaazi C: 2); the drop in numbers became more serious at A' level. However, for this level, the statistics to illustrate the attrition rate at national level are yet to be compiled.

Since 2007, researchers interested in the French teaching and learning at Secondary level have been trying to understand the causes of this phenomenon. Muhangyi J. (2011:3) for example singles out the unfavourable education system as the main cause of declining interest. As Kikide A.M. (2011) talks about the inappropriate methods used by

---

[2] The senior secondary level in Uganda is divided into two parts: Ordinary level (O level), starting from Senior 1 to Senior 4 and the Advanced Level (A Level), stretching from Senior 5 to Senior 6.

some teachers, Eyotaru B. (2011:14) appreciates the initiative of the French Embassy for the local scholarship scheme, which it introduced in the Academic year 2008/2009 in universities, but notes that it limits the learners to the teaching profession and ends up pushing off other potential learners of the French language. However, while the drop in the number of learners in secondary schools is relatively well documented, not much research exists, to address the causes of the low numbers of French learners at the University level. We also note that the available French related reports are written in French and that their findings and recommendations may not reach Ugandan policy makers because of the language barrier. This study was prompted by the lack of literature on the topic and by the fact that the French programme of Diploma in Education Secondary (DES), which had been in existence since the 1970s during the times of National Teacher College Kyambogo, was shelved in 2014 due to... (Among other reasons was) in-sufficient numbers of applicants. Another French programme, Bachelor of Arts in Arts, which enabled students to combine for example French and Development studies has had no candidates admitted for the last three consecutive years.

This picture is in contrast with what is happening in neighbouring Kenya, where according to Nginye M. (2007), the number of learners in French is increasing at the university level.[3] Nginye reminds his readers that French is the only language other than English that is spoken on five continents and that its relevance stems from the fact that, it is used in international organizations such as the United Nations, UNESCO, the International Labour organizations (ILO), the Inter-national Olympic committee, the Red Cross etc. He does not forget to remind us that, with the rebirth of the East African Community, which has been joined by Rwanda and Burundi, policy makers will have serious deliberations to do on the status of French in the sub-regional community. In addition to the earlier reasons stated, also this discrepancy between Uganda and Kenya as far as the learning of French is concerned, prompted me to undertake this study in order to see if something went wrong somewhere in the teaching process at the French Section in Kyambogo University.

---

3   According to Nginye's article, in 2004, Kenya had a total 47,000 learners of French in Non-Francophone Sub-Saharan Africa. Out of those 2,500 were from universities. He derived this total from statistics released by The Francophone International Organization in its report of 2004. Out of the13 countries, which are listed a shaving embraced the learning of French, Uganda is not mentioned. Some of the countries listed include Angola, South Africa, and Eritrea etc.

6.2 Brief history of French language teaching and learning at Kyambogo University

Kyambogo University is an 11-year old public university. It was established by an act of parliament in 2003, as a merger of three institutions of higher learning namely Uganda Polytechnic Kyambogo (UPK), the Institute of Teacher Education (ITEK) and the National Institute of Special Education (UNISE). In the Academic year 2013/2014, Kyambogo University had a population of 30,000 students making it the second biggest public university after Makerere University. French language teaching at Degree level started under ITEK whose aim was to train teachers of different disciplines including languages. As far as the French language is concerned, from the Academic year 1987/1988 up to 2000/2001, only two programmes were offered (Diploma Double Main, Bachelor of Education, also as a Double main). On average, the DES programme would attract 15 students per year. Upon completion of the DES programme, which was 2 years, the students would go to the field and teach for a minimum of 3 years and come back to upgrade by joining the Bachelor of Education programme (BED). However, the numbers of students admitted to the DES programme kept on decreasing until 2013, when only two students were admitted in Year I. In the table below, we indicate the number of final year students per programme from 2008 to 2014.

Table 6.2.1: Number of French students in the graduating class since August 2008

S/N	Academic Year	Programme	No. of final year students per programme.	Total no. Of final year students in the section.
1	2008/2009	DES	17	28
		BED	5	
		BAED	6	
		BAA	-	
2	2009/2010	DES	6	18
		BED	5	
		BAED	7	
		BAA	-	

3	2010/2011	DES	**15**	40
		BED	5	
		BAED	17	
		BAA	3	
4	2011/2012	DES	**8**	16
		BED	1	
		BAED	7	
		BAA	-	
5	2012/2013	DES	**6**	21
		BED	5	
		BAED	10	
		BAA	-	
6	2013/2014	DES	**5**	17
		BED	2	
		BAED	10	
		BAA	-	
7	2014/2015	DES	**1**	7
		BAED	4	
		BED	2	
		BAA	-	

Source: *French Section records, Kyambogo University*

As it can be seen in the above table, the number of students in the graduating class is low. It is only in Academic year 2010/2011 that the numbers went slightly higher following the introduction of the local scholarship scheme by the French embassy talked about above. The impact of the scheme has been documented by Eyotaru B. (2011: 15) in her report titled *L'impact des bourses sur le choix du français*.[4] However, the preceding low numbers did not come overnight. When the members of staff realized it, they drafted a Bachelor of Arts with Education (BAED) and a Bachelor of Arts in Arts (BAA) syllabi to open the scope of the French combinations and enable the students to access more choices. With BAA and BAED, it became possible to combine French and subjects like History, Economics, Geography, Religious Studies, and Development Studies in

---

4 In English: The Impact of Scholarships on the Selection of French.

Kyambogo University. But, it seems that these initiatives towards widening the scope of combinations did not go far enough to satisfy the aspirations of potential students in the subsequent years.

Alongside the reviews of the Advanced French syllabi, French for Beginners was also introduced in the departments of Home Economics, Business Studies, Development Studies and Engineering but the curriculum content is usually too restricted by the time table to be of any meaningful purpose in the job market. Typically, in the above departments, only one or two course units lasting 30 hours each are offered in a 3 or 4 year course. Interestingly, the number of students registering for this French for Beginners is usually big. For instance, in 2013/2014, in the Development Studies class alone, the researcher had a class of 75 third year students choosing it because they had taken the International Relations option. The colleagues handling similar groups in Business Studies and Home Economics have observed a similar scenario. What we can learn from this is that the demand for French learning exists. The question is how to effectively service it.

6.3 Statement of the problem

The French Embassy has been supporting the teaching and learning of French at Kyambogo University. The members of staff have tried to diversify the French subject combinations by designing new programmes namely, The Bachelor of Arts with Education and The Bachelor of Arts in Arts and a Certificate in Business French. In the same vein, course units for beginners have been introduced in some professional programmes (Business studies, Home economics and Engineering). Despite these efforts, the numbers of learners choosing to study French Advanced at Kyambogo University level remain low. In this study, we therefore wanted to ascertain the causes of this phenomenon by focusing mainly on issues of subject combination and institutional support to French teaching and research.

6.4 General and Specific Objectives of the Study

The general objective of this study was to find out the causes of the low numbers of students choosing to study Advanced French at Kyambogo University. The specific objectives of this study were as follows;
- Find out whether the French studies programs are well designed to suit the demands of the current job market.
- Find out whether Kyambogo University has enough institutional support from the government of Uganda and from the French Embassy, to enable it popularize the study of the French language and related research.
- Make recommendations to government, French Embassy, teachers and lecturers of French so as to reverse the trend.

6.5 Hypothesis, Justification and Scope

The low numbers of students choosing to study French at Kyambogo University are due to a narrow scope of the subject combination and insufficient institutional support from the Ugandan Government and the French Embassy. This study may be of use to curriculum developers, language policy makers and career guidance masters. It covers only the teaching of French at Kyambogo University. Other institutions are mentioned for comparison purposes. The study also covers the period from 2009 to 2014.

6.6 Definition of key terms

A foreign language: A language acquired by those for who it is not a mother tongue in an Educational set up through a process that is more or less voluntary (Cuq & Graca, 2003:94).

Institutional support: It includes support, which comes from institutions in form of infrastructure, training, study trips, supply of instructional materials (equipment, books, CDs...etc.

6.7 Review of Related Literature

In this section, we make a brief review of what other researchers have had to say on the issue of limited numbers of learners of French language in Ugandan schools. The topic has attracted the attention of researchers especially in the teaching and learning of French in secondary schools. At the tertiary level though, little has been done on the topic. We shall therefore review some of the principles, which are fol-lowed by successful universities in order to attract a reason-able number of French learners.

6.8 Lack of successful models to emulate

According to Kayanja (2011: 1), while the economic value of the study of English is obvious to every Ugandan child, the relevance of French for many children in Uganda is not very clear: *"the average young Ugandan knows very few successful graduates of French, who owe their success to their mastery of the French language"*. Universities which have an efficient foreign language department usually organize open days where the Department invites bilingual people from different professional backgrounds, to talk about how they have benefited from their knowledge of languages.

According to its website (www.reading.ac.uk), the University of Reading in the United Kingdom does it every year in order to inform its new students. In addition, it has a career orientation programme and its language options are diversified. The French combinations we have in Kyambogo exist there too but they add the following innovative combinations: French and Politics, French and International relations, French and German, French and Italian, French and English literature, French and Management, French and history of Art. Secondly, the career prospects of the French graduates are clearly indicated on the university website for students to make an informed decision during the choice of programmes. The following economic sectors are mentioned on the University of Reading website as potential employers of their graduates in the fields of telecommunication, insurance, communication, diplomacy, teaching, translation and interpretation, research etc. During open days, the department invites successful alumni to talk to students so as to widen their world vision and appreciate the economic and cultural importance of the foreign languages they study. We note that at Kyambogo, all this information is lacking and the students are operating in a vacuum with no role models to emulate.

6.8.1 Unfriendly language policy

In a recent study conducted by Avako (2014:19-23) in the boarder district of Arua in Uganda, the researcher reports that the number of learners of French remains low because "the Ugandan language policy does not give enough support to the teaching of French". She explains that the reduction of the number of subjects to be studied at 'A' level from 4 to 3 was frequently quoted by her respondents as having negatively impacted on the choice of the French language by learners in Senior 5. The other reason she recorded was the insufficient number of competent teachers of French. The above reasons can also be found in research reports done in other districts of Uganda such as Kisoro, Wakiso, Luwero, Kampala and Mbarara. These studies were carried out in different years. For example Naluboka (2011:) notes that, "the teaching of French as well as that of other foreign languages is in a permanent state of insecurity because it is only compulsory in the first two years of secondary and becomes optional from the third year onwards". She reports that 50% of the people she interviewed did not know whether Uganda had a language policy or not. The idea of giving a clear status to each language spoken in Uganda was not familiar to them.

The most systematic study on the impact of an unfriendly language policy on the teaching of French in Uganda was carried out by Muhangyi (2011: 3). He notes that in 1973, when the then dictator General Idi Amin Dada declared Kiswahili as a national language, many headteachers decided to substitute French with Kiswahili. This, according to him, seems to have signaled the beginning of the challenges foreign languages are facing today. He goes ahead to explain that in 1987, with the Kajubi Report and later the Government White paper on Education of 1992, the necessity of promoting a national language was reinforced. This implies that since that time, the space left for the French language as well as other foreign languages in the Ugandan Education system became problematic. It was to be observed that later in 2007, headteachers of all secondary schools received a circular in which Kiswahili and other seven compulsory subjects were listed but French was not mentioned among the optional subjects. After the above circular, Muhangyi (2011:3) asserts with examples to illustrate his point that "some headmasters simply decided to scrap the French subject from their programmes". He concludes that this state of affairs, combined with the fact that very few teachers of French have been absorbed into the Public Service since 2006. It leads to job insecurity. Put together with the lack of sensitization of learners on the importance of French in Uganda, these conditions eventually lead to the decline in the number of students opting to study French in secondary schools.

Olebo (2013) also mentions the Ugandan language policy as a major cause of the drop in numbers at 'Level. The study deals with the challenges teachers encounter as they try to encourage learners to continue with their French career path at A' level. It was carried out in Jinja district in 2013. Olebo (2013:48) observed that in the whole district, only two schools had students in the candidate classes and the two schools combined had only 5 candidates! He noted also that the decline at 'A' level is affecting the number of learners of French in lower classes as well. He explained that this is due to the fact that, when it comes to the grouping of subjects at A 'level, the headteachers do not bother to inform the students of French about the subjects, which can be combined with French. The students are left to make their own choices without guidance and many of them end up dropping French.

6.8.2 Inappropriate methods and insufficient teaching materials.

The poor mastery of the methods recommended by experts in the teaching of foreign languages is also another cause often cited by researchers to explain the drop in numbers of learners of French in secondary schools and at Kyambogo University. According to Kikide M.A. (2011: 14), Nassazi C. (2014: 28) and Luswata B. (2014:22), French is consistently labeled by different learners as "a difficult language", pointing to the fact that the best practices scientifically proven as effective in teaching foreign languages, may not be used consistently leading to the disappointment and discouragement of the learners. This situation is also caused, according to Avako (2014: 24) by lack of reading materials in lower classes. In the schools she investigated in Arua district, the ratio of books to learners in one of the schools was 14: 337. In such a context, how can a student opt to continue studying French when there are other subjects with a variety of textbooks? It is not therefore surprising that many learners drop French at the end of Senior 2 and Senior 4 due to poor performance as Olebo notes in his report (2013:51).

The few who persevere with French also face the same challenge of lack of sufficient teaching materials at university. In her report titled *The impact of the lack of teaching materials on performance in Kyambogo University*, Kansiime (2012: 14-16) singled out the fact that the French section has no Internet connection; it has a TV set but cannot access francophone TV programmes due to non-payment of subscription fees to service providers. It does not have plays written in French nor does it have French songs for the students to sharpen their listening skills. She also reports that due to lack of space, even the available materials cannot be put in accessible shelves so that students can see them and borrow them easily. She concludes by saying that "if the current situation continues, the students will not have a solid foundation in French".

6.8.3   Insufficient incentives

According to Eyotaru (2011:15), the local scholarship scheme introduced by the French Embassy in Kyambogo, Makerere and Kabale universities has had a positive impact on students' enrollment. However, it had limitations because the scholar-ships were few and they were limited only to students preparing for the teaching profession. Disappointed, some of the unsuccessful applicants went for courses in other professional profiles such as Business administration, Human Resource Management and International Relations. She concludes that it is merely "getting the scholarship, which became the aim of studying French in Ugandan Universities".

6.8.4   Incompetent teachers

Kikide (2011:14) asserts that some teachers in the secondary schools where she carried out her study in Kampala and Wakiso districts were not skilled enough in the methods recommended by experts in the teaching of French as a foreign language. Meanwhile, Mfitumukiza (2013:1) noted that in Kisoro district, due to lack of recruitment of French teachers by the Ministry of education and sports, there are still many untrained teachers of French. Such teachers cannot motivate the learners to continue with the study of the French language when they reach university. Many learners from such schools drop it at the first opportunity they get.

In conclusion to this section, we can say that the above causes already investigated in secondary schools in different districts point to the fact that the issue of low numbers of French learners faced by Kyambogo University stem from earlier on at the secondary level and that any effort to address it will have to be done in conjunction with the stakeholders right from Senior Secondary 1.

6.9 Lessons from successful universities in Africa and beyond
6.10 Importance of designing courses in tandem with market trends

According to Gilbert Nganga,[5] in his article titled "Kenya: cashing in on foreign language learning" observes that "leading universities in Kenya such as Nairobi, Kenyatta, Moi and Maseno have added French to their curricula as pressure on them mounts to offer courses in tandem with market needs". The same author reports that in 2012, Maseno University alone had 1500 students in its Department of Hospitality and Tourism Management. He also reports that, there are 500 students in different Kenyan Polytechnic Institutes. He finally says, there is stiff competition as each university tries to attract as many students as possible to its foreign language offer. It is because of these high figures that Kenya managed to attract funding from FIPF (International Federation of Teachers of French) through a project called *Fond de Solidarité Prioritaire*[6] (FSP), which has enabled it to put up French Resource Centers and train the manpower needed to run them efficiently. According to Milcah Chokah (2013), this project ran from 2008 to 2013, and it enabled Kenyan Universities to diversify their options. Teach French for Specific Purposes, and design appropriate programmes and train teachers in this relatively new area of French for professionals. In this study, we shall assess whether Kyambogo University is getting enough institutional support from the French Embassy and the Government of Uganda for the promotion of French language teaching and research.

6.11 The Importance of a strong lobby from the Associations of teachers of French

According to Fafouna International Journal of Education (www.fafouna foundation.tripod.com), Nigerians managed to get a friendly foreign language policy, due to the strong lobby done by the Associations of Nigerian Teachers of Foreign Languages including the Association of Nigerian Teachers of French (NATF). Consequently, the government recognized the importance of French. According to the Nigerian policy in education, it is desirable for every Nigerian to speak French for smooth interaction with Nigeria's francophone neighbours. The question here is: Is the Association of Teachers of French in Uganda's lobby strong enough to influence language policy reforms? The association of French Teachers in Uganda (APFO) organizes in-service training programmes for

---

5   www.universityworldnews.co/article.php

6   In English: Funds for Priority Solidarity.

the teaching of French and maintains a register of French Teachers in Uganda. It has also conducted sensitization visits to schools, to lobby for the maintenance of the French Subject, produce a francophone bulletin (*Liaison*) and mobilize through its regional representatives, cultural activities around 'Francophone' related events. The question still remains: are these activities strong enough to make an impact on the language policy makers in Uganda?

6.10 The Importance of multilingualism and partnerships with French universities and Francophone Organizations.

According to sources available on the South African language policy in Education (www.education.gov.za. linkclick.asp), South Africa respects all languages in order to foster national unity. This respect encompasses foreign languages such as French, Spanish and Latin, which are important for international trade and communication. Having recognized this as a principle, the country is bound to facilitate the teaching of such languages. For this reason, South African universities have formed partnerships with French universities such as Grenoble, Rouen, and Strasbourg in order to modernize the teaching of French in their country. South African students have study trips organized to go to France, enabling them to get a linguistic and cultural immersion in the French language. Some South African universities are also members of the Association d'Universités Francophones (AUF)[7] an organization, which supports French teaching, learning and research in the universities, which are affiliated to it. The question one may ask here is: have Ugandan universities like Kyambogo and the Government of Uganda developed the same attitude as South African universities and their Government towards foreign languages?

6.11 Partial Conclusion

The literature identified tends to show that behind the low numbers of students opting to study French in Kyambogo University lay other questions of motivation of the teacher, dissemination of information to the learner and the need to modernize the teaching of the French language in secondary schools, which serve as a springboard for universities. When the numbers of learners of French drop in secondary schools, there is a drop in universities. This is unavoidable. The aim of this study is to investigate the other possible causes of the drop in numbers beyond this obvious reason.

---

7   This is the Agency for Francophone or Partially Francophone Universities.

6.12 Methodology

6.13 Sample size and Selection

A total number of 35 subjects participated in this study (30 advanced learners of French, 3 lecturers and two executive members of the Association of Teachers of French in Uganda. Given the nature of Kyambogo programmes where some students come directly from Senior 6, while others come to upgrade after a certain number of years in practice, it was not possible to get a homogeneous sample. Some were DES students (Year I and II), Bachelor of Arts with education students (Year I, II and II) while the rest were BED students Year I and II).The latter are mature students who have worked as teachers for more than five years. Nine students out of the 30 students who received the questionnaires were beneficiaries of the French scholarship scheme, which we have mentioned before. Two of them first completed a degree in International Business in Makerere University Business School, while one was concurrently doing DES (French) in Kyambogo University and a Degree in Journalism from Uganda Christian University. These three (3) typical cases already show that, there is a problem at design level as far as French teaching and learning at Kyambogo University is concerned.

6.14 Data collection procedures

Questionnaires, interview guides and documentary analysis were used to collect quantitative and qualitative data. The questionnaires were pre-tested and then administered to students of the French Section at Kyambogo University (KYU). Each participant was given a week within which to think about the issues raised and to respond freely. The researcher interviewed 3 lecturers of French and 2 members of the Board of the French Teachers' Association APFO on a face to face basis. She carefully noted the remarks for content analysis. The documents, which were subjected to documentary analysis were mainly research reports produced by students of the French Section KYU between 2011 and 2014 on the factors affecting French teaching and learning in Uganda. The administration of questionnaires and interviews was done from the 15th May to 31st may 2014. Data analysis was done in June 2014 and a first draft prepared in August 2014 and presented as a paper at the Foreign Languages Conference organized by Makerere University. In the paper the researcher identified emerging themes and interpreted them in this article as causes of the low numbers of learners of French in Kyambogo University.

6.15 Method of data analysis

Data was analyzed using a descriptive qualitative design. For easy reading and interpretation, it is presented in tables where frequencies and percentages are indicated. Quotations have also been integrated from the qualitative data through the process of content analysis.

6.16 Presentation and interpretation of data

6.16.1 Numbers of learners of French at Kyambogo University
Presentation of data.

We asked the learners how many they were when they sat their A` level examinations. The data collected indicates that the highest class of French at A' level had 8 students and only one respondent out of the 30 who returned the questionnaire indicated that, half of his classmates continued learning French at university. The remaining 29 said that their friends opted for programmes other than education. The majority believe that, their friends were influenced by the negative perceptions; that the teaching profession leads to poverty and is therefore not attractive to young people. Some other interesting causes were noted as findings from the study.

Table 6.16.1: Causes of the low numbers of French learners at Kyambogo University

Causes	Frequency	Percentages
French in Kyambogo only leads to one career, teaching.	18	60%
The officers at the ministry of education do not understand the importance of foreign languages.	2	6%
Pressure from parents. They discourage us from choosing French but encourage us to take subjects perceived as more marketable.	2	6%
Emphasis of government on science subjects and the policy of only 3 subjects at A Level.	5	18%
Fear of unemployment at the end of DES, BED and BAED programmes.	5	18%
Promotion of Kiswahili as the second official language.	3	10%

Lack of knowledge on the opportunities offered by the mastery of the French language in the job market.	4	13
Lack of government initiatives to encourage the learning of French.	1	3%
The myth that French is a difficult language.	1	3%
Total	41	100%

Table 6.16.1 shows that the major cause mentioned is the lack of diversification in French studies with 60% of the respondents citing this reason. Note is taken of the 18% who indicate the fact that French studies have become synonymous to the teaching career and this has rendered the subject unpopular. The other reasons given by the other 18 % of the advanced learners of French at KYU, is the emphasis put by government on the teaching of sciences and the fear of unemployment. According to these findings studying French seems not to have clear career prospects.

We also asked the subjects to suggest ways to reverse the trend and their responses are summarized in the Table 6.16.2 below:

Table 6.16.2: Suggestions made by the students on strategies to reverse the trend

Strategy	**Frequency**	**Percentage**
Restoring trips to France or French speaking countries for the best performing students and practicing teachers.	18	60%
Giving enough teaching materials to schools	10	33%
Making French learning compulsory from Senior 1 to senior 4.	10	33%
Making the knowledge of a foreign language an essential subject for all candidates for entry in programmes such as Political Science, Home Economics, Business Studies, and Economics.	15	50%
Increase the number of course units in French for beginners to at least 3 per programmes to make the French content more meaningful in the job market.	5	16%

Foreign language lecturers should form an association with the aim of lobbying the government for reforms in the country's language policy.	2	6%
The government should treat the teachers fairly so that they can access the government payroll like teachers of other disciplines.	10	33%
Introducing more effective ways of teaching French.	15	50%
Universities should seek partnerships/ exchanges with French speaking universities.	3	10%

Table 6.16.2 above shows that the most outstanding concerns in the teaching of French at KYU are: the restoration of incentives, the introduction of innovative ways of teaching French and making the knowledge of a foreign language an entry requirement for the most marketable university pro-grammes. These were mentioned by 50 to 60% of the respondents interviewed.

6.16.2 Perspectives of lecturers and representatives of APFO on the topic

This data was collected from three lecturers selected out of the 8 staff available at the French section, and two executive members of Association of Teachers of French in Uganda (APFO), through interviews on a one to one basis. The reasons they gave are summarized in **Table 6.16.3**.

Table 6.16.3: Reasons given by lecturers and executive members of APFO for the low numbers of learners of French

Reasons	**Frequency**	**Percentage**
Lack of a clear language policy.	5	100%
Wrong perceptions that French is a language for foreigners (refugees).	3	60%
Decrease in incentives from the French Embassy in terms of scholarships, teaching materials, trips to France and other French speaking countries.	5	100

| Wider exposure of students to other attractive careers. This is due to print and electronic media. | 4 | 80% |
| Ignorance on the job prospects available for French graduates in Uganda and abroad. | 4 | 80% |

From **Table 6.16.3** above, it is evident that the lack of a clear language policy is seen as a big roadblock in the teaching and learning of French in Kyambogo University. This concern is at the same level of importance as the decrease in incentives by the French Embassy. The 3 reasons above are followed by the wide exposure of students to other more attractive career prospects. It should however be noted that, this exposure does not stretch to job prospects offered to French graduates. That kind of exposure would inform young people on this important advantage of French communication skills in the regional economic activity and beyond.

6.17 Interpretation of the Findings

From our analysis, it has emerged that students are silently protesting against the lack of diversification in the design of the current French programmes available at KYU. It is true that the Bachelor of Arts with Education programme allows students to combine French with another discipline such as Economics, but this is not enough because the career envisaged is still Education. The students would love to see openings to disciplines such as Political Science, Management Science, Business Studies and Secretarial Sciences. Combining with French also makes sense in the Telecommunication and Marketing sectors. In other words, the whole area of humanities should be open to foreign languages in order to have a good integration of subjects, which would enable language specialists to fit in different profiles available in the job market.

It has also emerged that the institutional support the French section is getting from the University Administration and the French Embassy is not enough to continue attracting consistent numbers of students. We must however acknowledge here that the Embassy in the recent past funded fully the doctoral studies of 3 members of staff, of the Section in French universities and 2 others up to Master of philosophy level (although two of the staff members have since left the University to look for better opportunities elsewhere). The French Embassy in Uganda also provides and pays the salaries of two French lecturers, who teach specifically Listening, Speaking skills and French Language Teaching Methods. This is in conformity with a Memorandum of Understanding, which was signed between the Embassy and Kyambogo University. All this seem to imply that the current capacity building alone is not enough to attract students to the French language study. More needs to be done. The section needs for example space where to display the available textbooks, Internet connection to enable learners to download e-documents and materials in order to update and sharpen their language skills in French. In other words, rather than blaming the dwindling number only on the drop in numbers at the secondary level, or the lack of marketing language skills on the part of lecturers of French, all stakeholders need to devise serious innovative strategies to attract the majority of the learners who pass well French Exams at A Level. If this is not done, learners in the lower levels of French will unfortunately also be discouraged in taking up the subject at the tertiary level.

Finally, it has emerged that limiting the French Embassy scholarship to Education students alone, is not enough as it does not market well the French language at the university level. The scope of the scheme may need to be broadened to other areas such as French for Political Science, for Sociology, for Demography, for Institutional Catering, and for Development Studies. Note has been taken of the fact that the French Embassy has so far broadened the scheme to Bachelor of Journalism and Bachelor of Tourism in other universities in Uganda but Kyambogo University has not yet started those programmes. Other incentives apart from scholarships, such as laptops, text book funding and other pedagogical materials need also to be explored. The possibility of writing proposals to diversify sponsorship for the teaching of French at the university level also needs to be explored. This is especially linked to the relevance of French for other countries and private companies, which have shown interest elsewhere in developing communications skills in French.

6.18 Summary of findings and recommendations

The objective of this study was to find out the causes of the low and dwindling number of learners opting to study French at Kyambogo University. The questionnaires, interviews and documentary analysis revealed the following main causes: lack of a clear national language policy, lack of diversification in the existing university programmes, insufficient institutional support, lack of knowledge on job opportunities available for French graduates outside the teaching profession, the wrong perception right from its inception in Uganda that French is for foreigners (meaning refugees), the misconception that it is a difficult language and the exposure to social media, which have increased exposure to career prospects and pushed students and their parents to more attractive career choices. This exposure it was noted, excludes contemporary French career prospects.

Recommendations to the Government of Uganda

The government of Uganda should give a clear status to all the languages used in the country, including foreign languages deemed vital for regional and international cooperation. The learning of one international language should be made compulsory from Senior 1 to Senior 4. Having done that, the Government of Uganda should recruit a fair share to teachers of foreign languages teachers to the Education Service. It should also give logistical support to schools and universities offering French rather than leaving this responsibility to the French Government, through its Embassy in Uganda. The Ministry of education should also prevail on head teachers who threaten to close the French departments at the slightest excuse. The issue of subject combinations at A 'level, which is seriously reducing the numbers of learners in the French classes at Advanced level and consequently, at Kyambogo university should be seriously discussed by educational policy makers and stakeholders at all levels, so that measures can be taken to introduce better reforms in the education system of Uganda.

6.19 Recommendations to the Association of French Teachers in Uganda (APFO)

The Association of French Teachers in Uganda should strongly lobby the government so that their jobs are protected by a clear language policy. They have already tried through their other programmes and by choosing a Patron who is the current Prime minister of Uganda but this is not enough. They should seize systematically opportunities during career guidance sessions in schools to inform adequately the learners and the headteachers of modern job prospects available with French. They can record and project prominent Ugandan personalities who have economically and professionally benefited from their knowledge of the French language. They can also invite such prominent role models to talk to students as they join senior 3 and senior 5. This sensitization could also be made through the media (radio, TV, Internet). University lecturers of French, especially those of Kyambogo University, should play a more active role in this sensitization because if the number of learners increases in secondary schools, the universities will also benefit by getting sufficient numbers.

6.20 Recommendations to Kyambogo University Administration

Kyambogo University should support the redesigning of French Studies by allowing a wider combination with subjects like Political Science, Business Studies, Sociology, Economics etc. which do not exist in the current programmes. In other words, emphasis should now be put on French for Specific Purposes. The training in French must be adjusted in tandem with market needs like it has been done in Kenyan universities. It should allow for the introduction of short courses at different levels to enable its students acquire basic communication skills in French. French for Beginners should increase its content in programmes, where it is offered to make it more relevant to the job market. Adequate infrastructures and up to-date teaching materials such as books, magazines and CDs should be provided to the French Section, so that it can get enough space for students and staff. Such facilities, when provided can be maximized by being shared by all the languages units currently operating at the university. Finally, Kyambogo University should invest in partnership with Francophone organizations like the International Federation of French Teachers and The Agency for Francophone Universities so as to benefit from the international services of such bodies. This in turn will attract more students to French studies as they will compete for study trips or scholarships and access to an immersion into the French language and culture. In order to demystify the perceived difficulty of French, efforts should be made to modernize its teaching through the use of modern information technology. This can only take place if the members of staff are trained in the usage of the new technologies. Partnerships would enable the French Section staff to access those training opportunities once Kyambogo University becomes a member of the Agency of Francophone Universities.

6.22 Recommendations to the French Embassy and other Sponsors

The French Embassy in Uganda should also diversify the beneficiaries of the scholarship scheme to universities by opening it to other professional profiles. It has already opened it to Journalism and Tourism but the number of beneficiaries is still too low to make a significant impact on the numbers of learners of French. As Universities open up more programmes to the French language, sponsors like the French Embassy and French companies operating in Uganda (Orange for example) should show their willingness to support the Language like it has happened in Kenya and South Africa. This presumes that Kyambogo and other universities in Uganda should be ready to diversify their sources of sponsorship for French teaching. Sponsors could in turn restore study trips to francophone universities in Reunion Island, Bujumbura, Vichy, Besançon etc. They could also invest more in the purchase of pedagogical supports, teaching materials, learners' equipment and the training of staff.

References

Avako F. (2014), *Impact de la politique linguistique sur L'enseignement et l'apprentissage du FLE dans les écoles sélectionnées dans le district d'Arua*, Kyambogo University, Research report, unpublished.

Eyotaru B. (2011), *Impact des bourses sur le choix du Français langue étrangère dans les universités en Ouganda*, Kyambogo University, Research report, unpublished.

Chokah M. (2013), *Fifty years of teaching French as a foreign language in Kenya: challenges for teachers and learners*, International journal of education, Vol I, No 3 (www.iejern.com/images/march-2013) Fafouna International Journal of Education (www.fafounafoundation.tripod.com) Accessed 25/07/2014.

Kansiime B. (2012), *Impact du manque de matériel scolaire sur la performance des étudiants de l'Université de Kyambogo*, Kyambogo University, Research report, unpublished.

Kikide M.A. (2012), *Les Méthodes utilisées par les professeurs de français langue étrangères et l'effectif des apprenants en Ouganda*, Kyambogo University, Research Report, unpublished.

Kayanja S. (2011), *Les représentations du français dans les districts de Wakiso et de Kampala: Etude basée sur un échantillon d'élèves et d'employés*, Kyambogo University, Research Report, unpublished. Language in education policy, South Africa. (www.education.gov.za/linkclick.asp 25-7-2014)

Luswata B. (2014), *Les causes de la chute du nombre d'apprenants de français dans le district de Mbarara*, Kyambogo University, Research Report, unpublished.

Mfitumukiza B. (2013) *L'impact des professeurs non-qualifiés en didactique du FLE sur la performance des élèves secondaires dans le district de Kisoro*, Kyambogo University, Research Report, unpublished.

Muhangyi J. (2011) *Influence du système éducatif sur l'apprentissage du français langue étrangère(FLE) dans les districts de Kisoro, Mpigi, Luwero et Kampala en Ouganda*, Kyambogo University, Research Report, unpublished.

Naluboka H. (2011), *L'attitude des politiciens et des spécialistes de l'éducation sur l'enseignement de la langue française en Ouganda*, Kyambogo University, Research Report, unpublished.

Nassaazi C. (2014), *Enquête sur l'impact des Méthodologies utilisées par les professeurs sur le choix du FLE par les apprenants de niveau ordinaire en Ouganda dans le district de Wakiso*, Kyambogo University, Research Report, unpublished.

Gilbert Nganga www.universityworldnews.co/article.php, *Kenya: cashing in on foreign language learning* Accessed 25/01/2015.

Nginye M. (2007), *The learning of French in Kenya Universities: The Relevance of French*, Journal of Language, Technology and Entrepreneurship, Vol. 1, no 1(www.ajol.info/index.php/jolte/article/viewfile/41758/9022)

Olebo C. (2013), *Les défis de l'augmentation de l'effectif des* élèves de français langue étrangère dans les écoles secondaires sélectionnées dans le district de Jinja, Kyambogo University, Research report, unpublished. University of Reading: www. Reading.ac.uk Accessed 25/07/2014

CHAPTER SEVEN
ANALYZING PEDAGOGICAL VALENCES OF INTER-CULTURAL COMMUNICATION IN THE TEACHING OF FRENCH AS A FOREIGN LANGUAGE: THE CASE OF SECONDARY SCHOOLS IN KENYA

Crispus Mwakundia[1]

Abstract

Given the fact that the majority of teachers of French in Kenya teach forms from a culture in which they are not personally living, and given that the context of their training was not in a French-speaking country, they need effective training in Inter-cultural communication, to do their work efficiently. This is lacking in the training curriculum of foreign language and yet it is necessary for the teachers to acquire themselves Inter-cultural competency, before they can inculcate the same in their learners. The purpose of this paper is to give an overview of the role of foreign cultures in the teaching of foreign language, in a largely English-speaking country and a globalization world. It discusses methods and techniques that are appropriate in the teaching of French as a foreign language (FFL) with the aim of making suggestions for developing new materials for foreign language teaching in Kenya. This paper examines the course books *Parlons Français* and *Entre Copains* in order to illustrate how the curriculum in French can be revised to keep up with the changes brought about by globalization trends. These revisions could help the teacher of the French language plan better for enabling the learner to acquire the "interpretive know-how" of cultural and Civilization issues.

Key words: *Valence, French as a Foreign Language, Inter-cultural communication, pedagogy, otherness, interpretive know-how*

---

[1] The author is a part-time lecturer in French language at the Technical University of Mombasa with a vast experience spanning over six years in the teaching of French as a Foreign Language (FFL). He is also a teacher of Kiswahili and a conference interpreter/ translator. His research interests include Inter-cultural communication, curriculum development, translation & interpretation. He is interested in the study of Inter-cultural communication through language education, in order to understand how cultures interact and create synergies aimed at achieving international understanding and peace in a globalized world.

7.1 Introduction

The issue of improving teaching approach in order to enhance students' academic performance, is closely correlated with teachers' concerns of the perfection of their professional and pedagogical skills. It is a well-known fact that the performances of the students in school activities are correlated with the strategies used by teachers to impart knowledge (Ticusan, 2013). In this article, I link the teachers' competence in Inter-cultural communication with their efficacy in teaching French as a foreign language. This approach considers providing an effective alternative to the French language curriculum as a possibility of changing pedagogical practice; a pedagogical valence, enriching the life experience of the learners and stimulating their creative potential. But before I go into the analysis of the current French methods, it seems fitting to begin with an overview of the role of cultures in successful foreign language teaching and more specifically, the role of culture in the teaching of French as a foreign language in secondary schools in Kenya. French is the first foreign language taught in the country. It is taught in 350 secondary schools, of which 20% are private schools. It is irregularly distributed all over the country and there are nearly 400 teachers and approximately 30, 000 pupils involved in the teaching and learning French respectively. (www.frenchin-kenya.com). Three quarters of the teachers are employed by the national Teachers Service Commission (TSC) and enjoy the status of civil servants. The others are directly recruited by Boards of Governors (BOG) of the various institutions and have a less enviable status. Approximately 30 lecturers teach French in the universities including 4 Kenyan PhD holders, 2 Congolese PhD holders and 5 PhD students sponsored by the French Government. (www.frenchinkenya.com). The teaching of French as a Foreign Language is also strongly present in the 20 national schools, which admit the best pupils in Kenya. In addition to the foregoing, more than 2, 000 pupils learn French in 25 major international schools in Nairobi and Mombasa in preparation of their International General Certificate of Education (IGCSE) or International Baccalaureate (IB). (www.frenchinkenya.com)

At the tertiary level, French is present in the four largest public universities, in 5 private universities and in 20 Institutes of Technology where it is selected by more than 2, 500 students. The four public universities as well as the Teachers' Colleges offer training for future Teachers of French as a Foreign Language (through a 4 years Bachelor of Education - French at the university or a 3 years Diploma in Education- French at a Teachers College) also offer French. In 2007/2008, Kenya's four public universities had approximately 150 students who studied French under a Bachelor of

Arts, (French), 350 students under Bachelor of Education, Arts, (French); 5 were preparing for a Masters of Arts and 3 a Doctorate in French linguistics (www.frenchinkenya.com). The various polytechnics and technical institutes also offer French language courses under the departments of Tourism, Hospitality and Secretarial Studies and have approximately 1,500 students taking French. Besides these adult French learners, more than 400 military personnel have been trained in French language since 1999 under the French-Kenya Cooperation with its branches. The Alliance Française in Kenya with its network in Nairobi, Mombasa, Eldoret and Kisumu hosts more than 4, 000 students (www.frenchinkenya.com/lecturers.php). In Nairobi itself, with the presence of many international organizations where French is the statutory language, as well as headquarters of regional companies and NGOs covering francophone countries, the attraction for the language has greatly increased among the Kenyan working class.

The general picture therefore of French teaching in Kenya is that of a blooming discipline, with numbers on the increase. Apart from the foregoing job market explanations, one can probably find a political inclination to French in the recent integration of Rwanda and Burundi in East African Community, and the resumption of the exchanges with the Democratic Republic of Congo. Indeed, the teacher-student ratios suggest that Kenya is fast opening towards the French-speaking countries of Africa, thus reinforcing the position and demand for the French language. Considering the sociological status of the French language in Kenya, based on the number of its learners as compared to those of other languages, (Chokah, 2013) it is fitting to discuss its cultural link with the society and to re-think its teaching in a globalization world. It seems to be the right time to revisit the teachers' long held self-distancing views from the "other" cultures, which they try to convey to the learner who has never been exposed to it.

In essence, this paper poses the following research questions: if the facilitator is teaching an imaginary concept, how effective can s/he be in training in cross-cultural communication? How much of the cross-cultural competence acquisition is included in the current training curriculum of FFL teaching? In this era of globalization, how much does the international media, migrations and foreign travels influence and enrich our French learners' experience?

The Universal Declaration of Human Rights, Article 26[2] states that, "Education shall be directed to the full development of the human personality and to strengthening of respect for human rights and fundamental freedoms". Improving cross-cultural communication competence seems to provide one way of realizing this because it "opens a vast opportunity for identity growth, [since] in order to speak to the other, you must speak about yourself. The foreign language makes it possible to "move away" from your long-held view about your culture and that of the other person" (O'Neil, 1993). Since foreign language theorists claim that all teaching methodologies are born out of new societal needs and aspirations (Puren, 1998), this paper explores ways to make the 21st century teacher's teaching methods innovative and creative so as to keep up with modern approaches like e-learning.

7.2 Inter-cultural Approaches: Theoretical issues

By introducing cross-cultural communication in foreign language teaching, we are opening the door to the source culture; in this case the French culture. The class and minds of teachers and learners according to the classical curriculum were used to the triangular teaching model juxtaposing the Learner, the Language and the Teacher. But recent teaching models that can be explored by French teachers in Kenya are four-sided; that is to say that they bring into interaction the Learner, the Language, the Teacher and "the Other" (Verrier, 1997). Given that the language, the teacher and the learner are tangible realities in the Kenya learning environment, the linguistic perspective changes in terms of points of reference as soon as French language and the learner are placed into a different communicative context. In the old practices, we placed the learner, the teacher and the language in an arbitrary context of the textbooks as can be illustrated by this schema inspired by Lesson 6 in the *Parlons Français* Student Book I.

Figure 7.2.1: The Classical teaching example

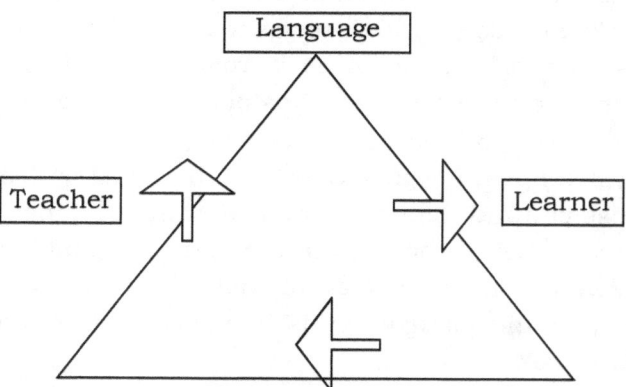

In the classical communication situation above, the teacher had to explain the cultural issues of the foreign culture in order to bring to the mind of the learner the image of the native speaker and his culture in the class in Kenya. In this classical curriculum, the fictional character of the textbook, like the student in the song 'Le Lycée de Bopol', Mansiamina, who accompanies every lesson, guides it and serves as a model throughout the learning. According to Zarate (1986:86), "the character found in the textbook is not considered as representative of the whole group but as an ideal type with unique attributes which cannot be found in everyday life".

By bringing simulations and speech acts into the communication situation through the use of photographs or a video clip or a film, the teacher can expand the image of the native French-speaker the learners' minds. Simulations which are enhanced by information technology can currently be expanded to include, the new dimension involving the speech of the native speaker. This can be illustrated by the figure below:

Figure 7.2.2: Simulated Communication Situations

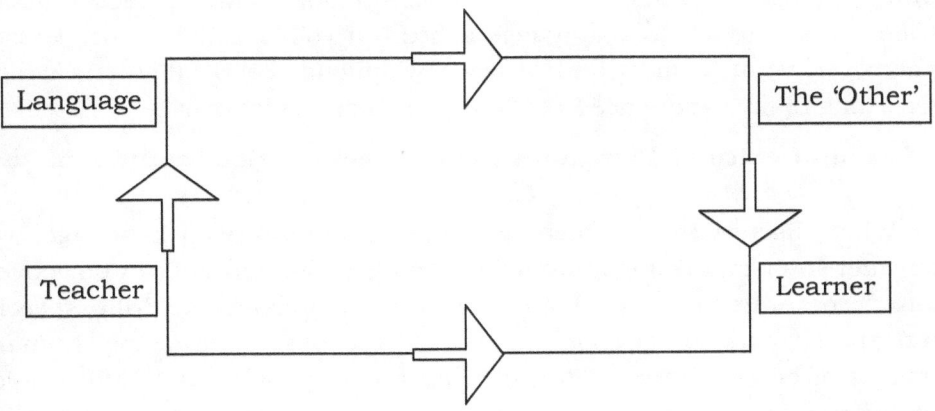

Although the *'Other'* in *Figure 2*, the native speaker, is physically absent from the class, his psychological presence hangs over the learners' minds. This interlocutor is an intermediary who the teacher can call back into the class (by replay) and with whom the learner can try to speak in future communicative contexts. In the simulated scenario, the learners in communication find themselves shifting between a real geographic-cultural space defined by the classroom context in Kenya and the cultural environment of the mother tongue, supported by a geographic-cultural space representing the collective imagination of the French people. This latter version of foreign language learning enhances chances of interactivity.

7.3 "Inter-cultural communication" and "Inter-culturality": Definitional Issues

The adjective 'Inter-cultural', (used very frequently) has a noun equivalent "Inter-culturality" (used much less). The prefix 'inter' is more complex than the prefix 'multi', which refers to juxtaposing or putting cultural aspects side by side. The prefix 'inter' denotes a relationship, a bridge or a system that has been established by blending two cultural elements. 'Inter-culturality' is the sum total of psychological, interpersonal and institutional processes brought about by an interrelation between cultures in reciprocal exchanges, with the aim of safeguarding a relative cultural identity of partners in the relationship (Clanet, 1989:21).

In the teaching of FFL, we open the doors to an 'international' dimension. We set the pace for an 'intersection' between the learner's Kenyan culture and the source culture of the language and we should be able to create adventures from the 'inter-language' 'metissage' set in motion.[2] The expression Inter-cultural introduces the idea of reciprocity in terms of exchanges and a level of complexity in the relationship between cultures. It is these interferences that revitalize relationships. The Inter-cultural communication, like in the simulation context, seems more evident if we attach to a language a head, a voice, a smile or a person whom you want to meet and discover (Capucho, 2008). If this is done, according to my experience in FFL, it motivates the learner.

7.4 Inter-cultural Communication versus Multiculturalism in the Classroom

When discussing the teaching of French as a Foreign Language, we consider Inter-cultural communication both as an end and an objective. Directly or indirectly, we find ourselves working on language drills, speech and speech acts to "develop the capacity to assimilate deeply human aspects of other cultures". 'A multicultural' angle applied to FFL would be different from an 'Inter-cultural' one: multi-culturalism would bring in the language class the co-existence many cultures rather than symbiosis between cultures. This co-existence may sometimes lead to a good mixture (symbiosis), but more often, it gives rise to tension, which can lead to violence. When multicultural methods have led in many cases to an uncontrollable and unmanageable complexity, teachers have deemed it necessary to seek a unifying or dominant factor chosen within or without this attested plurality. This has led to the use of the term 'Inter-cultural communication' (Coste et al, 1997:11).

7.5 The Inter-cultural Enigma

First, it is clear that a cultural representation involves having an idea or a structure or reality organized around simple symbolic elements shared with an individual or a collective unit (Preiswork & Perrot 1975). Consequently, in the French class, the sharing has two dimensions, both

---

2 'Metissage' in English : half- casteship

individual and social. At the individual level the student is faced with the challenge of overcoming stereotypes of the French culture, which stress the differences and at the same time, the student is making an effort to embrace the reality of the cultural diversity, the whole class as a group is discovering through the learning context. Students identify the images of the culture of origin and those of the target culture now being diffused through the language class. The FFL lesson becomes, for the learner a constant interplay between identification and detachment (Bourdieu 1979). The balance in our view, is only achieved when the learner attains the Inter-cultural competency, which allows one to choose "to be like the other person while maintaining your personality" (Ricoeur, 1992) or better still, "to be diverse while remaining unique" (Besse, 1993).

However, the interplay between images of diverse linguistic and socio-cultural contexts can be conflictual and that would be a cause for concerns for all of us. So for the teacher of FFl, it is important to note that linguistic competence alone is not enough. The communication process itself is not linear in practice; some students overcome the cultural stereotypes quickly and others will need much more time. In addition, the transmission of information is never neutral; linguistic and non-linguistic barriers will constantly interrupt the transmission process. The attainment of a satisfactory understanding between the class as a social group and the 'other' culture is not self-evident; the 'intent' as the teacher is describing and the 'representation' to the group of receivers will affect the interpretation of the information. This is why it is vital that the teacher who is handling the Inter-cultural communication in the classroom, masters the art of representing that target culture using the best instruments available for the task.

7.6 The Pedagogy of Inter-cultural Communication

In as much as the effort to master Inter-cultural skills leads the teacher to spread to areas beyond linguistic competences, areas like literature, history, philosophy, political economy, geography, science etc. It requires as well a certain level of understanding cross-cutting features that underlie the FFL curriculum. That is what Louis Porcher et al (1996) have termed "pedagogy of Inter-cultural communication".

According to Porcher (1997, p.48), the pedagogy of intercultural communication takes into account (cultural) diversity as a characteristic of school population today and relies on the mutual enrichment of the learners. In my FFL class at the Technical University of Mombasa for instance, I have to handle several cultural identities and bring them to appreciate a cultural image like wishing a person **'Bon appétit'** through ways, which enrich their understanding of 'having a meal' "à la française".

My message therefore will not only be focusing on the culinary vocabulary of the meal, it will also set the stage for students to discover the practices that accompany that meal. As a result, the idea of Inter-cultural competence will be reducing the importance given to the acquisition of knowledge per say about other countries and cultures; as Trim says, it introduces attitudes and skills necessary in order to discover the others and develop a relationship with "the other" (Trim, 1997:56). That orientation towards "otherness" or inculcating "the openness towards the other" is what Porcher proposes as "the fundamental feature of the effective teacher in Inter-cultural communication" (Porcher, 1997:48)

7.7 The Inter-cultural Approach

At the beginning of this article, I hypothesized that since the teachers of French in Kenya are not exposed to the culture they are trying to present, they encounter difficulties in orienting the FFL class towards that openness towards the 'other'. The question which we try to answer in this section is: what are the basic principles of that Inter-cultural approach to FFL? According to Martine Abdallah-Pretceille (2004), the following, in a paraphrased version, are the tenets for the pedagogy of Inter-cultural exchanges in foreign language teaching:

- Analysis of the encounters and exchanges with a view to training the understanding of other cultures.
- Demystifying cross-cultural exchanges of myths relating to real life communication, mutual friendship and understanding, spontaneity and dialogue between cultures.
- De-emphasizing cultural differences to the benefit of similarities, coherence and common characteristics among the cultures in order to go beyond the level of detail, intuition and subjectivity.
- Learning is objective about the 'Other's being French, German, etc. focusing on the interpersonal exchanges in the communicative situation.
- Evaluating the exchanges to ascertain that the inter-national encounters are meeting points par excellence for Inter-cultural communication.

In summary therefore, we can consider the Inter-cultural approach as basically training in observation, understanding and applying cultural relativism to the foreign culture under study. In other words, when I talk of applying the Inter-cultural mode to FFL, I am encouraging all of us teachers of French to open our classes to a dialogue of cultures.

7.8 Possible Objectives to Facilitate an Inter-cultural Approach

There are few general objectives that can be suggested for FFL teachers to integrate Inter-cultural communication in a language classroom. To use the inspiration of Myriam Denis, (2000:62), these are objectives that are aimed at achieving the Inter-cultural approach:

- ***Moving away from the centre:*** we learn to look at our groups and ourselves from the outside, to be objective about our own system of cultural references and to distance ourselves from our own culture without denying it, thus accepting other points of view.
- ***Putting ourselves in other people shoes:*** we aim at developing empathy, putting ourselves into another person's perspective or point of view, and appreciating the characteristics of other cultures.
- ***Opening to cooperation:*** we must overcome the prejudices and attempt to understand the other, how one perceives reality and so we must learn how to effectively describe the messages transmitted.

7.9 Teaching Methods that usher in the Inter-cultural Approach

Having looked at the pedagogy, at the objectives that facilitate its application, we have to discuss the methods that can allow us to practice it. Some of these have been suggested by Louis Porcher (1988:49).

1. ***Learner-centered and cooperative teaching methods:*** these take into account the learner's needs: self-image, values, beliefs, perception of good and bad. They go beyond theory, basic analysis and comparison since knowledge on cultures alone does not guarantee development of Inter-cultural competence when the learner is faced with the reality of the new culture. Role plays in the teaching of French, other simulations and participatory observations serve as examples of knowledge co-developed by both the teacher and the learners, whereby the classroom observations are to be applied in real life situations.

2. ***Experiential learning methods:*** in this case, one of the French speakers interacts with the learners in a communicative situation and as social players. The teacher as in the classroom scenario works together with the learners for the collective benefit. The learners perform actions themselves in the communicative situation to develop communicative competence for the benefit of all. Here, simulation is not enough to train a social player. The teacher through experiential learning methods seeks to train independent individuals who are also creative, responsible, active and cooperative citizens. These methods include interdisciplinary and extra-curricular Inter-cultural classroom experiences.

3. **Autonomous methods of teaching:** the role of the teacher under the Inter-cultural approach could completely evolve due to the progress in the area of approach to teaching of communicative behaviours. The teaching of language and cultures give the opportunity to the learners to acquire a foreign language outside the classroom, hence allowing for autonomy of the learner while expanding the learning horizons. The teacher in this case will no longer be the sole dispenser or giver of knowledge but a guide, an informant and Inter-cultural mediator, or the linguistic go-between of the teaching-learning process of language and cultures (Cuq & Gruca, 2003: 118). After having awakened the intellectual curiosity of the learner on the linguistic and cultural aspects of the target language, the teacher will guide and support progressively the learning needs.

In brief, these methods rely upon trust as the central pillar for interpersonal exchanges and getting to know each other better when placed in a conducive environment As teachers though, we must note from the above teaching methods that "we do not receive Inter-cultural communication ready-made, we manufacture it"(Porcher, 1988:49).The teacher who will achieve best the Inter-cultural approach must be willing to take risks, to ask the difficult questions about culture, to be sincere in ex-pressing deep feelings before asking the learners to share their own observations.

7.10 Inter-cultural Communication and the Teaching/Learning of French as a Foreign Language

The major assumption we made in this article is that language is the carrier and container of culture on the one hand and on the other hand, language is influenced and shaped by culture; it reflects culture (Liu Kun, 2013). In the same vein, "learning a language is learning or attempting to penetrate a culture". (*Le Français Dans le Monde.*1977: n° 131). The challenge of the teacher of French as a foreign language is not only to teach the foreign language and culture, but also to show the learner how native culture interacts with the culture of French or the Francophone person. That is the main challenge in the lesson, which integrates culture or Civilization. The foregoing discussion has shown that in order to develop their capacity to communicate effectively with those who are different from them, teachers of FFL must develop methods and techniques that transcend theoretical, analytical and comparative levels since we know that knowledge alone does not guarantee skills development in the context of intercultural communication.

The transmission of purely informative knowledge will not allow the learner to develop an aptitude in observing the foreign reality, so long as the learners have not acquired what Geneviève Zarate (1993) calls the "interpretative know-how" of other cultures. This 'skill' needs time to sensitize the learner on the efforts one has to make to effect the transition from one cultural system to another, despite the different nature of the native cultural competence and that of the foreigner.

When dealing with a learning point that is of a topical nature in FFL, the objective of cultural awareness is therefore to make the learners interrogate reality with more acuity and to exploit the Civilization issues without being judgemental. This presupposes that the teacher of French as a Foreign Language accepts to learn and to teach theory and practice of his own culture and that of the foreign culture. It is an obligation that we should first look at our own culture in the mirror before looking through the window of other cultures. It is in one way, as the sayings go, of trying to 'sweep in front of our own door' or 'removing the speck in our own eyes'.

7.11 Tools for Bringing Inter-cultural communication into the French Class

By now we know, that as teachers in French as Foreign Language classroom, we should teach the learners to reflect upon what culture is and the way we use to reveal the cultural knowledge to the learners will conditions our actions. In order to make it easier to impart this awareness to the learners, a systematic progressive move from the classical teaching tool more effective ones in communicative terms is vital. The teacher may start this endeavour with observable cultural elements (e.g. architecture, clothes, foods, symbols etc). The teacher can subsequently introduce the cultural implicit knowledge, which conditions our behaviour as social players from the most visible to the less visible elements: gestures, the management of space and time, relationships and feelings, social status indicators, methods of work, etc.

Besides, the group actions in class, in order to sensitize the learners to Inter-cultural communication, audio-visual supports like the Internet also put at our disposal a great quantity of original documents such as photos, radio programmes, statistics, newspapers, films etc., which could serve as stimuli for Inter-cultural classroom activities. In the Inter-cultural teaching model, these tools and documents should not be used in a purely descriptive approach, but should guide the learners to think about the reasons which condition our different habits and behaviour.

However, the best way to initiate the learners to Inter-cultural communication seems to be bringing them into direct communication with other speakers of the target language. This is what the exchange and collaborative programmes can help us to achieve. It is important for teachers of FFL to engage in projects that allow the learners to know each other and to communicate amongst themselves on topics related to their day to day life vis-à-vis the life of the French or Francophone peers: their school, their estate, their meals, their leisure activities, their holidays, their tales and legends, etc. Such exchanges put the learners in a dialogue situation with the language they are studying for example, through letters or correspondence or study visits with the native speakers, and this reinforces mutual cultural understanding. Since inter-cultural communication is a product of interaction between two cultures, the impact of such programmes should be observed, analyzed and documented in order to prepare both teachers and learners to cope with global trends towards multi-lingualism and multiculturalism.

7.12 Inter-cultural Communication Content in the current Curriculum of French in Kenya.

As noted at the beginning of this article, FFL teaching today in Kenya is characterized by two main pedagogical orientations: the classical language teaching and the more recent communication simulation trend. However, the textbooks available in the market are the major sources of information in the classroom because of constraints being experienced with other teaching tools and materials. It is in this context that I place my analysis of the sociological relevance of the text-books of teaching the French language and the cultural, how we can adapt Inter-cultural communication to the local situation and render it more current and relevant.

It is evident that no course book for French as a Foreign Language developed for use for more than five years can include all the topicality and modernity of the society. *Parlons Français,* and *'Entre copains'*, the French Course books currently in use in secondary schools, have texts and activities to do in a language classroom, which are part of Civilization issues. Some good examples have been extracted in the Figures below:

Figure 7.12.1: Cultural aspects in Parlons Français

Student Book I: Map, greetings, language registers, francophone calendar, currencies, expressions of politeness, simulation (in a restaurant), advertisements, song (Bopol Mansiamina).

Student Book II: Welcoming a guest, education system, cars and registration numbers, transport system in France, time table, poems, proverbs, horoscope, meteorology, road signs, foods and vegetables, types of shops.

> **Student Book III:** Games and sports, poems, recipes, proverbs, tourist activities and attractions, transport systems in France and in Mali, poems, signage/ road signs, rural-urban lifestyles, advertisement, environmental issues.
>
> **Student Book IV:** Professions/ careers, proverbs, poems, advertisements, gender issues (at workplace), acronyms and abbreviations, domestic consumption of goods, domestic animals, French television, radio and print media, vocabularies of the French–speaking world.

Figure 7.12.2: Cultural aspects in Entre Copains

> **Student Book I:** Photos, advertisements, time table.
>
> **Student Book II:** School bags, towns, poems, transport system, tourist attractions, photos, traditional / staple foods.
>
> **Student Book III:** Photos, sport celebrities, poems, diseases, television/ cinema/ film, cars, fashion, communication system, song, horoscope, advertisements, tourist attractions, pastimes, environmental issues, personalities, town versus village.
>
> **Student Book IV:** Celebrities, sports, tourist attractions, photos, songs, poems, education systems, currencies (the Euro), advertisements, occupations, pastimes.

The analysis above shows the cultural aspects extracted from the Table of Content of *Parlons Français* and the aspects from that one of *Entre Copains*, represent approximately 35% and 28% respectively of the total content of the 2 selected text books of FFL at secondary school level. Unfortunately, they constitute components of cultural knowledge only. Creative and comparative approaches must therefore be used to go beyond this current scope and bring in more information on the French culture and Civilization.

An analysis of the Table of Content also shows that about 30% and 25% of the Kenyan or African cultures was included in this curriculum of FFL. In terms of balancing the learner's indigenous cultures and the target foreign culture a lot more has to be done. In order to make this a real inter-cultural approach, it is absolutely necessary that the course book uses information, which is accessible in order to help the teacher to communicate to the learner current and familiar information from the French-speaking world. Given the paucity of such information in the curriculum of the 2 text books selected, the teacher Kenyan teacher of FFL at the secondary school level has the responsibility of enriching his course content with supports like audio-visual additions or even 'Civilization issues' or 'topics' extracted from authentic francophone documents.

Available authentic documents to explore include:

1. **Songs:** these constitute a very important source of Civilization information in today's world. They are also a good example of original documents to be introduced in the teaching of French as Foreign language. Since learning a language is to learn or attempt to penetrate a culture, and that songs among other elements constitute culture, their pedagogical importance should be reconsidered. Songs should not be used only as sources of motivation but they should be part of complete language lessons. They should be pleasant to the learners, either their words or their melody, preferably by all these elements. They should be able to study the imagination and creativity of the artists and compare their visions. It is edifying and interesting.

2. **The press:** A section of international print media is published in French every week. Thanks to the francophone press reviews, laden with opinions expressed in other countries, learners are able to enrich their cultural knowledge.

3. **Films:** they are complete aids in themselves and have been favourably received by many teachers. It is important however to watch out for stereotypes, which they some-times pass on. If they are identified and discussed, they make an interesting study of the target culture and civilization.

4. **Sections of travel guides:** The contexts vary a lot depending on the "spirit" of the collection. The FFL teacher can watch out for the commonest clichés and preconceived ideas for their discussion and sensitization of the learners.

5. **Collections of pictures / photographs:** these are usually, based on themes and depicting the rituals of different countries, they constitute a good starting point for classroom study. The teacher has to facilitate their appreciation taking into account the origin of the learners.

The Kenyan FFL teacher could also explore more cultural awareness activities like francophone national events and artistic performances where possible. Since Inter-cultural communication is designed as a process, exchange programmes between students in indigenous culture settings and those using French as native or official language should be developed. These collaborative projects, as, Coste et al (1997), ob-serve, will help remove social barriers, and strengthen cultural reciprocity and solidarity. The learners themselves in this case can act as cultural interpreters and using their capacity to decipher coded messages in the target culture.

Other resources and statistics provide original tools for comparison of lifestyles. Always, the teacher is called upon to be creative and innovative in order to make his lesson more relevant.

7.13 Conclusion and Recommendations

Being a new value to add to the overall educational objective, Inter-cultural communication does not only aim at making the learner understand better the foreign language in all its linguistic and cultural dimensions but it facilitates opening up to the other and increases mutual respect for the other. The principle of "dialogism", otherness and "intercorporeity" so dear to Bakthine (1975) where the role of the teacher-media-tor in the teaching of language and cultures, is to inculcate the spirit of dialogue and humanism in a language class and unite human beings can be expanded to become a humanistic en-deavour for the mutual understanding between people and mutual enrichment of cultures. In the context of FFL in Kenya, it helps us to challenge the social stereotypes, fight xenophobia and racism as we have seen them recently erupt into terrorist atrocities in our territory.[3]

For this to happen, a few suggestions are made here as recommendations:

- Kenyan teachers should think much more outside the box in the teaching of French as foreign language, ready to adapt their teaching methods to those that critique objectively our own system of cultural references, enable us to appreciate the characteristics of other cultures and be open to cooperation.
- Even as they make use of the course book, teachers at the secondary school level can enrich this course content with materials for activities based on inter-cultural communication like 'Civilization issues' or 'topics' extracted from authentic francophone documents such as songs, media excerpts, films, travel guides, photograph collections etc. or those present on the Internet.
- The course books for French as a Foreign Language in Kenya, like *Parlons Français* or *Entre Copains* developed in the 1990s, have not been revised to keep pace with the globalization trends worldwide. They need to be reviewed with a view to producing a new edition.
- The texts and activities currently proposed in the FFL curriculum, should be studied in a classroom situation using a cooperative and experiential approach in order to create in the learner the 'interpretive know-how' of cultural and Civilization matters.

---

3 Like some media reports of the last terrorist attacks on Westland Mall in Nairobi.

- Cultural activities evolved around proverbs, sayings, poems, songs, tales and legends, can be studied in a comparative approach in respect of the indigenous cultures of the learners and the foreign language culture to encourage cultural dialogue and mutual understanding.
- Teachers of French at the secondary level are encouraged to engage in collaborative exchange projects, which can allow the learners to know each other and to communicate amongst themselves on topics related to their day to day life vis-à-vis the life of the French or Francophone peers.

References

Abdallah-Pretceille M., Porcher L. (1996) (2nd ed.2001): Éducationet communication interculturelle, Paris, PUF

Abdallah-Pretceille M.(1999): *L'éducation interculturelle,* PUF, Collection Que sais-je? n° 30487

Bakhtin, M. (1975): *The Dialogic imagination: Chronotope, Heteroglossia:* University of Texas Press.

Byram, M. (1992): *Culture et éducation en langue étrangère,* Collection LAL, Paris, Hatier-Didier

Besse, H. (1984): «Éduquer la perception interculturelle», in *Le Français Dans le Monde,* n°188

Besse, H. (1993) :« Cultiver une identité plurielle», in *Le Français Dans le Monde,* n° 254

Bourdieu P. (1979): *La Distinction: Critique sociale du Jugement,* Les Éditions de Minuit, 670 pages, Paris.

Capucho M.F (2008) « Quel plurilinguisme pour quel Environnement professionnel multilingue? Un nouvel atout dans le monde professionnel», in *L'Intercompréhension en action,* Repères Do RiF n. 4 CECC – Universidade Católica Portuguesa, Lisbonne, Universidade Católica Portuguesa : Projet INTERMAR.

Chokah, M. (2013):"Training of teachers of French in Kenya: Redefining the needs of an increasingly demanding context", In *International Journal of Education and Research.* Vol. I no9: 2013.

Chokah, M. (2013):"Fifty years of the teaching/learning of French as a Foreign Language in Kenya: challenges for teachers and learners" in *International Journal of Education and Research.* Vol.I,no. 3, 2013.

Clanet C. (1989), *L'interculturel. Introduction aux approaches interculturelle en Éducation et en Sciences Humaines,* Toulouse, Presses universitaires du Mirail (http://questionsdecommunication.revues.org/4510)

Coste et al (1997): *Compétence plurilingue et pluriculturelle. Versun cadre commun de référence pour l'enseignement et l'apprentissage des langues vivantes: études préparatoires*, Strasbourg: éditions du Conseil de l'Europe.

Cuq, J.P. (2003): *Dictionnaire de didactique du français langue étrangère et seconde*, Paris, CLE international, ASDIFLE

Cuq, J.P., Gruca, I. (2002): *Cours de didactique du français Langue étrangère et seconde*, Grenoble, Presses Universitaires de Grenoble.

Denis M. (2000): Appréhender l'interculturel dans un Establishment secondaire au Portugal in Dialogues et cultures, no 44

Iraki, F. (ed.) (2006): «Research on French Teaching in Eastern Africa, Opportunities and Challenges», Nairobi, USIU

Loccidal, M. (2001): "La pluriculturalité en milieu scolaire", *Cahiers Pédagogiques*, n°395, pp 66-67

O'Neil, C. (1993): *Les enfants et l'enseignement des langues* étrangères, Paris, Didier-Hatier

Porcher L. et al (1996): *L'apprentissage précoce des langues*, PUF, Collection Que sais-je ?

Porcher Louis. (1998): « De l'interculturel », in *Cahiers pédagogiques*, n°360 : éditions du Conseil de l'Europe.

Puren, C. (1988): *Histoire des méthodologies de l'enseignement des langues*, Paris, Nathan.

Preiswork & Perrot. (1975).(1975): *Ethnocentrisme et histoire*. Paris: Anthropos.

Reboullet, A., Tétu, M. (eds) (1977) : *Guide Culturel, Civilizations et littératures d'expression française*, Paris, Hachette

Ricoeur P. (1992): Oneself as another http://www.newworldencyclopedia.org/entry/Paul_Ricoeur Accessed 19/01/2015

Trim, J.M. (1997): Language learning for European citizenship: Council of Europe Publications.

Verrier, J. (1997): « Cinqquestions sur l'enseignement du FLE en milieu scolaire », in *Le Français Dans Le Monde*n °291, pp27-28.

Ticusan (2013): "Psycho-pedagogical Formative Valences of the Geographical Game" in *Procedia - Social and Behavioural Sciences*, Volume 83, 4 July, Pages 234–237.

Zarate, G. (1993): *Représentations de l'étranger et didactique des langues*, Coll. Essais, Paris, Didier- CREDIF.

Zarate, G. (1986): *Enseigner une culture étrangère*, Paris, Hachette, F-Recherches et applications.

Internet Sources

http://www.didierfle.com/didier_fle/publications/41922.htm Accessed 12/12/2014

http://www.fdlm.org/fle/article/358/Kenya.php Accessed 12/12/2014

www.frenchinkenya.com/view_content.php?contid=4 Directory of the Teaching of French in Kenya. (n.d.) Retrieved 14/01/2015

http://www.millenaire3.com/contenus/ouvrages/lexique8/multicult.pdf Accessed 12/12/2014

http://resources-cla.univ-fcompte.fr/gerflint/Baltique2/Inter-culturalte.pdf Accessed 12/12/2014

http://casnav.ac-dijon.fr/article.php3?id_article=78, as retrieved on 28th august 2008

http://franc-parler.org (Lettre d'information, été 2008) as retrieved on 28th august 2008

http://www.rifeff.org/pdf/Ouvrage_fef_2_additif2.pdf Accessed 12/12/2014

http://questionsdecommunication.revues.org/4510%3Flang%3Den Accessed 12/12/2014

http://www.portaldeperiodicos.unisul.br/index.php/Poiesis/article/download/1166/962 Accessed 12/01/2015

PART THREE
TRANSLATION AND INTERPRETATION

PART THREE

CHAPTER EIGHT
NOMENCLATURE AND AUTHENTICITY OF TRANSLATED PLAYS FROM ENGLISH TO LUSOGA

Cornelius Wambi Gulere[1]

Abstract

Translation of literary texts from European and Oriental Languages into African Languages is a worthwhile under-taking for bridging the gap between the cultures involved. However, due to poor translation strategies and decision-making processes, such translations fail to capture the dynamics of both the Source Language (SL) and Target Language (TL) because of nomenclature. As a result, most translations communicate more the SL culture than the intended messages and themes. I argue that authenticity of literary translations is obtained when a text speaks directly to the TL audience as it did to the SL audience without any cultural and contextual barriers. My argument is based on my experience of translating five plays from English into Lusoga Language: Austin Bukenya's *The Bride*, Wole Soyinka's *The Trials of Brother Jero*, and Francis Imbuga's *Betrayal in the City*, Sophocles' *Antigone* and William Shakespeare's *King Lear*. I find that all the five texts speak directly to their audiences in Lusoga when people and place names, the relevant imagery and contexts are totally adapted to the Lusoga language and culture. Instances like in *Trials of Brother Jero* where characters are foreign the message is equally treated as foreign although prevalent in Busoga. Similarly, events like that initiation in *The Bride* or inheritance in *King Lear*, not part of Kisoga culture are authenticated in the Lusoga language and culture through a creative transformation of the literary texts.

Key words: *Lusoga, nomenclature, context, translation, adaptation, interpretation, performance*

---

1 Cornelius Wambi Gulere has written and translated over 200 works in Lusoga. The books and articles he has authored include: Riddling and Taboos: Exploring Boundaries in Discussing Reproductive Health; Eibwanio: The Lusoga - English Dictionary; Riddle Performance: The Evasive, the Popular and the Enigmatic in the Written Form; The Popular Form and Structure of Riddle Discourse in Lusoga; Lusoga-English Riddle Performance: Diikuula's Love Riddles. He is a Doctoral Fellow of the AHP/ACLS and MakNUFU Folklore Linkage Project 2007-2012.

8.1 Introduction

"Juliet: ...that which we call a rose/by any other name would smell as sweet; So Romeo would, were he not Romeo call'd,/Retain that dear perfection which he owes/without that title. *William Shakespeare's play: Romeo and Juliet (1600)*"

"Namwendwa: ...ekyo ekyetweta loozi/na liina lindi kyandiwunha kaghoogho nga kyo; Kale Mpomyewo yandibaire, waire tiyandibaire ayetebwa Mpomyewo,/ Yandisigaiza obwamufu obwo bw'aghola/nga azira ntwiko eyo. (Cornelius Gulere: Mpomyewo ni Namwendwa (2014)"

The translator and critic have to grapple with the challenge of translating and interpreting Literatures in languages different from the Source Languages (SL) and cultures. The translator's audience, time and place are often quite different from the Source Text (ST) writer's audience. As such, any good translation must have a particular audience, time and place constantly in mind. Hence, much attention needs to be made to imagery and nomenclature, which determine how an original work of art or its translation is to be categorized, appreciated and analyzed. In this perspective, I have been theoretically guided by what Louis Kelly, cited in Venuti (2012: 4), has said of a complete theory of translation: basing ourselves on the three components of "specification of function and goal", "description and analysis of operations", as well as "critical comment on relationships between goal and operation". Whereas I have focused on the translation of Kisoga nomenclature as the main goal, I have endeavoured to describe and analyze how the meaning of these names impact on the message and understanding of the plays that have been translated. I have also critiqued the socio-cultural, ideological and pedagogical relationship between those names in the source text and how they are perceived in the receiving culture.

In this article, I share first hand experiences of translating five plays from English into Lusoga, namely (1) Austin Bukenya's *The Bride* (2) Sophocles' *Antigone* (3) Wole Soyinka's *Trials of Brother Jero* (4) Francis Imbuga's *Betrayal in the City* and (5) William Shakespeare's *King Lear*. I transformed these ST in terms of nomenclature, imagery and contexts and created five Lusoga plays, entitled, (1) *Omugole,* (2) *Nantameigwa* (3) *Ebikemo by'Owoluganda Yero,* (4) *Nkwe mu Kibuga* and (5) *Kyabazinga Mukama.*

I pay particular attention to nomenclature because in Busoga culture, nomenclature plays a major role in the characterization of people and places and in cross-cultural communication. This is because unlike the English names, which may only be an individual's label, a name in the

Kisoga culture indicates a historical context, social affiliation status and to some extent the personality of the bearer. Name is an embodiment of one's identity. The interpretation of meaning of a work of art is therefore enriched by the names and imagery used to communicate its message. The audience has in most cases, to grapple with the challenge of interpreting Literatures in translation, which carry much of the SL culture into the TL. For example, a name like Oedipus that means 'big foot' in Greek where used in an African context would immediately carry with it that foreign connotation. For audiences that are not familiar with this meaning, the meta-communication in the name would be missed. This leads the translated literature to "occupy a referral position" (Tamar Even-Zohar, in Lawrence Venuti, 2000:197) because it does not serve the full purpose of emancipating the TL rather it serves the SL.

In culturally authentic translation, texts, names, imagery and contexts have to fit within the context of the TL. In particular, the naming of people, places and things as well as the imagery used should be localized to the TL context(s). Imagery and names are in most cases not just artificial. Since they carry diverging connotations from one language to another, they communicate differently from one culture to another. It therefore matters so much "how they communicate" (Pilkington, 2000: 89)" [Quoted in Xiao 2011:80]. Important stylistic features in the original such as metaphor can help us to evaluate how close or how far removed is the translation from the original. Metaphorical expressions need to be localized and not simply stated literally. When names and imagery are not placed appropriately into the context of the target language, they distort messages and as a result the meaning and interpretation of the work is flawed. The naming of people, places and things whether in symbolism or style, needs to be localized to the new language context(s).

The matter of transformational translation remains of interest to linguists especially because total comprehension of literary translations is problematic to the TL audience necessitating constant reference to the SL culture. This article focuses on the problematic of translating nomenclature, from one language to another while maintaining the primary intention of the text. Four of the five plays, namely, *The Bride, Trials of Brother Jeroboam, Betrayal in the City* and *King Lear* were originally written in the English Language, although it is only King Lear that is an English play. Antigone is a Greek play originally written in the Greek Language and the Lusoga translation is made from an English translation making the translation into Lusoga far removed from the original text hence a completely new literary creation.

Baker's taxonomy: Mona Baker (1992: 26-42) quoted in Zohre Owji (2013:17) lists eight translation strategies:

> Translation by a more general word.
> Translation by a more neutral or less expressive word.
> Translation by cultural substitution.
> Translation using a loan word or loan word plus explanation.
> Translation by paraphrase using a related word.
> Translation by paraphrase using unrelated words.
> Translation by omission.
> Translation by illustration.

I mostly applied the strategy of translation by cultural substitution that "involves replacing a culture-specific item or expression with a target language item considering its impact on the target reader."(Zohre Owji 2013:17) The decision to use this strategy depended on my personal desire to create plays in Lusoga that would be "more natural, more understandable and more familiar to the target reader." (n.d) I argue that, for the text to remain authentic with regards to the SL and TL, the nomenclature and imagery has to be changed as demonstrated in the following examples.

8.2 The nomenclature in the play: Omugole

Omugole, a translation of *The Bride* by Austin Bukenya is a play about the family and the state. It reflects the state of marriage in a post-colonial setting of which Busoga is a part. Transforming the title *The Bride* to *Omugole* and adopting new names that conform to the title and culture of Busoga makes the text easy to receive. The new title *Omugole* is as connotative and symbolic as the English title as it suggests, 'one whose finest hairs have been shaved off from their forehead'. In Lusoga, this does not only mean smartness and beauty but submitting to the shaver and subordinating oneself to the world of the onlookers, which is exactly what Namaadhi does without necessarily being circumcised. In order to complete this meaning in the play, other names of places and of the characters have to be transformed into Lusoga too. Simply translating words from the Source text (ST) to the Target text (TT) does not achieve the goal of validating the text as a Lusoga text.

I have taken Austin Bukenya's personal elaboration of meaning attached to the characters and came up with the following matching names in Lusoga. (This information was shared in an email communication with the author on Tuesday, June 12 2012 at 4:28 PM).

Figure 8.2.1: Nomenclature in the play: Omugole

Name	Metaphoric Projection	Literal rendition	Authentic Translation into Lusoga
Namvua	"image of innocence, generosity, regeneration"	Daughter of the Rains	*Namaadhi*
Lekindo	"an articulate revolutionary, symbol of a new generation; also element of reckless youthfulness	Arguer	*Mughakanhi*
Shundu	"thick, stubborn and aggressive conservative	Die-hard	*Byantaka*
Mkumbu	"pathetically trapped in the past and her total refusal to accept the death of her son."	Memory woman	*Byaidho*
Lerema	"a dual personality: divinely, he is the image of wisdom and power (when possessed); humanly, a tired, sluggish and disillusioned man."	Heavy One	*Isegya*
Lesijore	"a man with an identity crisis: neither youth nor elder; anxious to be accepted as an adult with wisdom"	Pretender	*Mulobole*
Merio	"a humble but cunning little man, with the sharpened survival instincts of the self-conscious 'outsider'"	Shrewd one	*Magezi*
Tatu	"a loud domineering woman, with an ethnic superiority complex over her husband and daughter"	Triple Woman	*Kwemanha*
Sikitu	"friendly worldly-wise mature woman delighted to play her 'senga' role to the hilt"	No-matter/ Never mind	*Nziransonga* from which is derive *Songa*
Nghaghenya	an ancient relic, peddling out dated and unconvincing heroics"	Inciter	*Ngaghenha*
Kajiru	a "nasty, self-assured snob, fiercely jealous of Namvua" is conceived as Kasiru	Insidious One	*Mpalampa*

Foreign Languages: Lessons

Replacing the Kiswahili names with Kisoga names takes the play from its original set culture to that of the target Lusoga language. The meanings and metaphoric connotation embedded in the names of the characters both in the SL and TL are culturally appropriated for the play to communicate its authentic message. In particular, Kisoga names that carry meaning in Lusoga are a great resource for the play.

Foreign names in an indigenous text like this are sometimes treated lightly, and not deserving seriousness because they place the character outside the context of performance. For instance, names like Mtuta and Nyagwede transformed as *Mutwita* and *Nagwere* respectively, gain admittance into Lusoga for their identifiable meanings "smashing beauty" and "a lady belonging to the Gwere clan". On the contrary, Mtuta and Nyagwede inserted into a translation without adapting or "lusogasing" them will be nothing but undecipherable references. Similarly, the rituals, songs and dances had to be adapted to Kisoga culture to meet the theme of the play. The "rika of the Albinos" is conceived as clan "*kika kya Beerupe*", which completes the historical and traditional sense of the play.

The Bride as *Omugole* with all these transformations in nomenclature and imagery is from this linguistic perspective an authentic text in translation. A failure to re-align the text with the culture of the TL renders the play *Omugole* ineffective in Lusoga because the embedded meanings are compromised.

8.3 The nomenclature in the play: Nantameigwa

Similarly, translating *Antigone* into Lusoga without using the local flavour, imagery and nomenclature only makes it a play in Lusoga. Watching "*Nantameigwa*" on stage should neither betray its foreign origin (Greek – English) nor is its present transformation into Lusoga. This goal is achieved by fully adjusting the socio-historical-literary account of its nomenclature to suit the TL. Leaving communication gaps hidden in the names, imagery, setting, and other literary features of a work of art betrays the essence of transforming the text to communicate and entertain the targeted audience in the TL.

In the English text, *Antigone*, the name of the central character is Oedipus' daughter. It is the same name as that of the Greek text but in Lusoga, this name does not make sense. It becomes a barrier to the appreciation of the message. Suitable names and imagery used in the Lusoga play *Nantameigwa* matching those in Sophocles' *Antigone* are as follows:

Figure 8.3.1: Nomenclature in the play: Nantameigwa

Name in Greek	Metaphoric Projection	Literal rendition	Authentic Translation into Lusoga
Antigone, daughter of Oedipus	Invincible	*Worthy of one's parents; unbending*	*Nantameigwa mughala Kigereigu*
Isemene, daughter of Oedipus	Knowable	Self-conceited person	*Naimanhe - mughala wa Kigereigu*
Oedipus	Big foot	Proverbial name meaning, a heavy foot is not too heavy for its owner	*Kigereigu*
King Creon	Chief	One who presides	*Mwami*
Euridice, wife to Creon	Truthful	Honest person	*Mazima muka Mwami*
Haemon, son of Creon	Bloody	Tainted with blood	*Lwamusaayi mutabane wa Mwami*
Polynices	Quarrelsome	Never at peace with others	*Muyombi*
Teiresias, the blind prophet	Foreteller	Soothsayer	*Mulaguzi Taire omutulu*
The Guards	Keepers	*Soldiers or battalions*	*Baisirukale or Abakuumi*
Eteocles	Agreeable	One who is always in agreement with others	*Basakana*
Messenger	Carrier of news	Servant	*Mugheereza*
Chorus	Group of commentators with one voice	Players and singers	*Bazaanhi, Bembi Basungirizi*

In terms of nomenclature, there is hardly anything in the play *Nantameigwa* that betrays a foreign origin of the story. By doing so, the Lusoga translation achieves what I consider a complete transformation. According to Greek mythology, Thebes is the birthplace of Dionysus, the god of wine and pleasure, and Heracles. It was also the place of mythical king Oedipus and mythical creature Sphinx (See, Greek gods.org). It would be ridiculous to localize Thebes as *Thebusi* or *Sebusi* because physically and metaphorically, those two alternatives evoke nothing to a Kisoga speaking audience. Instead, the setting was made Sigulu Islands, which is a part of Busoga in the eastern part of the Lake Victoria and has similar physical features as those of Thebes, namely a rocky island. Sigulu Island has its own stories about a minotaur and snakes with two heads but these have not been researched and documented to support this choice of name.

Sigulu Islands is a realistic setting for the play in the TL context, rather than just creating an unknown place by just localizing the foreign names. The Sigulu Island set instead of Thebes makes all the other adaptations and actions natural and meaningful. In this way, the play *Nantameigwa* is authenticated as a Lusoga play on the language level as it conveys Sophocles' universal message about how love is unshakable, while at the same time communicating the culture of the people of Busoga and not necessarily that of the Greeks.

8.4 The nomenclature in the play: Ebikemo by Owoluganda Yero

In this next play, Wole Soyinka does not use names, imagery and settings, to convey his message to the same degree as either Bukenya or Sophocles does in *The Bride* and *Antigone*. For that matter, the transformation of the play The *Trials of Brother Jero* is not so profound. The names and places are translatable without having to make great inventions because they are common place to the TL community. The play is set at a beach – *Omwaalo* and Jero's compound – *Oluya lwa Yerobowamu*. The main characters, Amope and Chume are treated as foreigners to this part of the community. The original meaning of Chume in Igbo is linked to God, who is known as "Chi" (God the spiritual being). It could be a short form of Chimaka, "God is beautiful" (www.behindthenames.com/names/igbo/). Amupe, on the other hand makes reference to unfortunate tongue. Most probably, the names were crafted to beseech God's providence and mercy to the foreigners. These names are therefore used to create the impression that, this is a story of errant foreigners who have come into Busoga following a foreign religion and culture; the names of the characters are not translated into Lusoga. This thinking is partly in line with Wole Soyinka's own thinking.

Although such nomenclature leaves loopholes in the message to the **'Amopes'** and **'Chumes'** in Busoga, it is realistic that Amope is conceived as a woman from one of the settler families coming in Busoga in the advent of foreign religions. Likewise, Chume and Jeroboam are identified as foreigners thus distancing their ill character from the TL culture. This point of view safeguards the integrity of the TL culture and society, making the play accurate in terms of the desirable invincibility of the Basoga as a nation.

Some other language aspects like the religious incantations of "Abraka" and "Hebra" in the following prayer are left without being translated into Lusoga so that the foreignness of the new culture being conveyed remains prominent:

> **KYUME:** Y-e-e-e-e-su. Y-e-e-e-su, mwambe mulundi mulala
> Y-e-ee-e-e-su.
> **YEROBOWAAMU**: Abraka, Abraka, Abraka.
> **KYUME**: [yeyungamu] Abraka, Abraka. Abraka.
> Abraka, Hebra [x8].

These incantations have come along with the new religious movements sweeping across Africa. We therefore use them in the Lusoga text in recognition of the fact that, they too are localized in contemporary Americanized worship. This is part of the mystery of "speaking in tongues "in some contemporary churches. The mystery of the power of the Holy Spirit in this case seems to be more important than the actual communication between the pastor and the worshippers. The dialogue is a linguistic anomaly, which we have decided to keep "as is", in other words as an anomaly in Lusoga. Replacing them with tradition incantations like "*hemu hemu hemu!*" would remove the play from the thematic critique on religion and the dramatic concerns that Soyinka wanted to convey thus making the play less authentic in that regard.

8.5 The nomenclature in the play: Nkwe mu Kibuga

The universality of African's post-colonial city woes and terrors makes *Betrayal in the City* by Francis Imbuga easily adaptable into various languages. Just like the plays discussed earlier, "*Nkwe mu Kibuga*" would be inauthentic if the nomenclature was not transformed to meet the needs of the TL culture. This was achieved with slight adjustments in name spellings but the impact is to totally offer complete effects and meaning in the Lusoga play.

For example, the name Adika that carries no meaning in Lusoga was first adapted as *Azika,* meaning the one who gets wild or bushy but with further analysis, the connotatively richer *Aizika,* meaning the one who is returnable was adapted. In the Lusoga version of the play, the name *Aizika* captures both meanings of one gone wild and returned home. The pun is suggested in the line:

> There is nothing we shall do that will return Adika.
> *Ghazira kye tunaakola kinaiza Aizika.* (9)

The statement in Lusoga is richer because of the internal rhyme in "*kinaiza Aizika*", which is suggestive of eternal hope as reflected in the name *Aizika*. Similarly, the irony of rottenness of the system needed to be sustained in the name '*Kyagaga*' for '*Chagaga*' to mean something going stale; a choice opposed to '*Kigaiga*' [it is rich], which is suggested in the character of '*Chagaga*'.

In addition, the pun on 'Jusper', 'Jupiter' and 'justice' (10) is embedded in *Mayengo, Mayingo* and *Mayungo* (11) respectively. The statement: "*ekyo kyendi, Mayingo Mu-wendo*" make much sense and beauty in Lusoga compared to "*Ekyo kyendi, Jasipa Wendo*", which is a mere corruption of the SL text.

Likewise, the state of Kafira is named *Kafiirwa* because of its double entrendre in Lusoga. The prefix *ka-* denotes a diminutive relationship with regards to loss and bereavement. *Kafiirwa* also means a small man who is impotent. Combining these two views give the name Kafiira a greater aesthetic appeal in the TL compared to Kafira that would not carry any significant meaning.

Language mannerisms linked to characters like the use of "gonna join", "we gotta restore" (11) used by *Mayingo* have been translated through the forcefulness of the written Lusoga language rather than the spoken word. In a theatrical performance however, the stress syllables and the drawl of spoken Lusoga have to be leveled out in time.

Vainly, the degree 'BA' is not easy to translate and it is a glaring communication gap. An appropriate acronym needs to be obtained in the Lusoga. Maintaining BA in the Lusoga play adds to the cynicism that, the playwright has over this paper qualification.

Similarly, Mulili's grammatical errors have been replicated in Lusoga but not to the same degree of effect as in the original English text. This is because the errors in English are the result of direct translation of his local language interference with the English. I have nonetheless attributed some ridiculous phrases, to Mulili that may not be as obvious as the English text showing that Mulili is not well (in) formed. For example;

> **MAYINGO:** *(adhugumira / atiire) Isebo, ate ebidhuuba?*
> **KIBUTO:** *Omughasi yetwakobeje okukola emuntu akaali kudhikola.*

Other names I have modified include *Baaleka* [they left] for Kaleka, *Ndoga* [I bewitch] for Doga, *Niinia* [bring it up] for Nina, *Musesi* [laughing one] for Mosese, *Kibuto* [large stomach] for Tumbo and *Kabitiro* [by pass] for Kabito. In this way, the names speak directly to the new context and reinforce the meaning of the play in Lusoga.

8.6 The nomenclature in the play: Kyabazinga Mukama

In the previous play, *Nkwe nu Kibuga* and in this *Kyabazinga mukama*, the transformations are quite elaborate because of the ideological orientations of the original plays. It is therefore not just the names and imagery that necessitated changing but some ideas had to be reconstructed in order to suit the new contexts. In keeping with this, the translations are not just linguistic and literary fits, but ideological re-orientation of the texts.

For that matter, King *Lear* is versioned as *"Kyabazinga Mukama"* not as *"Kyabazinga Liya"* because of the need to capture part of the history of Busoga while maintaining the historicity of both texts. Although having daughters like Nangobi and Walugono inheriting Busoga Kingdom may appear unauthentic, it reinforces the problem of the girl child in Busoga not only inheriting land but Kingship too. Considering that the Kyabazinga Mukama had only eight sons, does not mean he had no daughter but because of tradition, daughters were not named. In the play, *Kyabazinga Mukama*, his decision to give part of his kingdom to three of his most beloved daughters WALUGONO, NANGOBI, and MUTESI maintains coherence with the structure of King Lear and the known fact that Kyabazinga Mukama bequeathed his kingdom to his sons and servants.

The cast is therefore conceived as royals, chiefs and commoners from Busoga and the neighbouring kingdoms in Uganda as indicated in Figure 8.3.

Figure 8.6.1: Summary of Nomenclature in Kyabazinga Mukama

Name in English	Sound / Metaphoric Projection	Literal rendition	Authentic Translation into Lusoga
LEAR, King of Britain	Crying - lira; Mukama - milker	Believed to be the first King of Busoga	*Kyabazinga MUKAMA, wa Busoga*
Duke of Burgundy	Burgandy - Buganda	Buganda was originally known as Muhwahwa	*KABAKA WA BUGANDA*

Duke of Cornwall	Cornwall - Bunholo	Bunyoro-Kitara was the greatest Kingdom in the region and Bunyoro is a part	*MUTONGOLE WA BUNHOLO*
Earl of Kent	Kent - Kaliro	Fire place meaning the origin of the Basoga where Lusoga Lupakoyo is spoken.	*MUTONGOLE WA KALIRO*
Duke of Albany	Albany - Kigulu	Place of the heavens or the big firm leg	*Mutongole wa Kigulu*
King of France	France - Kisiki	Tree stamp or the accommodative kingdom	*Mulangira wa Kisiki*
Earl of Gloucester	Gloucester - Bugabula	Bugabula means distributor and it is the place with majority speakers of Lusoga Lutenga	*Mutongole wa Bugabula,*
EDGAR: Son to Gloucester	NDUGA	Ndhuga - am at peace but sounds like I shake – I wonder about	*NDHUGA: Mutabane wa Bugabula*
EDMUND: bastard son to Gloucester	MUDYOPE	Budyope was annexed to Bugabula to make kamuli district	*MUDYOPE: mutabane wa Bugabula atali wa mukazi mumpeta.*

CURAN: a courtier	MUGALIMU	teacher	*MUGHALIMU: mukozi mu mbuga*
Old Man: tenant to Gloucester	MUZEYI	man of experience	*Muzeeyi: mutyamye wa Bugabula*
Doctor	MUYIGHA	healer	*Musawo (Muyigha)*
Fool	DIIKUULA	wise and daring	*Musiru (Diikuula)*
OSWALD: Steward to Goneril	MUSIIWUUFU	One with tainted habits	*MUSIIWUUFU: Mupakasi wa Walugono*
A Captain employed by Edmund	OMUSIRIKARE	Soldier	*Omusirikale omukozi wa Mudyope*
Gentleman attendant on Cordelia		man of virtue	*Omusaadha alabirira Mutesi*
Servants to Cornwall	ABAGHEREEZA	obedient	*Abagheereza ba Bunholo*
A Herald	OWAMAKOBO	journalistic	*Owamakobo*
Goneril	WALUGONO of Bukono	Possessed by spirits of inadequacy	*WALUGONO mughala wa Mukama, omuberi*
Regan	NANGOBI of Bugweri	One who sends away	*NANGOBI mughala wa Mukama, ow'okubiri*
Cordelia	MUTESI of Kigulu	One who settles	*MUTESI mughala wa Mukama, nkoma*
Knights of Lear's train, Captains, Messengers, Soldiers and Attendants	ABAMBOWA ABAGHEREEZA ABASIRIKARE ABAKUUMI	Dependants and helpers	*Abambowa, na Abagheereza Abakuumi abambowa ba Mukama abamugoberera, Abasirukale, Abatumwa*

Some of the names in Lusoga are preferred partly because of their tonal closeness for example; Buganda and Burgandy, Bunholo and Cornwall, while others are ideological. Portraying Cordelia as Mutesi of Kigulu, Regan as Nangobi of Bugweri, and Goneril as Walugono of Bukono is informed by their respective characters. Mutesi means pacifier while Nangobi has connotation of divisiveness (derived from *okugoba* meaning sending away). Walugono is popularly used to refer to deformity in the limbs because of being possessed by evil spirits. Since the name Goneril sounds like the gonorrhea, a disease that affects the reproductive system. I chose the names Walugono to echo the disease that affects the lower limbs making the person crippled. These two names, Walugono and Nangobi speak to the Lusoga reader better than Goneril and Regan would. Similarly, the suitors, Mulangira wa Kisiki of Busiki, King of Buganda and Mutongole wa Bunholo though selected for tonal effects are also historically known to have engaged in similar conflicts and tensions as those portrayed in the original play of King Lear. It is therefore befitting that, such relationships are artistically transformed to echo the social-political conflicts in the play.

Adapting names of Busoga's Chiefdoms and chiefs easily achieves the goal of Localization and total transformation of the text because it brings the story closer to the home of the target audience. I did not translate France into "Bufalansa" and Lear into "Liya" as is commonly the practice simply because that style would require a good knowledge of the history of France and England. If that option was chosen, the TL audience would be at a loss looking for equivalences in the play. In contrast, conceiving Cornwall as Bunholo, for example, is true to the fact that there is an existing relationship between "the Mukama" of Busoga and Bunholo (Bunyoro), which the historical context of the play espouses. Busoga looks onto Bunyoro for the coronation of their Kyabazinga because of this historical attachment.

Also, poetic nuances in the relationships between chiefs shown in their infighting for the throne of Kyabazinga are apparent thus making the translation authentic. It is also a fact that, the Kisiki conquered the Nkono and allowed Chief Nkono to establish Bukono chiefdom within Busiki chiefdom. Therefore likening Kisiki to France who allows King Lear and Cordelia's captors to reign within the French territory is in context.

The positive side of such a total transformation of the play into Lusoga is that the lessons drawn can be fully owned and utilized by the target audience as original to their situations. This radical move makes the play *Kyabazinga Mukama*, a realistic literary experience for the Lusoga speaking audience and Busoga in general. They can thus draw political and ideological lessons from reading it and it can be performed without any gaps in production. The physical environment is also well adapted to that of Busoga. The satire on the triple meaning in "Mukama" as king, leader and exploiter is also achieved. At several instances in the history of the TL, the "leader" who is also expected to be the provider has turned into an "exploiter" that the society has had to fight bitterly to withdraw from power. An example can be given here of many leaders in Africa who have abused the people's trust like King Lear or who had a similar dilemma of possession of power at the end of his mandate.

Where horses and chariots are mentioned, bulls, donkeys and bicycles which are familiar to Busoga's transport system are used. They can be easily feed into a theatrical rendition of the kingdom in its capital Idhindha (Jinja). Incorporating a political history of Busoga into an historical play completes the transformational role of translation of such a work of art.

Since Karamoja was as feared among the Basoga, as Hitler's Germany was feared by the British, hence the speculation that the exiled Kent (Kaliro) had gone with Cornelia (Mutesi) to Germany (Karamoja). These nuances in the relationship between Busoga's chiefs and Busoga's neighbours are helped by the apparent infighting for the throne of *Kyabazinga,* thus making this present text a poetic representation of Busoga's present cultural terrain.

The positive side of total transformation of the play *King Lear* into *Kyabazinga Mukama* is that the target audience can effortlessly identify with the message and draw lessons for their own use just like any play is intended to do. This radical style of translation makes *Kyabazinga Mukama*, a true literary experience.

8.7 Conclusions and Recommendations

The language of expression plays a major role in transmission of messages and interpretation of meaning of a work of art. In particular, imagery and nomenclature determine how a work of art is to be categorized, appreciated and analyzed. It is therefore important that names and imagery are fully translated in order to appropriately place the text into the context of the TL.

The naming of people, places and things as well as the use of localized imagery in new language context(s) raises some conceptual challenges especially with regards to contextualization, categorization and authorship of the primary and secondary texts. However, since a work in translation is indeed a new piece of work, then it should go miles to prove its newness by its ability to exist without necessarily antagonizing the original text. A good translation needs to transform the original text into a radically acceptable original in the TL.

A translation is therefore a new creation in its own right and should for that matter stand without relying heavily on the ST. The argument that "transformational translation" drains the original play of its originality and historicity can be dispensed with as it makes the play more informative in the TL through cultural substitution. Localized text communicate better and eliminate the hanging meanings embedded in names and imagery that carry obscure meanings from ST to TL.

Changes in nomenclature, imagery and contexts suggest that novel realities and forms of Literatures evolve when either indigenous or hybrid literatures are translated from one language into another. Works that are merely written in a second or third language without rooting their aesthetics into that language diminish the message in the TL.

Translation produces innovative literary realities in the TL having been adorned with new language settings, contexts and style. Although the works translated from English to an African language would ideally be categorized as "works in translation," such works make greater impact if they are accurately conveyed in the culture of the TL. The effect of such authentic translations in Africa, is intended to create a movement socio-cultural activism, sow seeds of political critique of literary texts in foreign languages and serve as avant-garde advocacy for national literatures.

Names of people and places portray the context of any text. Unless appropriate names are given to all characters and sets in the plays, the play reads and sounds unrealistic. The authenticity of the text is compromised when a translated text does not radically transform the ST into an original text. Simply translating the culture of the ST into the TL without transforming its nomenclature, imagery and context leaves artistic gaps in the resulting text, thus rendering it pedagogically inaccessible to other cultures and other audiences, which would have enabled it to expand its readership and its dissemination.

Cultures where nomenclature and imagery are embedded with meta-communication, complete translation strategies that help to refine the adaptations to dramatisable concrete levels of communication are desired. To qualify to be seen as original texts and performances in the TL, texts in translation need to be totally integrated in their new cultural context. To do this, translators need to access adequate information on the ST cultures and TL in order to effectively effect the translations. This is an ongoing project and can by no means be accomplished at one go.

References

Bukenya, Austin (1987). *The Bride*. East African Publishing Kampala.

Gulere, Wambi Cornelius. (2013). *Ebikemo by'owoluganda Yero*. Mpolyabigere RC-RICED Center, Kampala.

Gulere, Wambi Cornelius. (2013). *Kyabazinga Mukama*. Mpolyabigere RC-RICED Center, Kampala.

Gulere, Wambi Cornelius. (2013). *Nantameigwa*. Mpolyabigere RC-RICED Center, Kampala.

Gulere, Wambi Cornelius. (2013). Nkwe *mu Kibuga*. Mpolyabigere RC-RICED Center, Kampala.

Gulere, Wambi Cornelius. (2013). *Omugole*. Mpolyabigere RC-RICED Center, Kampala.

Imbuga, Francis. (1976). *Betrayal in the City*. East African Publishing Kenya

Shakespeare, William. (1997). *King Lear*. Electronic Classic Series Publication, PSU

Sophocles. (442 BC) *Antigone* Classic Series Publication, London.

Soyinka, Wole. (1964). *Trials of Brother Jero*. Ibadan.

Vanuti Lawrence (Ed). (2000): Translation Studies Reader, Routledge. London.

Xiao Cong Huang (2011). Stylistic approaches to literary translation: With particular reference to English-Chinese and Chinese-English translation. Ph.D. Thesis Birmingham, http://etheses.bham.ac.uk/2949/1/Huang_X_11_PhD.pdf. Accessed 22/7/2014.

Internet Sources

http://nameberry.com/babyname/Antigone Accessed on 11/1/2015

http://www.babynamewizard.com/baby-name/girl/antigone Accessed on 11/1/2015

http://www.greekgods.org/ancientgreece/thebes.php Accessed on 11/1/2015

http://www.merriam-webster.com/dictionary/greek%20chorus Accessed on 1/1/2015

www.behindthename.com/names/igbo; Cambridge scholars; Accessed on 1/1/2015

Zohre Owji *(2013)* Translation Strategies: A Review and Comparison of Theories *Translation Journal*. URL: http://translationjournal.net/journal/63theory.html Accessed on 1/1/2015

CHAPTER NINE
ANIMAL FARM ACROSS CULTURES: CHALLENGES OF TRANSLATING ASPECTS OF CULTURE

Isaac Ssettuba[1]

Abstract

Since publication in 1945, the novel *Animal Farm*, by British author George Orwell, has enjoyed global acclaim as a satire of greed and selfish manipulation, in revolutionary politics, thus its translation in several world languages. This study contrasts approaches and challenges of rendering aspects of culture in two translations of *Animal Farm*; the French *La Ferme des animaux* (1981) by J. Quéval and the Luganda *Amaka ga Bawansolo* (1988) by C. Kalinda. The methods and procedures variably adopted by the translators reflect a central concern with the width of the cultural gap between the source and target languages neighbourly French against faraway Luganda.

Cultural proximity affords the French direct transfer of common social culture, with simple modulation, where referents are recognizable despite difference in world view. 'Midsummer's Eve' is 'à la veille de la Saint-Jean', and 'playing an ace of spade simultaneously' is rendered as 'abattre un as de pique en même temps.' In both cases, the Luganda text, perhaps for reasons of cultural remoteness or belief in 'untranslatability', opts for omission.

The Luganda translation, in an effort to conform to Ganda orality in narration and literary norm, abounds in 'munange (s)' (my dear one), where narrator calls for reader's/listener's involvement in the unfolding tale, as well as proverbs and similes, to condition transfer of meaning. Here the word is re-worked, leaving the link to the source text only situational. The animals' lamenting the sale of Clover's foals is painted in the proverb '*Olukula... (The old animal that ends up suckling its very children), for the phrase 'support and pleasure of your old age', that the French freely modulates into 'la consolation de tes vieux jours.'*

---

[1] Isaac Ssettuba is a multilingual language consultant with an active private practice as a conference translator and interpreter. He is also active as a researcher and has published on language studies, culture, gender and development.

Justifications are debatable and defensible, when translations, such as the above two, strive to achieve readability through making significant allowance to capture the target language's natural usage.

Key Words: *Cultural distance, Cultural proximity, orality, literary norms, translatability, untranslatability.*

9.1 Measure of Cultural Distance

The novel *Animal Farm* by British author Eric Arthur Blair, more popularly known by his pen name, George Orwell, was first published in 1945. Interpreted as a subtle satire of greed and selfish manipulation in revolutionary politics, the novel has over the years enjoyed global acclaim, and thus its translation in several world languages.

This paper contrasts approaches and challenges of rendering some aspects of culture in two translations of *Animal Farm*: the French *La Ferme des animaux* by French translator Jean Queval, published in 1981, and the Luganda, *Amaka ga Bawansolo*, by Ugandan translator Cranimer Kalinda, in 1988.

The two recipient languages in question are quite distant from each other, and accordingly the cultures they represent. Luganda is an African indigenous Bantu language, spoken by the Baganda (Muganda-singular) people of modern Uganda, who inhabit the north-western shores of Lake Victoria, and are one of the most populous ethnic groups in the country. French is a European Romance language, language of the people of France and the global Francophony cultural family. This cultural grouping brings together diverse peoples whose language of adoption, culture or education, is French (Crystal, 1992/1994, pp.39, 155, 335).

However, the more interesting issue is rather the cultural distance between each of the translations and the original English text. On the one hand, Romance French is comparatively 'next door' vis-à-vis Germanic English, with which it shares geographical proximity as well as cultural and linguistic affinity. In a long history of interactive neighbourliness, involving conquest and exchange, the English and French cultures have mutually influenced each other. This is manifest in the presence of loan words on either side, though older etymologies suggest more French influence over the English while presently, French is fighting English intrusion. Both languages also have a common European base-culture and environment, observable in aspects such as the rhythm of the four seasons, farming practices and modes of leisure.

On the other hand, Bantu Luganda is definitely farther from English, geographically and culturally. Expressing aspects of English and European culture in 'faraway' Luganda is therefore more of a challenge, as compared to French. Luganda is more attuned to realities of the tropics, with seasons described as dry or wet, and a corresponding social culture. Where aspects of borrowed culture exist, they still pose translation difficulties, for they are rarely fully assimilated. For instance, appropriate farming tools differ according to the local environment and foreign games may not be universally known to given recipient society. Nonetheless, we note that the colonial experience somewhat narrows the cultural gulf between Luganda and English.[2] Literacy came to Luganda speakers, in the company of English in Latin script. There are many borrowings of English words into Luganda, especially for items and concepts that were traditionally inexistent. *Saati* is from 'shirt' and *puliida* (pleader), the word for 'lawyer or advocate.'

The degree of difficulty in expressing aspects of culture in translation is, to a certain extent, proportional to the cultural gap between the language of the original text and the respective recipient languages.

9.2 What Might Be in a Name?

Animal Farm's translation into French is entitled 'La Ferme des animaux'. A renaming in direct translation, probably meant to keep to the spirit of the original, in so far as to what a title may suggest at first sight. There are two earlier French translations of the novel, namely 'Les Animaux partout' (Animals Everywhere) and 'La République des animaux' (Animals' Republic), published in 1947 and 1964, respectively. Whereas the first title is rather neutral, even with a picture of animals all over the place, the second decidedly implies a book with political undertones. Queval's literal title keeps to the mystery of the original one, in that it overtly suggests nothing to do with politics. Moreover, in offering a new translation despite two older ones, he has his reasons that could be appreciated through a contrastive study of all three, which are outside the scope of this paper.

The Luganda translation bears the title 'Amaka ga Bawansolo' (Animal Home). By substituting the literal equivalent of 'farm' (eddundiro) with 'home' (amaka), Kalinda manages to avoid a title that would suggest obvious human agency to Luganda readers. He also uses 'bawansolo' for 'animals', instead of 'nsolo', the direct connotation-free word for 'animals' in Luganda. He has thus borrowed from the Ganda folkloric personification tradition, where 'nsolo' becomes 'wansolo' (bawansolo, in plural), to indicate that the animals are intelligent role-playing characters in a tale. The Luganda title intuitively takes us back to the author's very first title 'Animal Farm; A Fairy Story.' The subtitle was eventually dropped for good in subsequent editions of the novel. This mark of economy in titling is not really justifiable.

---

2 Uganda was a British Protectorate from 1894 to 1962.

From the name of book, we move on to the translation of names in *Animal Farm*, and their implication as a means of cultural transference. In the French text, names of persons are left the way they are in the English original; 'Messrs Jones, Pilkington, Frederick and Whymper', are all re-written with 'Mr', shunning the expected 'M' (Monsieur) (pp. 1,7,23,40), and similarly 'Mrs Jones' does not become 'Mme (Madame) Jones'(pp. 7,45,74). This apparently serves to retain some degree of 'Englishness' in the translation, reminding the reader that the novel is set in English (sub) culture.

The Luganda translation almost exclusively settles for pronounceable corruptions to ease articulation for the target language readership. With the exception of 'Mwami (Mr)' and 'Mukyala (Mrs) Jones', which should read 'Jonizi', all person names are corrupted to fit Luganda phonology; Frederick and Pilkington are contracted to become 'Fuleedi' (Fred) and 'Pili', and Whymper is 'Wimpa' (pp.1,27,43).

Animal names are also treated the same way; Old Major 'namukadde wambizzi Meeja', the three dogs Bluebell, Jessie and Picher 'bawambwa Bululu, Poliisi ne (and) Picha', the cart-horses Boxer and Clover- 'bawandogoyi Bokisa ne Kilova', the goat Muriel 'wambuzi Miriyeeri', the donkey Benjamin 'endogoyi Benya', the mare Mollie 'endogoyi enkazi Mole', the raven Moses 'Musa', the pigs Napoleon and Snowball 'bawambizzi Napoliyooni ne Sinoboolo', the small fat pig Squealer 'akabizzi ka Sikwira', and the young pig in charge of tasting food Pinkey 'Pinke'. The few inconsistencies with the corruption could be simply editable oversights, like leaving 'Jones' intact. However, some the translator's choices, such as having 'Poliisi' for Jessie, are quite arbitrary. (Orwell: 1,2,3,9,10,59) (Kalinda: 1,2,3,4,12,59)

The above examples could serve to illustrate Catford's phonological translation where, 'the Source Language (SL) phonology of a text is replaced by equivalent Target Language (TL) phonology. The grammar and lexis of the SL text remains unchanged, except in so far as random grammatical or lexical deviations are entailed in the process (1964/1993: 59).'

The Luganda versions of names in *Animal Farm* generally obey the phonological rules of the recipient tongue, of which we will cite the in existence of closed syllables, and the 'interchangeability' of the liquid sounds /l/ and /r/, depending on the preceding vowel sound. In the 'phonological translation', Snowball and Muriel take a vowel at the end, to read 'Sinoboolo' and 'Miriyeeri', while for Fred (Frederick) and Muriel again, /r/ turns into /l/ in 'Fuleedi', and /l/ into /r/ in 'Miriyeeri', because the preceding vowels are /u/ and /i/, respectively. In 'akabizzi ka-Swikira', the diminutive marker 'ka' has to reappear, for correct grammatical concordance. The choice to corrupt or translate phonologically confirms some degree of appropriation of the text by the recipient culture. This contrasts with transliteration, which aims at correct pronunciation of foreign words through adopting indigenous orthography, implying less desire to own.

On the other hand, the French translator opts to render most with culturally equivalent names. Unlike the Luganda text, which remains textually oblivious of the connotation aspect in certain names, the French one attempts, where applicable, to find culturally equivalent French names, for the English animal names, and other names given to the personified animal characters. Here the functioning of the Luganda translation could be due to the wide cultural gap separating it from the English original or a conscious effort to avoid venturing into 'splitting' a name. To confidently propose names that are likely to suggest similar connotation, one would presuppose cultural familiarity and affinity among the recipient readership, in relation to the original.

In the French text, we have old pig 'Sage l'Ancien', the three dogs 'Filou, Fleur et Constance', the two horses 'Malabar et Douce', the goat 'Edmée', the donkey 'Benjamin', the mare 'Lubie', the raven 'Moïse', the popular pigs 'Boule de neige et Napoléon', the talkative little pig 'Brille Babil' and the young pig 'Oeil Rose.'(Queval: 7, 8, 9,1020,21,102). Literary critics have generally perceived political meaning in the names given to major characters in *Animal Farm*. Napoleon's conduct is akin to French General Napoléon politics in 18th century. The name and real life character are common knowledge in both cultures, and there is no translation problem around naming. 'Sage l'Ancien' for Old Major, paints the image of an old wise man, explaining what Major really is. The name Snowball is actually translated to give the French literal and right equivalent 'Boule de neige'; European audiences could probably see some hidden meaning, invisible to distant readerships. 'Malabar' suggest strength, 'Filou' mischievousness, 'Lubie' craziness, 'Brille Babil' talkativeness, and 'Oeil Rose', the colour pink. To dig further into the deep meanings would require thorough anchorage in French and English cultures, of a native-speaker level. In opting for French substitute-names, the translator is apparently after 'equivalent effect', though running the risk of limiting the text's full accessibility to a 'French' rather than 'Francophone' audience. The latter audience could lack some cultural keys necessary for fair readability. As Newmark puts it, achieving 'equivalent effect' is, in some instances, a crucial end in translation.

It has sometimes been said that the overriding purpose of any translation should be to 'equivalent effect', i.e. to produce the same effect (or one close as possible) on the readership of the translation as was obtained on the readership of the original (1988: 48).

As for nations and places, the French text uses old universally accepted equivalents, takes the original forms, or offers either direct or explanatory translation. England is 'Angleterre', so the animals' song 'Beasts of England' is entitled 'Bêtes d'Angleterre'. 'Manor Farm' is directly translated as 'La Ferme du Manoir', since the large feudal home of old, 'Manor/Manoir', is known to both cultures. The other farms, 'Pinchfield' and 'Foxwood,' keep their English names. The same applies to other localities, such as Willington, and this helps retain the Englishness of the novel's setting. We get to know that 'The Red Lion' is a pub/inn (taverne), in the explanatory and direct 'La Taverne du Lion-Rouge.' This translating option (Lion-Rouge for Red Lion) points to a common leisure culture and tradition for naming pubs.

Despite existence of the Luganda equivalent 'Bungereza' for 'England/Britain', the Luganda text titles the song 'Ensolo za Bulondaganyi', using an old name of Buganda's Bugerere County, for England.[3] The intention seems to be placing the translation farther into the recipient culture. Apart from the farm 'Mena', all names of farms, bars and towns are omitted. Such omissions confirm the adaptation's desire to replace an English setting with a Ganda one. (Orwell: 1, 7, 11, 23, 40) (Queval: 11, 17, 24.44, 45) (Kalinda: 1, 9).

9.3 Renderings of Social Culture

In the transference of elements of social culture, the distance between the original and recipient culture again comes into play. The closer culture is relatively more at ease with finding appropriate equivalents than the farther one. However, the daunting translating difficulties resulting from the cultural gulf should not in any way imply untranslatability or hinder a translator search for proper re-expressions of alien culture.

Beast of England's tune is 'something between Clementine and La Cucaracha.' The culturally nearer French proposes, 'l'air tenait d'Amour toujours et de la Cucaracha', for the popular love lyrics of 'Clementine' and 'Amour toujours'. Sung in English, both songs, are common knowledge to the native French and English readers. Here, the Luganda text chooses omission.

---

3   Buganda Kingdom, presently a political traditional entity within Uganda, is composed of 18 counties; Bugerere, formerly Bulondoganyi, being one of them.

Elements to a common European agricultural tradition are quite findable in French, 'Wheat and barley, oats and hay/Clover, beans, and mangel Wurzels' translates as, 'D'orge et de blé, de foin; oui da/De trèfle; de pois et de rave', whereas Luganda gives, 'Emmere mayuni, balugu, kyeban-dula, lusumba/Ennyama, byanyanja, ddoodo.' (Orwell; 7(Queval; 17, 18) (Kalinda; 9, 10).

The Luganda translator attempts an adaptation to suit the local agricultural environment. In the first line, the 'unknown' plant items are substituted with tuber foods widely eaten in southern Uganda, and in the second line even meat (ennyama) and fish (byanyanja) are included. Without wishing to dictate direction of an adaptation, we believe that closer equivalents are findable in Luganda, as wheat-bread and barley beer have been known to Luganda speakers for some time, and exit from the plant world is not very justifiable.

Seasons unknown to tropical Africa pose no translation problem in the French, we read 'tout l'été' for 'all through the summer.' Common agricultural practices are rendered in acceptable 'modulation'; such as, 'bien tôt la fenaison' for 'the hay was almost ready for cutting.' 'Modulation' is a translation procedure explained as, 'variation through a change of viewpoint, of perspective (éclairage) and very often of category of thought' (1988: 88) by Newmark, and 'changement de point de view' (change of viewpoint) (1987: 26) by Chuquet and Paillard. Both explanations are inspired by original definition proposed by Vinay and Darbelnet which goes: 'La modulation est une variation dans le message, obtenue en changeant de point de vue' (Modulation is variation in a message through change of viewpoint or lighting perspective) (1958/1977: 51). The Luganda is caught in between omission and inclusion of season, month or the corresponding seasonal farming activity. (Orwell: 11, 21) (Queval: 24, 34)(Kalinda: 19).

For instance, 'early in October, when the corn is cut' is translated into Luganda as 'musenene, nga gunaatera okutandika', mentioning the month while leaving out the 'cutting' activity, unlike French, which renders it in full as 'au début d'octobre, une fois le blé coupé.' (Orwell: 24) (Queval; 47) (Kalinda: 28)

The 'raging southwest winds of November' (novembre et les vents déchaînés) that lead to the suspension of windmill construction work, are absent in the Ganda setting, and the reason for halting the work in the month of 'ntenvu' (November), is 'nnamutikkwa wa nkuba' (heavy rains). (Orwell: 44) (Queval: 78) (Kalinda: 46). We note another mark of cultural appropriation in the translator's decision to use traditional Ganda names for months (ntenvu, museenene) instead of the commonly used corrupted forms (okitobba, noovemba). The 'bitter winter' followed by 'sleet and snow' then 'hard frost', that 'did not break till well into February', is pictured in French in corresponding modulated terms; 'rude hiver', 'la neige et la neige fondue' and 'qui ne cèda que courant février'. Luganda omits the month, given the different nature of tropical African Februaries, but describes the weather conditions in a contracted modulation 'obudde (...) bwa mpewo ya mugganda' (bitterly cold weather) (Orwell: 45) (Queval: 82) (Kalinda: 48). Luganda grapples with some disconnection because, for Europe and Africa, corresponding period of year, does not necessarily mean similar climatic conditions or weather dependent farming activity.

In addition, probably for reasons of achieving coherence in adaptation, the Luganda text omits other details like 'the Midsummer Eve' (la veille de la Saint-Jean), a day celebrated in many European countries to mark Saint John the Baptist's martyrdom. The encounter between Napoleon (a pig) and Mr. Pilkington (a man), where they attempt to cheat each other by playing 'an ace of spades simultaneously' (abattre 'un as de pique en même temps'), is also left out. (Orwell: 89) (Queval: 151) (Kalinda: 84). This episode, a symbol of insincerity, is too central to the novel's theme to be omitted. Besides, many European card games have been widely played in Africa.

Elsewhere, Luganda again favours omission where French translates with generalized descriptive equivalents and explanation. Titles of well-known English newspapers and manuals are simply described; 'un hebdomadaire à sensation' for '*News of the World*', 'des hebdomadaires rigolos et un quotidien populaire' for '*John Bull, Tit Bit,* and *Daily Mirror*', and 'un manuel de bricoleur, un autre de maçon, un coursd'électricitépour débutants' for '*One Thousand Useful Things to Do about the House, Everyman His Bricklayer* and *Electricity for beginners.*'(Orwell: 11, 25, 30, 85) (Queval: 25, 57,144). The translation guides us by specifying the periodicity and character of a given piece of writing. The newspapers are 'quotidien' (daily) or 'hebdomadaire' (weekly), with a character that qualifies them to be 'à sensation or rigolo' (tabloid) or 'populaire' (popular/people's). The self-instructional books are 'manuel' (manual/handbook) and 'cours' (lesson/course).

Getting rid of an old toothless dog by drowning it in a pond is so strange in a Ganda context that it turns into 'kuwa butwa, olufa ng'asuula ku jjirikiti' (poisoning, and deposit of remains at the foot of a *jjirikiti* tree), in observance of Ganda rite for disposal of deceased dogs. (Orwell: 5) (Queval: 14) (Kalinda: 6, 7).[4]

---

4 '*Jjirikiti*' is a thorny flame tree; the eternal abode of deceased dogs among the Baganda.

The representation of error, however, illustrates justifiable use of adaptation for equivalent effect. In the English original, the error in writing the animals' seven commandments is misspelling 'friend' as 'freind' and writing 'one of the 'S's (...) the wrong way round.' The French relocates the mistake onto the phrase 'tout volatile' (whatever has wings), to read 'vole t il' (so it/he flies or steals), keeping the easily identifiable inverted 'S'. In Luganda, the error is transposed onto commandment six, 'tewali wansolo yenna ateekwa kutta...' (No animal shall kill...); the animals' drop a 't' on the verb 'kutta' (to kill), spelling it 'kuta' (to free). (Orwell: 15) (Queval: 30, 31) (Kalinda: 19). Luganda speakers joke about their kings of old, ordering 'kuta', for prisoners under vassal chiefs' custody, who would instead understand 'kutta', having misheard the stress on the 't', and go on to execute the detainees. In French, there is a pun in the double-meaning of the verb 'voler' (fly/steal).

In both translations, the adaptation allows for easily perceivable error, an effect that would have been harder to achieve had the translators stuck to 'friend.' Thus within such limited range adaptation is translation.

9.4 Reworking Word and Idea

On the one hand, *La Ferme des animaux* and *Amaka ga Bawansolo* are translations that variably demonstrate a reworking of both word (letter) and idea (spirit) in quest of suitable equivalence. A stanza of Beasts of England that goes, 'Beasts of every land and clime/Hearken to the joyful tidings/ Of the golden future time,' reads, 'Animaux de tous pays/Prêtez l'oreille à l'espérance/Un âge d'or vous est promis,' in French, and 'Ensolo ze bule n'e Bweya/Mutege amatu mwe muwulire ebirungi/Mu biseera eby'omumaaso ebirungi nfaafa,' in Luganda. (Orwell: 7)(Queval: 17) (Kalinda: 9).

Both renderings manage to carry across 'letter' and 'spirit', with or without keeping to the idiomatic original. 'De tous les pays' is the plain equivalent of 'of every land and clime,' which equates the Luganda idiom in alliteration 'eze bule ne bweya, 'freely translatable as 'of far and wide.' The verb 'hearken' is also rendered in idiomatic expression in both languages; 'prêter l'oreille' (lend an ear), and 'kutega matu,' literally meaning 'lay ears'- as though they were a trap, to mean 'listen carefully/lend an ear.'

On the other hand, the Luganda translation has many cases where 'idea' is redone in quasi suspension of 'word', in an effort to conform to the target language's penchant for orality in all narration, and to some established Ganda literary norm. Luganda creative prose is predominantly rich in imagery and idioms, with many marks of orality, borrowed from tradition.

In many episodes, *Amaka ga Bawansolo* contains proverbs, similes and interjections where none exists in the original. The animals' lament about the sale of Clover's four foals is rendered in modulation into both French and Luganda, but a Ganda proverb is added to further colour the situation. 'Who should have been the support and pleasure of your old age,' goes, 'qui auraient été la consolation de tes vieux jours,' and 'balikuyamba (abaana) mu bukadde bwo anti munnange baalugera dda 'Olukula...'

'La consolation de tes vieux jours (consolation in your latter years) and 'balikuyamba mu bukadde bwo' (helpers in your old age), could suffice in translating the original phrase. Luganda adds, 'anti munnange baalugera dda' (oh' dear one, the old proverbs says), and the introductory part of the proverb, 'Olukula...' (The old animal...) The utterance is naturally completed by a participative interlocutor, who gives the concluding part; 'luyonka baana baalwo' (ends up suck-ling its very children). In conformity with conversational norms, the text calls upon the reader/listener's active involvement in the unfolding tale, with a friendly interjection and a test of general knowledge.

Furthermore, many other witticisms in the Luganda text would only have a situational link with the original if they were to be traced back. Mr Jones drunken state is described in rather culture-specific extended similes. 'Was too drunk', put into French in equally few words, 'était bien trop saoul', is amplified in Luganda to give, 'yakomawo embwa agiyita ŋŋwa olw'omulangira Ssegamwenge gwe yali okongozze', meaning 'he returns home calling *embwa* (dog) 'ŋŋwa', having lifted prince Ssegamwenge shoulder high,' in direct translation. The culturally-bound pointers to drunkenness are the drunk man's 'heavy tongue' and the royal name containing the Luganda word for alcohol/beer, *mwenge*. When Mr Jones' drinking becomes habitual, it is depicted in 'Omumbejja Namaalwa amuwasizza' (getting married to princess Namaalwa). The reference to ebriosity is again the particle *malwa* (millet beer) in the royal name 'Namaalwa', and power of the princess, assumed stronger than her husband. (Orwel: 1)(Queval: 7)(Kalinda: 1, 15).

9.5 Translatability and Adaptation

In our analysis of the translation of cultural aspects in *Animal Farm* into French and Luganda, it is apparent that issues of translatability and adaptation are often of great concern in literary translation. Indeed, both matters have always been debated in translation circles. In debating the question of whether 'all' can be translated, scholars of translation have generally spoken in relative terms even where they feel that there could be a limit to translatability.

Catford says that with total translation (text), translatability 'appears intuitively, to be a *refined* rather than a clear-cut dichotomy. SL texts and items are *more* or *less* translatable rather than absolutely *translatable* or *untranslatable.*' He also distinguishes linguistic untranslatability where, 'the functionally relevant features include (...) form features of the language of the SL text. If the TL has no formally corresponding feature, the text or the item is (relatively) untranslatable,' from cultural untranslatability, 'when a situational feature, functionally relevant for the SL text, is completely absent from the culture of which the TL is part. This may lead to what we have called cultural untranslatability. This type of translatability is usually less 'absolute' than linguistic untransalatability' (1964/1993: 93, 94, 99).

Newmark is sceptical about considering 'language as a component of culture,' for had it been so, 'translation would be impossible.' He also warns against, 'making generalizations about the translation of serious novels,' since a host of form and culture related problems 'have to be settled for each text' (1988: 95, 171).

Lederer assert that, 'with text, all is translatable, for words get linked up and build into re-expressible meaning,' and advises that in cases of apparent lack of certain correspondences between languages, 'lexical gaps' (vides lexicaux) should be 'compensated with rephrasing of idea.' (1994: 33, 77)[5]

Nida and Taber believe that, 'anything that can be said in one language can be said in another, unless the form is an essential element of the message' (1969/1982: 4, 134, 199, and 203). It is interesting to note that, their theorizing is contemporary (of the 60s) to Catford's, when some limited room is still accorded to the possibility of untranslatability. Further, in their typology of translation, they also oppose a 'linguistic translation' to a 'cultural translation' or 'adaptation', the former being more legitimate than the latter. In a linguistic translation, 'only information, which is linguistically implicit is made explicit,' whereas in a cultural one, 'content of the message is changed to conform to the receptor culture in some way, and in which information is introduced, which is not linguistically implicit in the original.'

We now turn to the acceptability of adaptation as a translation method. Above, Nida and Taber have taken 'adaptation' to be synonymous with what they view as 'cultural translation.' And elsewhere, Newmark describes

---

5   Original French original : « Au niveau texte, tout est traduisible car les mots s'articulent et se fondent en des sens ré-exprimables »/ « comblée par la reformulation de l'idée »/NB. Translations into English by this writer.

adaptation as 'the freest form of translation,' which he defines as 'the SL culture converted to the TL culture and the text re-written' (1988: 46). He is of the view that its practical utility is mainly in the area of drama.

In discussing the tension between 'author-centred' and 'reader-centred' translating, Hatim and Mason opine that for the reader-centred, 'priority is accorded to aiming at a kind of reader response. Given that, in any case, translating involves a conflict of, interest, it is a question of where one's priorities lie.' Nevertheless, they also wonder if it is of any use, 'to debate whether or not **adaptation** is still translation,' it being 'a procedure appropriate to particular circumstances, (e.g. translating for stage)' (1990: 17, 18; authors' emphasis).

Chuquet and Paillard are equally wary about including adaptation in procedures of translation. They find it difficult, 'to consider adaptation as a separate translation procedure, since it brings into play subjective socio-cultural factors, beside the linguistic ones' (1987, p. 10).[6]

On cultural transference in foreign literature, Lederer thinks that readers are rarely knowledgeable enough to understand foreign culture through literal translation, and it is therefore the translator's duty to offer some minimum but sufficient information, to open up the door leading to discovering 'the other.' In her suggestion for the transference of foreign culture, she discusses the case of 'ethnocentrism', where the translator, 'mindful of having the other accepted, sometimes goes beyond the mere concern of exposure, substituting aspects of the original text with features of his own culture, and thus "naturalizing" the foreign text.' In defense of a cautious middle course, Lederer suggests that, 'a good translator should equally guard against *naturalizing* the culture of the original and leaving in the dark what ought to be clarified' (1994, p. 126, 127).[7]

Such 'ethnocentrism' is akin to what Steiner, in his presentation of Goethe's scheme for classifying translations, calls appropriation 'through surrogate', in that 'a native garb is imposed on the alien form.' Steiner

---

6   French Original : «...quant à l'adaptation il parait difficile de l'isoler en tant que procédé de traduction, dans la mesure où elle fait entrer en jeu des facteurs socioculturels et subjectifs autant que lingistiques »

---

7   French original: « Le souci de faire accepter l'autre va parfois au-delà de la préoccupation de la faire connaître et il arrive que le traducteur substitue des faits de sa propre culture à ceux qu'évoque le texte ; il le naturalise. » / « Le bon traducteur s'interdit de 'naturaliser' la culture de l'original, comme il s'interdit de laisser dans l'ombre ce qu'il convient de faire comprendre : » Writer's translation into English.

views the craft of the translator as 'deeply ambivalent,' because, 'it is exercised in radical tension between impulses to facsimile and impulses to appropriate recreation' (1975/1988: 241, 271). This suggests that since forces of conformity and difference are both at work in translation, there should be a balance between faithfulness to original and acceptability before an audience.

Commenting on Gideon Toury's 'target-text theory of translation,' and the weight of 'local cultural constraints' in determining the character of a translation, Gentzler concludes:

Inescapable infidelity is presumed as a condition of the process; translators do not work in ideal and abstract situations nor desire to be innocent, but have vested literary and cultural interests of their own, and want their work to be accepted within another culture. Thus they manipulate the source text to inform and conform to the existing cultural constraints. (2001: 131)

La Ferme des animaux and *Amaka ga Bawansolo* are translations that could serve to illustrate the theoretical and practical culture-related issues addressed by the above-cited scholars of translation. Both translations contain elements of 'adaptation'; the French text being a more of a translation, with instances of 'adaptation' as a translating procedure, and the Luganda one, a translation that can bear the label 'adaptation', for it is the overriding translating approach for the entire text. We have seen that the farther away the culture of a recipient text, the more challenging the rendering, but all is findable in a foreign tongue, if we strive to centre the translation task on re-expression of meaning, and thus adaptation would be only a choice.

Both books are cases of reader-centred translation that display varying degree of decisive textual manipulations that depend on the translator's peculiar tendencies and his perception of the intended audience, with the ultimate aim of enhancing readability and acceptability within the recipient culture.

References

Catford J.C., (1964/1993), *A Linguistic Theory of Translation*, Nairobi (Reprint), OUP.

Chuquet H., and Paillard M., (1987), *Approche linguistique des problèmes de traduction*, Paris, Éditions Ophrys.

Crystal D., (1992/1994), *An Encyclopaedic Dictionary of Language and Languages*, London, Penguin.

Gentzler Edwin, (2001), *Contemporary Translation Theories*, Clevedon, Multilingual Matters.

Hatim B. and Mason I., (1990), *Discourse and the Translator*, London and New York, Longman.

Kalinda C., (1988), *Amaka ga Bawansolo*, (Luganda) - Kampala, Angelina Books.

Lederer M., (1994), *La Traduction aujourd'hui*, Paris, Hachette.

Newmark P., (1988), *A Textbook of Translation*, New York..., Phoenix ELT.

Nida A. E. and Taber R. Charles., (1969/1982), *The Theory and Practice of Translation*, Lieden, United Bible Societies.

Orwell George., (1945/1994) *Animal Farm*, Oxford, Heinemann.

Queval Jean., (1981) *La Ferme des animaux*, (French), Paris, Gallimard.

Steiner G., (1975/1988), *After Babel: Aspects of Language and Translation*, Oxford, OUP.

Vinay J.P. and Darbelnet J., (1958/1977), *Stylistique comparée du français et de l'anglais*, Paris, Didier.

CHAPTER TEN
TRANSLATION AND CONFLICT: A COMPARATIVE ANALYSIS OF CONFLICT DISCOURSE IN THE TRANSLATION OF GEORGE ORWELL'S ANIMAL FARM

Margaret Nanfuka Mbalule[1]

Abstract

Conflict is any type of verbal or nonverbal opposition ranging from disagreements to disputes in social interaction. It is an integral part of interactive discourse, for example in negotiations, meetings, arguments, or storytelling and it is fundamentally realized through language. A thorough under-standing of conflict therefore needs to be anchored in the analysis of interactive discourse, since language is a major component of the cause, course, end, or continuity of conflict.

Conflict is a distinctive component of the text, plot, characterization, themes, and other literary as well as linguistic aspects of the novel Animal Farm. These various forms of conflict were initially conceived and discursively expressed in English by the author of the novel. The translations into German and Luganda ought to reflect them. This paper will demonstrate whether the meaning, stance, as well as the textual rendering of the notion of conflict are maintained in the German and Luganda translations. It does not seek to provide a set of instructions for producing the ultimate translation, but rather to understand the internal and external structures operating within and around the translations, and how these can be of use in the pedagogy of foreign languages.

Key words: *Language, Cross-cultural Translation, Levels of Conflict, Conflict discourse.*

10.1 Introduction

This literature article, drawn from my doctoral study, focuses on the definitional issues, the theoretical approaches in translation and the semantic challenges as we encounter them in the translation of George Orwell's *Animal Farm* by Walter in German as *Farm der Tiere* (1982) and

---

1 Margaret Nanfuka Mbalule is an Assistant Lecturer teaching the subject of German at Makerere University. Currently she is a Ph.D. Candidate. Her area of research interest is Translation. She speaks German and English and Luganda is her mother tongue. This paper presents the work in progress of her Ph.D. Thesis especially the literature reviewed. Her publications include: Luganda - English Phrase book for Tourists, (1995) and *Awo Olwatuuka*: 10 Kurzgeschichten aus Afrika, (2013).

Kalinda in Luganda as *Amaka ga Bawansolo* (1988). These three axes of analysis have been chosen because of my interest in conflict discourse challenges involved in cross-cultural translations. Although the original work of George Orwell is in English, its translations into German and Luganda, two languages that are not related, constitutes an important basis for a cross- cultural investigation. My work is based on the premise that since the three artists come from three different cultures, they experience conflict differently and this has an impact on their documentation and translation of conflict in *Animal Farm*. This is why it will be the subject of our evaluation and appraisal of the rendering of conflict in the two cross-cultural translations.

10.2 The "narrative" of Animal Farm and its research undertakings

Animal Farm, by George Orwell, (1945), is an allegory that has enjoyed international readership and scholarly interest for a long time due to its universality. This is why it has been reproduced in many film versions. It has been a case study for discussion by different scholars over the years. It gained a lot of interest in political as well as language studies. It is a novel in which animals (people) keep changing their beliefs as a result of the greed for power.

The story begins with the oldest pig, Old Major, narrating a dream he had had in which the pigs revolt and throw their master, Mr. Jones out of the farm and manage it themselves. This allows them to eat whatever they please and get rid of all the instruments Mr. Jones had used to abuse them as summarized in the song 'Beasts of England', which Old Major teaches them after his revelation. Old Major dies a few days later, the animals' revolt not long afterwards and start managing the farm. However, the pigs take it upon themselves to be the masters and change all the rules agreed upon at the beginning. Verbal and non-verbal disagreements arise between the two leaders, Napoleon and Snowball as a result of which Snowball was chased out of the farm by Napoleon's guard dogs leaving Napoleon as the sole leader. Napoleon, however, ends up abusing fellow animals more than even the humans had done.

This "narrative" of *Animal Farm* is placed at the beginning of the article to demonstrate that "narratives constitute crucial means of generating, sustaining, mediating and presenting conflict at all levels of social organization" (Briggs, 1996:3 cited in Baker, 2006; 3) The presentation of this "story" as other scholars have elaborated, encompasses elements of social and political positioning in relation to other participants in the interaction. Our linguistic turn to the narratives of *Animal Farm* is meant to compare how the animals, the bearers of the representative identity, with singular sets of characteristics, have been made to mediate conflict in their social and political context in the two translations. (Whitebrook 2001; 5 quoted in Baker, 2011:4). It has also been noted by Ehrenhausm (1993:80) that a story is grounded in the social formations through which individuals as members of an interpretive community, understand the world they inhabit and reproduce it. The translators in this case reproduce their world through their discursive participation and imprint the overall performance of translation as a communicative act.

Animal Farm has been used as a case study by several researchers over the years. Wain, in Sewlall, (2002:81) testifies that there have been, are, and always will be pigs in every society and they will always grab power. Power grabbing and power relations lead to people changing ideologies and adapting others.

Whereas Kleinová (2012), who compares several novels to discuss the politics of the times shows how *Animal Farm* is used as a fable in medieval and modern English literature, Sewlall (2002) studying the political situation in South Africa, looks at *Animal Farm* as a metonym for a dictatorship and argues (2002: 85), that the discourse of Animal Farm possesses meaning at the point of articulation but also provokes feelings and emotions, which go beyond the immediate text. Sewlall's study concentrates on dictatorship, related to it, this study, however, is based on how language provokes feeling and emotions that can lead to conflict.

Both (Mehdizadeh, 2013: 1603) and (Fadaee 2011a) are interested in the language used in *Animal Farm*. The former investigates the similarities and differences in the patterns of English and Azeri Turkish grammatical collocations, while the latter is interested in symbols, metaphors and similes to find out the effect of using figures of speech on the writer's style and the addressee's understanding. Fadaee (2011b: 174), compares Figures of speech and multi-word expressions in *Animal Farm* and their Persian translations on the basis of Newmark's and Larson's theories of translation. Their main research interest is in the correspondence of English and Persian translation techniques of figures of speech and not conflict discourse. Conflict is a major theme in this novel, although it does not seem to have attracted great attention from scholars, thus creating a gap for this research.

10.3 Translation Studies: a cross-cultural perspective

Translation studies were originally looked at as just a branch of linguistics but dating from the 1980s, it has grown to be known as a separate discipline (Venuti: 2004, 7) and recognized by many scholars Holmes, (2004:173). Although the early principles of translation focused primarily on literary texts, the value and need for translation studies and services is today invaluable in different sectors all over the world, Nida (2006:14). Schleiermacher in (Venuti 2004:99), viewed translation as an important practice in the early nationalist movements. According to Kelly (1979:1), Western Europe owes its Civilization to translators: right from the Roman Empire to the European Common Market and its ramifications in international trade. This is recognition of how translation as a discipline crosses borders and brings people together.

Nida, (2006:14), comments that Luther made an important contribution to the theory and practice of translation through his own translation of the Bible. Lefevere, (1992:7), who refers to translation as rewriting, argues that since non-professional readers of literature are at present exposed to literature more often by means of rewritings than by means of writings, and since rewritings can be shown to have had a marked impact on the evolution of literatures in the past, the study of rewritings should no longer be neglected. Bernacka (2012: 1) goes on to add that the role of the translator in mediating source ideas across cultural and national boundaries places him or her in a unique position in particular for understanding a range of development issues.

How important then is translation in cross-cultural interaction? As both the process and product of transferring a written text from a source language to a target language, according to Newmark, often, translation is rendering the meaning of a text into another language, thus making it accessible to a bigger readership globally. Other early scholars in this field like Nida and Taber (1974:12), have summarized translation as consisting in "reproducing in the receptor language the closest natural equivalent of the source-language message, first in terms of meaning and secondly in terms of style." This is so important in cross-cultural interaction because as Venuti (2004: 468) puts it, communication is the primary aim and function of a translated text.

Toury's theory of translation (1980:24), seems to be the most relevant to cross-cultural interaction. He relates the translation process to the two cultures, the source and target cultures, with emphasis is on the target culture. He explains that "you translate from one culturally connected system into another, not just one language to another. Translations are facts of the culture which hosts them".

Toury's theory of the facts of the target culture is related to Lefevere's rewriting theory (1992), where the translator is seen to be using the original text only as a source of knowledge to help him write his text. Lefevere (1992 maintains that, the source text just provides information, which the translator uses to produce a target text in a target setting for a target purpose and target addressees in target circumstances. (Lefevere, 1992: 7). When a text is rewritten, chances are that content faces a different judgement considering the culture of the target language. This will be reflected through the choice of words in the translation that would be used to suit the target language acceptance.

From a different angle of cross-cultural interaction, the functionalist approaches, (Naudé 2002:50) have added to the mix, seeking to liberate translators from an excessively servile adherence to the source text. They have looked at translation as a new communicative act that must be purposeful with respect to the translator's client and readership.

From the discussion of such translation theories, we can see that translation is a series of decision making, selecting alternative vocabulary, positioning and narratives. Translators mediate and construct the textual world for us. As mediators, they are uniquely placed to initiate or diffuse discursive interventions. In our comparative study of the two translations of animal farm, we try to gauge how the notion of conflict is escalated, or diffused or is simply lost due to the decisions taken by the translator of the literary text.

10.4 Semantics and Discourse in Cross-Cultural Translation

Whereas Yule (2006: 100) considers semantics as the branch of linguistics dealing with the conventional meaning conveyed by the use of words, phrases and sentences of a language, Fromkin, Rodman and Hyams (2007:174), move a step further and define it as the study of the linguistic meaning of morphemes, words, phrases and sentences. O'Grady (1997: 268), on the other hand, more generically calls it the study of meaning in human language. This last definition brings in an aspect of universality, which is worth noting in the cross-cultural transfer of meaning.

The meaning of discourse, whether written or spoken, varies from culture to culture. What is positive in one culture may be negative in another. This difference therefore creates translation challenges when it comes to cross-cultural translation. Different cultures attach different meanings to what is seemingly the same thing. Fall (1996: 37), on translation across cultures, notes that *Gewisse Übersetzungsfehler sind auf den Mangel an Kenntnis der afrikanischen Kultur zurückzuführen.* (Some translation mistakes are attributed to limited knowledge of the African culture.)

Nida, (2006:13-14) argues that both culture and language are symbolic systems, but whereas language consists only in verbal symbols, culture includes all kinds of symbolic beliefs and practices. This, according to Hopkinson (2009: 25-26) makes the translator walk a tightrope between author, editor, publisher and reader. Where should the primary loyalty lie? Sometimes, if you are loyal to the author, the editor feels the text is inaccessible to the reader. But if you adapt to the limitations of the putative reader, you may feel you are being disloyal to the original text and the author.

Wang (2009: 109) contends that when the ancient Romans translated from Greek, they meant to obtain knowledge about cultures of other peoples speaking different languages. The carrier of knowledge in this case is meaning. In other words, when one translates, it means that the person intends to gain. A translator's core job therefore is to relay the meaning of a source text in the translation. When that meaning is relayed, then one can talk about a good translation, where one can never tell that, it is a translation because the translator becomes invisible. Shapiro in Venuti (2004: 1) explains what it means to have a good translation, which is like a pane of glass: you only notice that it's there when there are little imperfections [of] scratches [or] bubbles.

A translator must therefore understand the meaning of the words in the text, not just as individual words but what they mean in that context. Bell (1991: 79) confirms this saying that meaning is the kingpin of translation studies. Without understanding what the text to be translated means for the second language users, the translator would be hopelessly lost. This is why in the translation analysis, as scholars, we have are interested in the semantic of the works we are handling over and above everything else. Like Chesterman (2005: 4) we are interested in investigating whether different languages might give different weights to different features, highlighting one rather than another. On this same issue cultural balance, Masubelele (2011: 109) argues that, Makhambeni who translated *No Longer at Ease into Zulu*, effectively minimized the foreign culture and narrowed the gap between the foreign (source) and target culture, through the use of Zulu linguistic and cultural conventions. Makhambeni's translation is considered a good translation because it successfully naturalized the Igbo culture to make it conform more to what the Zulu reader is used to. In the two translations of *Animal Farm* under study was the cultural gap narrowed and the situations of conflict text successfully 'naturalized'?

Choi, Kushner, Mill, & Lai (2012: 656) go further to add that the translation process is not just about direct translation of the words; it also involves portraying as many layers of meaning as possible. According to Jirví Levý, (2004: 148)**, s**uppose an English translator has to render the title of the play *Der gute Mensch von Sezuan* by Bertold Brecht, he has to decide between **The Good Man of Sechuan** and **The Good Woman of Sechuan**. This decision will determine all other aspects of the play. If we substitute for the English translator the German word "***Bursche***", he would have to choose an equivalent from the group of synonymous expressions: boy, fellow, chap, youngster, lad, guy, lark, etc. The choice will depend on the term complying best according to the semantic paradigm; in this case corresponding to: "a young man". These are the layers of meaning in conflict discourse we would like to investigate in the two selected translations.

10.5 The Notion of Conflict in Animal Farm

While Kakava (2001: 650) defines conflict as any type of verbal or nonverbal opposition ranging from disagreements to disputes in social interaction and further notes that the term has for a long time been used to refer to physical and verbal disputes, Swanström & Weissmann (2005: 7) defines it as the result of opposing interests, where two or more parties strive to acquire the same scarce resources at the same time. On the other hand, Bousfield (2013: 43-44) defines it as a relation-ship in which each party perceives the other's goals, values, interests or behaviour as antithetical and Ramsbotham, Woodhouse & Miall (2011: 30) look at it as the pursuit of incompatible goals by different groups. In the context of this study, conflict will be seen as tension due to disagreement over all kinds of scarce resources including physical and material things and non-tangible positions that are of interest to an actor (Wallensteen, 2002: 15). The following is a demonstration of such a tension:

Figure 10.5.1: Comparing the notion of conflict

English Original	Translation in German	Translation in Luganda	Comment
One day, the order went forth that all the windfalls were to be collected and brought to the harness-room for the use of the pigs.	Eines Tages erging der Befehl, alles Fallobst sei einzusammeln und zur Verfügung der Schweine in die Geschirrkammer zu bringen.	Mu kiseera kyekimu, kyategeerekeka nti amata n'emmere endala nnyingi byali bya kuliibwanga bawambizzi bokka.	This resource, desired by all was assumed by one group, which considered itself better than others leading to tension among the rest.

The conflict in this case is not just about the milk and apples but about identity construction. The Oxford Advanced Learner's Dictionary (2006: 739) defines identity as 'the characteristics, feelings or beliefs that distinguish people from others. Dowling, (2011: 1) contends that constructing identity literally involves life experiences, relationships and connections. The pigs, which can now manage tasks that were before managed by humans, feel that they should eat "better" than others; thus the verbal distance they have created is causing non-verbal disagreement among the other animals. As a result of the scramble for scarce resources, actors resort to their abundant language resources, as demonstrated by the different animals in *Animal Farm*, which spark off the resulting conflict.

Asked what would happen to all the milk Napoleon replies that it would be taken care of. The hens mention that Jones used to mix it in some of their food. It is later discovered that the pigs are taking it. When the rest of the animals come back, the milk is noticeably not there. Below is their reaction to the pigs' taking care of the milk:

Figure 10.5.2: Reaction to pigs "taking care" of the milk

English Original	Translation in German	Translation in Luganda	Comment
At this some of the other animals murmured	Hierüber murrten einige der anderen Tiere...	Kyokka bawansolo abalala baasooka ne batolotooma...	Murmuring, *murren* and *okutolotooma* are signs of disagreement though all are at different levels.

This confirms Bousfeld's arguments (2013: 45) that one of the triggers of conflict is language in form of speech, comment or communication that incites an aggressive response.

In the broader, since the pigs had created for themselves a different group identity. The language they were using was generating discord just like in contexts where ethnic differences lead to ethnic conflicts. Commenting on the relationship between language and conflict Mabry (2011) contends that ethnic differences lead to ethnic conflict. The introduction of language differences: phrasings of "more equal" "better" as the "new" discourse of the pigs, can be associated with ethnic conflict. Napoleon for example considers himself above everybody else and does not take it lightly, when snowball develops plans for a windmill and is admired by the others.

At first the conflict is just "tension" (Page 19), 'Only Napoleon held aloof. He had declared himself against the windmill from the start' (translated into German as '*Nur Napoleon hielt sich abseits. Er hatte sich von Anfang an gegen die Windmühle ausgesprochen*). Luganda was translated as 'Naye Napoo-liyoni yaddanga mu kumukongoola bukongoozi'. (Napoleon simply mocked him). The rest of the text was left untranslated. It should be noted here that the Luganda translation is a note higher than the original hence alluding to mocking as opposed to indifference.

From tension, it escalates to "dispute" (pg. 19) 'He lifted his leg, urinated over the plans, and walked out without uttering a word.' (Translated into German as, 'dann hob er plötzlich das Bein, schlug sein Wasser über den Plänen ab und ging ohne ein Wort zu verlieren hinaus). This is untranslated in Luganda. The level of conflict in the German translation is reduced by the use of the word 'Wasser' (water) as opposed to urine.

It ends up in open conflict (pg. 20). 'Napoleon stood up and, casting a peculiar sidelong look at Snowball, uttered a high-pitched whimper of a kind no one had ever heard him utter before.' *German* In diesem Moment erhob sich Napoleon, bedachte Schneeball mit einem eigentümlichen Seitenblick und stieß ein hohes Quieken aus, wie es noch niemand von ihm gehört hatte. Luganda says: "Napooliyoni nayimirira, n'atunuulira sinoboolo nga bwamwenyinyimbwa, n'alyoka afuuwa akawa akeewunyisa buli wansolo yenna we yali". In this language of conflict, the look that Napoleon gave was peculiar, the Luganda translator looks at it as that expressing disgust which is a different thing. We see the mechanics of escalation get closer to that of ethnic conflict, though the process differs.

On a similar line of logic, Cohen (2001: 26), basing on the premise that language constitutes a community's shared stock of meaning, argues that the study of language may provide an excellent entry point for investigating how members of a group understand and handle conflict. Locutionary acts create illocutionary acts which lead to perlocutionary ones, a non-contentious statement or action carelessly made may be perceived as an insult and thus cause undue conflict. It may be a statement or a gesture that is misread. An example of this is when the animals realize that the pigs are sleeping in beds, yet there is a commandment against that. This, like many other things that are happening, causes uneasiness among them. Two words had been added to the commandment making it a different commandment all together. By using language, playing with words, the pigs are able to change the commandments, confuse the other animals thus fend off potential conflict. No animal shall sleep in a bed <u>with sheets</u>. This is translated into Luganda as: <u>*'Tewali nsolo eteekwa kusula mu buliri obuliko essuuka'*</u> and in German as <u>*'Kein Tier soll in einem Bett schlafen mit Leintüchern.'*</u>

In the above case, as the consequence of the animals' reaction to the commandment and realizing that this may cause conflict, Squealer attempts to defend the pigs and explains that they removed the sheets and the beds, like stalls, are just a place to sleep in thus putting them at ease. Evaluative expressions like criticisms, sarcasms, parody, and insults (Mateo & Yus, 2000: 87-112), are potential sources of conflict and when we realize a potential conflict, we can use language to fend off that conflict.

Different cultures use different kind of language to fend off conflict. Kakava (1993: 412) concurs with this argument noting that as many studies have shown, engagement in conflict may differ across cultural groups and different strategies may be used to avoid conflict. The Japanese, Kakava contends, tend to use silence to avoid confrontational topic shifts, whereas Americans tend to use verbal formulas to close such gaps. In Animal Farm, whenever a conflict is brewing, intimidating language and lies are used to fend it off, either by Napoleon or Squealer. Commandments are re-worded to mean something else that favours the pigs but not the rest of the animals. Whenever they want to protest, the animals are made to believe that they are mistaken.

Kakava (2001: 654) also suggests that silence has been found to be a strategy sometimes used to intensify a conflict. She cites Saunders' findings in an Italian village where silence is used in situations when the potential for conflict is high. The animals took Jones' mistreatment in silence for long but when they couldn't anymore, the impact of the rebellion was enough to send the men running.

Direct confrontation has also been reported by Kakava (2001:654) as likely to be used for the more trivial forms of conflict: and this was also noted in *Animal Farm* when animals made confessions to Napoleon and were immediately killed, pages 31-32.This shows that for each different layer of conflict a different strategy of diffusion or escalation is employed.

On conflict resolution, Kriesberg (2009: 7) notes that, as a conflict escalates and becomes increasingly destructive, various groups and people within one of the opposing sides, or external to the contending parties, may undertake conflict resolution practices that help limit, contain, or stop the escalation and help move towards a mutually acceptable accommodation. Such practices must include the use of conflict resolution rather than conflict escalation language. Boxer in *Animal Farm* is an expert of using conflict resolution language. We see this when for example, after confessing, animals are slaughtered by Napoleon, and Boxer says, 'It must be due to some fault in ourselves. The solution, as I see it is to work harder.' *'Der Fehler muss irgendwo bei uns selbst liegen. Die Lösung heißt, so wie ich das sehe, noch härter zu arbeiten.'* (This text is missing in the Luganda translation). Boxer prefers to use the language, which makes him to take the blame while encouraging others to see the situation in that way. Any potential rebellion it thus abated. In contrast, Napoleon seems to be an expert in using conflict escalation language. He always makes others uneasy by imposing policies and changing commandments to suit him, while leaving enough wording in the commandment to let it look as if it was never changed.

Translation and Conflict:

According to Cohen (2001: 26), conflict is a basic human activity articulated and conducted in forms that significantly vary across cultures. A good way to study these differences is through a comparative analysis of language. To confirm this, the following mini-inventory has been drawn from the terms conveying different layers of conflict in *Animal farm:*

Figure 10.5.3: Layers of Conflict in Animal Farm

English	German	Luganda	Comment
Murmer	Murren	Okutolotooma	Of the three, murmer expresses the lowest level of unease, followed by murren and then okutolotooma.
Protest	Protestieren	Okumukuba ku nsolobotto	Luganda idiom used to show disagreement.
Held aloof	hielt abseits	Akongoola	Luganda translation translates as mockery, what the original and the German version looks at as indifference.
Unease	Unbehagen	zeewuunya	Here the Luganda lowers the unease to surprise.
Napoleon and Snowball were in disagreement	Sie waren uneins	Baali kabwa na ngo	Luganda uses an idiom (they had a dog and leopard relationship). This is worse than being in disagreement as the English and German versions state.
They could not contain their rage	Vermochten ihre Wut nicht zu bremsen.	Kino kyanakuwaza bakama baazo.	Whereas English and German refer to rage, Luganda calls it sadness.

The inventory shows us that even though unease was translated as merely surprise here, Luganda feels stronger about conflict than English and German.

On a different note, one can say that the translation of conflict provides another means of comparing discourse functions in different languages. According to Myhill (2001: 169), this is useful in that it gives some idea of the functional similarity or difference between constructions in different languages. By understanding the functional closeness between the source and target language, the translator becomes aware of those nuances in meanings and makes appropriate decisions to avoid missing out on the source of conflict intended in the original text, or the creation of conflict in the target text that is inexistent in the source text.

One such example of lack of awareness of functional differences in languages is noted by Newmark, (1988:97) with regards to food is as the most sensitive and important expression of national culture. He notes that food terms are subjected to the widest variety of translation procedures. An example from *Animal Farm* is the translation of the disgruntlement, which arises when the pigs decide to keep all the windfalls for themselves.

Figure 10.5.4: Text of disgruntlement

> **Orwell (1945: 21)** The early apples were now ripening, and the grass of the orchard was littered with windfalls. The animals had assumed as a matter of course that these would be shared out equally; one day; however, the order went forth that all the windfalls were to be collected and brought to the harness-room for the use of the pigs. At this, some of the other animals murmured, but it was no use. All the pigs were in full agreement on this point, even Snowball and Napoleon. Squealer was sent to make the necessary explanations to the others.

Figure 10.5.5: Translation of disgruntlement

> **Walter (1982),** Die Frühäpfel reiften jetzt, und das Gras des Gartens war mit Fallobst übersät. Die Tiere hatten es als selbstverständlich angenommen, dass es zu gleichen Teilen unter ihnen aufgeteilt würde; eines Tages jedoch erging der Befehl, alles Fallobst sei einzusammeln und zur Verfügung der Schweine in die Geschirrkammer zu brigen. Hiermit murrten einige der anderen Tiere, doch es nutzte nichts. Alle Schweine waren sich in diesem Punkt völlig einig, selbst Schneeball und Napoleon. Schwatzwutz wurde ausgeschickt, um den übrigen die erforderlichenErklärung zu geben.

The translation in German reflects the special nature of the windfalls as 'Fallobst'. The translator also reflects the dis-parity between the animal's assumption as "*selbstverständlich*" (obvious) and their disillusionment when the apples are collected and taken for the exclusive use by pigs. The ensuing disgruntlement is noted as "murren" (grumbling). All this builds up to a situation of tension and dispute that are conveyed by the feelings of discrimination and disrespect by the pigs towards the other animals. This unease builds up with other occurrences.

In the Luganda translation, however, due to the absence of apples in the culture of the translator, everything related to apples is not mentioned. This is most unfortunate for the transfer of the important cultural information that is crucial for appreciating the conflict related text. Apples are a luxury in many cultures. That is why all the animals hope to get a share of the luxury after the revolution. Ironically, the pigs exploit the labour of the other animals to collect the apples and keep them exclusively for themselves.

The unfulfilled aspirations explain why the rest of the animals were disgruntled and why the sensitive aspect of food foments conflict among the animals. The extent of this conflict is not well captured in the Luganda translation because 'the apples' not 'naturalized' into an equivalent food in Buganda and therefore their value was not well articulated in Luganda. The comparative analysis has enabled us to see how flaws can be introduced into a translation. A possible remedy would be to look for alternatives like eggs. These too, are considered a luxury. This way, the readers of the Luganda translation will not miss out on information that has discursive importance.

10.6 Conclusion and Recommendations

All authors write with a purpose in mind. All the information that can be found on a book is a powerful resource before one embarks on a translation. This would enable the translator to analyze the text to be translated critically. Every single word, mood, the implicit and the explicit meaning, etc in the SL matters. This calls for a high level of understanding of not only the language but also the culture of the SL text.

It was noted that several texts were left out of the Luganda translation. Eliminating some of the text may be caused by several factors including untranslatability due to the text being cultural specific and lack of effort by the translator to find the right equivalents.

Translation, is important for the different sectors in development. it is therefore imperative that it is taught right from school to equip students with the technicalities of translation from an early stage. These include questions asked by Mundy, (2012: 16), Why this wording rather than another? What other choices did the writer have? What is the function of the writer's choice? What form of communication is produced by this choice?

This study looks at understanding and evaluating only the language of conflict in three languages for the novella *Animal Farm*. Conflict is just one of the themes. Using the evaluation and appraisal theory, future researchers can study other areas of discourse.

References

Baker M., (2006). *Translation and Conflict: A narrative Account*, Routledge, New York.

Bell, T. R., (1991). *Translation and Translating – Theory and Practice*. United Kingdom, Longman Group Limited.

Bernacka, A., (2012). *The Importance of Translation Studies for Development Education, Creating New Economic Paradigms: The Role of Development Education*, Centre for Global Education, Issue 14 http://www.developmenteducationreview.com/issue14-perspectives4

Bousfield, D., (2013). *Face in Conflict*. Journal of Language Aggression and Conflict. Volume 1, Number 1. Amsterdam, John Benjamin's Publishing Company.

Chesterman, A., (2005). *Interpreting the Meaning of Translation*. University of Helsinki

Choi, J., Kushner, K. E., Mill, J., & Lai, D. W. L., (2012). Understanding the Language, the Culture, and the Experience: Translation in Cross-Cultural Research. University of Alberta, International Journal of Qualitative Methods, 11(5)

Cohen, R., (2001). Language and *Conflict Resolution: The Limits of English Author(s)*. International Studies Review, Vol. 3, No. 1. United Kingdom, Blackwell Publishing.

Dowling, S. J., (2011). *Constructing Identity: Identity Construction*. Georgia State University, Editions Rodopi B.V.

Fadaee, E., (2011). *Symbols, metaphors and similes in literature: A case study of "Animal Farm*. Islamic Azad University of Bandar Abbas, Iran, Journal of English and Literature Vol. 2(2)

Fadaee, E., (2011). *Translation techniques of figures of speech: A case study of George Orwell's "1984 and Animal Farm"*. Mashhad, Iran, Journal of English and Literature Vol. 2(8)

Faghih, E. & Mehdizadeh, M., (2013). *A Contrastive Analysis of Patterns of Grammatical Collocations between the English "Animal Farm" and Its Azeri Turkish Translation*. Tehran, Iran, Theory and Practice in Language Studies, Vol. 3, No. 9.

Fall, K., (1996). *Eine Untersuchung zu Problemen einer literarischen Kommunikation zwischen Schwarz-Afrika und dem deutschen Sprachraum*. Frankfurt, Verlag für Interkulturellen Kommunikation.

Fromkin, Rodman & Hyams, (2007). *An Introduction to Language*, Eighth Edition (8th) By *Fromkin, Rodman, & Hyams*

Kakava, C., (1993). *Conflicting Argumentative Strategies in the Classroom*. Georgetown University Round Table on Languages and Linguistics

Kakava, C., (2001). *Discourse and Conflict*. In Schiffrin, D., Tannen, D. & Hamilton, E. H. (Eds), Discourse Analysis. United Kingdom, Blackwell Publishing Ltd.

Kalinda, C., (1988). *Amaka ga Bawansolo*. London, Longman.

Kelly, L. G., (1979). *The True Interpreter – A History of Translation Theory and Practice in the West*. Southampton, The Camelot Press Ltd.

Kleinová. D., (2012). *The Uses of the Fable in medieval and Modern English Literature*. Masaryk University

Kriesberg, L., (2009). *Constructive Conflict Transformation*. Syracuse University, Conflictology, Number 1.

Lefevere, A. (1992). *Translation, Rewriting, and the Manipulation of Literary Fame*. London, Routledge.

Levý, J., (2004). Translation as a Decision Making Process. In The Translation Studies Reader, London &New York, Taylor and Francis e-Library

Mabry, T. J., (2011). *Language and Conflict*. London, Sage Publishing.

Masubelele, M. R. *(2011)*. *A critical analysis of domestication in Makhambeni's translation of Chinua Achebe's novel No longer at ease (1960)*. Pretoria, Literator 32(3).

Myhill, J., (2003). *Typology and Discourse Analysis*. In Schiffrin, D., Tannen, D. & Hamilton, E. H. (Eds), Discourse Analysis. United Kingdom, Blackwell Publishing Ltd.

Naudé J. A., (2002). *An Overview of Recent Developments In Translation Studies With Special Reference To The Implications For Bible Translation*. South Africa, Acta Theologica Supplementum 2.

Newmark, P., (1988). *A textbook of translation*. Great Britain, Prentice Hall.

Nida, A. E. & Taber, R. C., (1969). *The Theory and Practice of Translation*. Leiden, E. J. Brill.

Nida, E. A., (2006). *Theories of Translation*. E-Version, Pliegos deYuste No 4, 1.

Noble, C., (2014). *I didn't mean it that way*. Cinergy, http://www.cinergycoaching.com/2014/03/i-didnt-   mean-it-that-way/

O'Grady W., (1997), Syntactic Development, University of Chicago Press ISBN: 9780226620756

Orwell, G., (1945). *Animal Farm*. Edinburgh Gate Harlow, Longman Group.

Orwell, G., Walter M., (1982). *Farm der Tiere*. Zürich, Diogenes Verlag AG.
Oxford Advanced Learner's Dictionary. (2006) Oxford, New York, Oxford University Press

Ramsbotham, O. Woodhouse, T. Miall, H., (2011) *Introduction to Conflict Resolution: Concepts and definitions*. (3rd Ed) Politybooks.com

Salama-Carr, M., (2012). *Translation and Interpreting Conflict*. Amsterdam, St. Jerome Publishing

Scollon, R. and Scollon, S.W., (2001). *Discourse and Inter-cultural Communication*. United Kingdom, Blackwell Publishers.

Sewlall, H., (2002). *George Orwell's Animal Farm: A metonym for a dictatorship*. Pretoria, Vista University Distance Education Campus. *Literator 23(3) Nov. 2002:81-96*

Swanström, N. L. P. & Weissman, M. S., (2005). *Conflict, Conflict Prevention, Conflict Management and Beyond:* Sweden, Uppsala University.

Toury, G., (1980). *In Search of a Theory of Translation*. Jerusalem, Academic Press.

Venuti, L., (2004). *The Translator's invisibility. A History of Translation*. Taylor & Francis E-Library.

Venuti, L., (2004). *Translation, Community, Utopia*, In The Translation Studies Reader, London &New York, Taylor and Francis e-Library

Wallensteen, P., (2002). *Understanding Conflict Resolution War, Peace and The Global System*

Wang, Z., (2009). "Universal Semantics in Translation". In *English Language Teaching*, Vol 2. No 3.

CHAPTER ELEVEN
ANALYZING INTER-CULTURAL COMMUNICATION THROUGH TRANSLATION: A CASE STUDY OF THE ARABIC LANGUAGE

Idris Mohamed Osman[1]

Abstract

Translation is one of the most important classical mechanisms of human communication and in modern times, its evolution has been a reflection of human evolution. This is linked to the debate of the evolution of Civilizations but it is faced with so many difficulties, for example:- the complexity of language itself and differences in cultures. The absence of complete equivalence among languages at all levels makes translation a difficult, if not almost an impossible task. But, does this mean that we should stop translation? Far from it!

This paper brings out the fact that, translation does not only stop at connecting human beings and interchanging knowledge between different Civilizations, but it also plays a basic role of enriching language with new words and vocabularies continuously. This is what exactly happened when Arabic became a language of international Civilization. With languages Inter-cultural and inter Civilization linkages are realized no matter how developed or underdeveloped the nations may be. Such are the lessons that we learn in life; arising from our analysis of Inter-cultural communication through translation. These vital lessons should be passed on to the younger generation.

11.1 Introduction

Translation is one of the most important classical mechanisms of human communication and in modern times, its evolution has been a reflection of human evolution. This is linked to the debate of the evolution of Civilizations. In our society, this has often been realized through technological, scientific, and social changes. Societies are varied in terms of their cultural bases and intellectual foundations of their development.

---

1   Dr. Idris Mohamed Osman is an Eritrean national holding a Ph.D. Degree in Arabic language studies from Islamic University in Uganda (I.U.I.U), a Master's Degree in Arabic Language and Islamic Studies, and a Bachelor of Arts Degree (Upper Second Honours) in Arabic Language and Islamic Studies from Islamic Call College, Tripoli, Libya. He has worked as a researcher in the Academic Research Centre in Tripoli and has taught Arabic Language at Makerere University for nine years (2006 – 2015).

Religions constitute one component that distinguishes societies. Through translation, we weave a global dialogue interconnecting world languages, ideologies and values. However, it is not easy to effect that weaving of languages, whether, it concerns Arabic and English or French and Tigrinya or any other set of languages that are brought face to face through an unequal interaction; one language is usually dominating the other in terms of cultural, intellectual and technological influence. One issue that this raises is the maintaining the privacy of the dominated Civilization. In this article, the author poses this important question: how can you make a leap in terms of the quality of the Arabic language through translation that lives up to the expectations of the individual and the nation, without excessive devaluation or disrespect of the set of cultural values embodied in the Arabic language when weaving it with other languages? With the high level of urbanization and cultural mixture, how does one manage to communicate effectively with the other within this framework of translation while at the same time, respect the cultural integrity of the Arabic language?

As a result of the lack of congruence between languages at both the individual and collective level, as well as lack of methods to make linguistic and rhetorical equivalence in the Arabic language, translation, for many people, is a very difficult process. This calls for some case study research to demonstrate how to overcome the difficulties encountered in the field of translation. Some researchers have come up with "Translation tricks" that can help the translator to come up with a text output that does not distort the language that conveys the meaning and respects the spirit of the text through the use of suitable expressions. These solutions in Arabic translation are cited as seven strategies, three of which are directly used in-translation and entail solutions so to speak, that use an "indirect" approach to the translation process. These solutions involve the use of modification, adaptation, equivalence, contrast and disposition. The indirect means will be resorted to in cases where the original text cannot fit in with the output text expressed in the target language (Hartmann and Stork, 1972:713).

11.2 Translation Concepts and Semantics

11.2.1 Definition of Translation in Arabic

The word translation in Arabic is derived from a quartet verb "targama", which means "translate". It is said that (Ebun Manzoor; Lisan Al Arab ; 2008:12/66) used to say that "torgoman" is the translator of the "tongue" and the translator is the one who conveys with his "tongue" somebody's statement from one language to another (Al Quran, 6/210). It's said

that this statement was translated from him into other languages with dictionaries of Arabic. From this statement we assume that, translation refers to four meanings in Arabic:
- to report the intended statement,
- to interpret the speech as it was in its original language,
- to interpret the statement in another language and not necessarily in its original form and
- to translate a statement from one language to another.

In spite of the multiplicity of meanings of the word in the Arabic language, the word translation in this paper is confined to the norm in the transfer of speech from one language to a second language in a manner, which convinces people that this speech is transferred originally with no increase or decrease in content.

The translation of the word in the English language entails a reflection on its image. The first part of the word 'translation', is the Latin preposition 'trans', which literally means "the other side"(Ebrahim Anees, Almugam Alwaseet: 2/371). In speech, translation either means "transporting meaning" along the lines of the word 'transport' (Ebun Manzoor; Lisan Al Arab, 2008: 426), just like in the Latin 'transfere'. The translator in this case, transfers the content of the text from one language to another, or shifts it from one form to another. He could also reconfigure the content using translation as an approach to 'transforming' the text (Lesley Brown, 1993:371).

This dictionary definition is therefore similar to the definition in the Arabic language where the word "translate" has the first meaning of translated speech. In the second meaning, it refers to the interpreted speech, and in the third one it connotes a translated text with the sense of moving it from one language to the other (Anis Ibrahim; 1995:83).

In general, it could be argued that, translation studies oscillate between these different meanings, depending on the various stakeholders to the translation. Translation Studies in Arabic vary between the formalism school with its rational direction where they see the translator as the instrument for the transfer of content that destined largely to another language, and the relative translation school, which believes that translation means switching to a new text, which has nothing to do with the original text. If we take into account these different schools of translation, it would allow us to look at translation as the transfer of linguistic content from one language to another. This would in turn enable us to understand the branch in language of "Stylistic Translation" that has been proposed by some Western scholars (Jackobson R; 1959; 232-235) as the so called new conceptualization of translation. This school of studies is interested in the reformulation of the translation method into another method that is not conceived in the original language of the text, but the language of the transfer itself. As such, this new school conceives the translation of a book, however complex as re-writing it into a new simplified text. By such an approach translation would mean resimplifying the books of science and philosophy, where we would be referring to the new version of the old text, even in the same language. In the Arabic language, this is what researchers in Modern Linguistics, have done by translating many of the heritage books to get them simplified and thus make it easier for the reader to follow the pattern of old Arabic poetry and prose.

Seen from another level, idiomatically, translations also express the transfer of knowledge from the words of one language to the other with the fulfilment of all its meanings and purposes (Ebun Manzoor; Lisan Al Arab, 2008:254). In this paper indeed, we see translation as the transfer of knowledge from one language to another through the written or spoken form or a series of referencing. With the knowledge transfer, the interpreter is able to shift the concepts of one language to the other language. This is why when the knowledge is partial or it does not fit with the ideas of the other language, we cannot have an effective translation. In Arabic translation, it has been observed that since translators are human and they come from different human groups, they can transfer knowledge that is at a different cultural level. This explains why, since ancient times of Civilization, research on translation in the Arabic language has continued in order to bring the translator to the same cultural level with that one of the language of translation.

11.3 Arabization and Localization

These are varying terms, which nonetheless are sometimes used synonymously. Arabization in the literal sense means translation from other languages into Arabic. The term however, in the modern sense was not used in the Arab Civilization. The term they used conveyed rather the sense of "transporting" When they read, wrote, or spoke of knowledge in various streets of the Arab world; it was mostly in the Arabic language. But later, on the contrary, when knowledge had to be put into Arabic from any other language, this came to be termed "Arabization" (*American Heritage Dictionary*: 2011). This transfer of knowledge to the Arabic language is what brought the feeling of a cultural victory over the Arabic language.

Localization on the other hand is the disposition of the word to become the norm, the scalable derivation from the Arabic language. This procedure enriches the language because it brings in new concepts and new terms.

But the translators who are "localizing" must be disciplined. He or she must respect the origins of linguistic terms so that they can be put in dictionaries and expressed on the basis of the roots from where they have been derived. This is where the Inter-cultural knowledge of the translator will prove relevant for expressing the new concepts and terms.

الأمثلة: Examples:
أولا: الألفاظ الأجنبية (التلفزيون) television (التلفون)
• telephone

• ثانيا: ترجمة جزء من التركيب المكون للمصطلح، واقتراض جزء منه، ونحو (PhoneticUnits)، اختيار مصطلح وحدات فونيماتية في مقابل (Phonological Sentence)، ومصطلح المحتوى الفونولوجي في مقابل (Phonemic Content (AhmedMokhtar ; DirasatAlsoutAllugawy ;1985,pp:368-369).مقابل (الفونيمي)

ثالثا: ترجمت جذر الكلمة مع إبقاء الصيغة الأجنبية على حالها، ونحو صوتيم•، وصرفيم، ووصفيم، والديم. هذه (طريقة الهتجنين) هي : طريقة التهجنين درسوسير.. المهتجنين هذه في تعريب بعض مصطلحات كتاب فردنان EME فتجرمانPHONEME) PHON من قبلـة الـلاحق ومن توصل، virtual ،بـالديم، Semantic unit بـ وصرفيم، بـ morpheme ،بصويتم unit بـفرضيم. (YusufGazi; MadkhalElaAlalson;1958:pp193)

• إعتبار اختيار المقابلات العربية للمصطلحات الأجنبية، وكتابات المصطلحات الأجنبية إذا بحروف عربية، وقد يكتب المصطلح بجانب كل غلبت عليه الألم مثل: الفونيتيك (phonetics) أو دراسة الأصوات، الديالكتولوجيا (Dialectology) أو دراسة اللهجات العامية، السيكولوجيا اللغوية Linguistics Psychology, أو علم النفس اللغوي، وهو دراسة العلاقات بين ظواهر اللغوية والظواهر النفسية بمختلف أنواعها، وبيان أثر كل منها في الآخر، والسيمنتيك (Semantics) أو دراسة اللغة من ناحية الدلالة. AbdulWahidWafi; ElmAlluga:pp:59))

خامسا: في حال المجرة والمجهر (microscope) ال نستطيع أن نمت بين اهما في النصوص العلمية التي شكلت ال فيها الألفاظ عادة.

11.4 Civilization and its Significance in Translation

Civilization is known as the human data, which enables the mind to innovate and provide appropriate responses to the challenges posed by the natural environment or social rights in order to facilitate access to life and upgrade to its ultimate level (Hashim Yahya Almalah; Alwasit: 2007:3). The concept of Civilization from the terminology of the modern and contemporary era is highly problematic. This is because it grew out of the schools and thinkers of various humanities, whose varied beliefs and opinions have made communities to respond in hundreds of ways to the natural challenges of life. These diverse scholars could not possibly agree on whose interest fits best in this area or which specific concept fits and applies to all Civilizations. Indeed, as Taha Khader Obide has observed, Civilization can cause people to differ in terms of upbringing, circumstances and characteristics. In translation, the scholar notes, this will play a role in their expression, their accuracy, and the role they assign to language.

Seen from this angle, Civilization consists of the accumulation of the achievements of the individual and the people of the community through the centuries in the different fields of life, whether administrative, economic, political, cultural, social, or religious. That accumulation in their own language will create their own peculiarities as an expression of their moral and material fiber. In turn, those peculiarities will reflect the achievements made by the people historically through the ages. In our view, when a translator in transferring content or knowledge from Arabic into another language, he or she is transferring the wealth of achievements accumulated through the ages. The question that arises here is: can translators from any other language effectively transfer the peculiarities of the Arab Civilization?

11.5 Translation Language and Society

There is no doubt that members of the community who speak one language and share one world-view, share their own way of projecting their culture to the outside world. This is why researchers in linguistics have observed that, the number of colours in the rainbow will differ according to different languages due to their varying modes of expression. Functions and affiliation for an individual or group for these formats will vary depending on the time and location where the occupier is, the levels of the individual and the community" (Alaa Abdel-Hadi: 2007: 36/1).

Does the language form the world of the individual? The first response is positive, and it links the evolution of human consciousness to the development of the human mind, which contributed to its unique abilities both linguistic and symbolic, and the use of tools to store information. This produced a Civilization and human history.

The second response is negative, arising from the enormous capacity needed and reflecting on the human biological and psychological status. Those forces have a special pattern that controls the human mind and take it towards a destination as perceived or predicted as change.

It also confirms the anthropological observations made at Boston University by Mysia Landau: "the revolution in linguistic studies in the twentieth century lies in recognizing that, language is not just a way to communicate ideas about the world, but rather a tool to make the world exist in the first place. It is not simply "sheltered" or "preserved" in the language, but it is actually generated by language"[2].

However, it is also said that it is possible for different cultural groups to share one language. Similarly, in the same cultural group, different language patterns have been found to be culturally dominant. This may explain why in the early twentieth century, language and gender were not perceived as problematic. This does not necessarily mean that they never mattered (Mohammed Alhanash; 2012:214).

In our opinion, language is a social phenomenon, and the changes that define it are also of a social nature. However, this does not mean that there is a symbiotic relationship between the linguistic structures and the community that uses those means to communicate. The linguistic structures in our view can remain intact, without changing, despite the changes that can occur in the cultural and social patterns. In this way, the real world of the individual is determined by those habits of different linguistic particularities and not necessarily of other systems in the society. Linguistically, one will be applying her or his own system. This view stands out as different from the opinion of one of the American researcher, Michel Zakaria, who affirms that language is not just a way you express ideas, but rather those ideas themselves. (Zakaria, 2001:223). Perhaps this conceptualization of language is the same as the one expressed by the French J. Vendreyes, who said that: "Speech opens the closed world to our inner life, and allows us to go out with it; it is the iconic manufacturer of social life" (Vendreyes, 1950: 5).

In a way then, language is a guide to the social reality of the individual; in framing speech, we indicate a range of linguistic views that are attributed to our cultural and social context. That is why in modern linguistics, the connection between language and cultural or social contexts cannot be analyzed in isolation as a linguistic phenomenon separated from the social structures, nor can one speculate on the linguistic roles and sufficiency of phrases in daily conversation without describing their structural format or distributional pattern. On this point, we agree with what has been said by an Arabic linguistics researcher Yahya Ahmed; the roots of the language extend to the depth of all kinds of social structures, which are as different and as diverse at the social, cultural, intellectual and ideological level to the speakers. Language is intended primarily to transfer feelings and

---

2 See: R. Lewin: In the Age of Mankind. New York: Smithsonian Institution, 1988, p. 80

desires that encapsulate phrases spoken by virtue of belonging to a set of environmental, cultural, religious and philosophical data (Yahya Ahmed; 1987:75). If we apply this to Arabic translation, we will find that the ideological structures of the translator will invariably affect the output text. One wonders therefore, how much a text will lose because its translator does not have access to the same cultural, intellectual and ideological set of data as those working from inside the Arabic social structures.

For example: 1. The man went home.

تتحكم في هذه الجملة المستوى الإدراكي: رجل ومكان يدعى: بالبيت وعملية حركة لذهاب، وأي خبار احتاج الحركة إلى. فيمكن ترجمة الجملة على الشكل التالي: ذهب الرجل إلى بيته، أو عاد الرجل إلى بيته.

2. John met his girlfriend at the station.

لقن هذه الجملة إلى اللغة العربية يكون صعبا بعض الشيء أن مضت كلمة girlfriend هي تشير إلى علاقة تدل على علاقة حميمة اجتماعية تقع بين الصادقة والخطوبة وهذه العلاقة "صديقة" قد مستخدم كلمة. فقد نستخدم "جون" بصديقته في المطعم لتفظ الصديقة إلى أقرب ال friend, العرب في المجتمع مكمصطلح أن هذه غير شرعية. فقنقول "التقى وبما استعمالها كون قد غير شيء محتوى اللغة في المستوى الإدراكي.

11.6 Language and Cultural Identity in Translation

The linguistic root of the word culture is a trio verb "thagafa" or "thagufa"in Arabic gives it the sense of resource-fulness, الثقافة» في اللغة or العربية» من «ثقف» أي حذق وفهم وحوي ام ثاقب، وكذلك تعني: فطن ذكي ثابت clever. Anyone who becomes proficient or skillful in Arabic, is "educated"; he has accessed "culture". He will retain elements of education and knowledge; such as human literature and translation. Associated with the verb "educate" are other meanings like to "illuminate our understanding" to "realize the person's full potential" or to "be polished" and "settled". The Arabic Language Academy recognizes culture as the "knowledge of science and the arts". This rimes well with UNESCO's definition of culture in 1985 as "all human knowledge about nature and society" (Taylor, 2011:23).

Maintaining the language without changing the pretext of communication, is, maintaining identity because the language is the identity. Language in this sense is the cultural property, without it, all phenomena become zero. Civilization as a formulation of words and traditions of historical significance would not have any meaning without their active and creative expression through language. Any additional, natural and renewable knowledge, which is inherited by generations as Civilization is channelled through language (Sello M. T.:2006; 13.)

In that sense then, culture is an intersection of the material and spiritual devised by man to control nature's behaviour while trying to improve the identity and the pattern of his life. Although, he would be exalting his present life, he would be actually engaging in the process of maintaining this life, and thus developing cultural sustainability; for instance, by preserving language for subsequent generations. In order for this to happen, he must maintain its dynamism whether it is modified or re-produced; this must be in accordance with the needs and conditions of its development.

In the light of the foregoing, we can say that language is an important aspect of the components of culture and its use has implications for the experiences and achievements of a Civilization. Its fields of expertise, when framed linguistically and cognitively, will form bases from which we distinguish identities! Most importantly, it is language, as an identity of institutions, which determines the affiliation of individuals of a particular culture, and may be the way we related to each individual language is the essence of the relationship. It is language, which will help an individual to have access to knowledge. This means that your language proficiency is indispensable to your access to culture. From this perspective then, language patterns are not just systems and forms, but are worlds of mankind, housing of forms of life. Accessing an Arabic translation in this sense would mean accessing the Arab world and forms of Arabic life; some form of facts or truth seen from the Arabic speakers' standpoint. (Al Jorjani, 1985; 33)

Identity, in this case looks like a structure inherited in the collective conscience, rooted deeply in oneself. In the words of Radwan Jawdat: this dimension of genetic identity in its relationship with the self should never be obscured from reality and restricted from the present moment. However, that observation is based on the inherited dimensions of culture; whereas linguistic identity should be based on active participation in the Civilization. Future research should show whether negative identity traits can be "de-educated" from an individual or positive ones can be consciously streamed through documentation. That is where translation and the transfer of identity traits would become important. If that is realized, then negative habits like cultural subordination and abuse of human rights could be targeted and reversed. Civilizations which feel threatened by subordination to others could also, through translation, defend themselves from the fall of their centres of power both internally and externally. The historic inventory or documentation in the Arabic language in this case would be their heritage weapon. (Radwan Jawdat, 2005: 186 - 187).

11.7 Language and Translation Problems

The multiplicity of visions and trends in translation studies are not well understood by many scholars and practitioners in this field. This multiplicity is not pure coincidence, or the result of the superficial differences, but it is a result of the complexity of the intellectual and philosophical perspectives of this discipline.

Translation Studies and philosophical studies are related. The nature of translation and the possibility of translation or its complexity depends on the relationship of language to meaning and hence the relativity of success of the translator. As a linguist, you may have the mastery of a language, however, each language has its peculiarities and uniqueness. It also has its specificity with regard to its relationship with the outside world. Therefore in certain instances, as noted by Quine, there may be the complexity of translating that relationship between languages. This is based on the observation of relative linguistic meaning and on the inability to prove the existence of moral synonymy or full synonymy between words, even within a single language.

ومما يصعب ترجمته من الشعر قولهم:
"رُبَّ حرْبٍ رُبْقَ بَرَقَ سيلُو ... رفِقَ ناكمب بِرحِ رُبَق.

But to balance this trend another direction is proposed to respond to the above claim on the grounds that systems and concepts can be different but they can explain to each other content without the need for a perfect match. This in a way confirms the possibility of translation and intersection between languages.

ويصعب ترجمة الشعر كقول الشاعر:
والشاعر الذفلي بين الناس *** سبتقم من حرال سفن من رعشال
حرمن

Subjects like these are difficult and complex. For instance, the issue of meaning in literature and language translation has remained unresolved. The word "meaning" has multiple meanings. There is the physical meaning, like when we say that "clouds" (مثل: فيالىن علم في أسه ران) means "rain" (مثل: (هيدوف باش) but there can be the linguistic meaning, or the social one, or the psychological meaning, and the aesthetic sense etc. Translation is a process is thus rendered complex because what comes goes in from one language has to go through the cultural and Civilization context of the person who wrote it in the original text on the one hand, and come out in the cultural and Civilization context of where the translated text is being received; which sometimes is the unknown modern reality. In this way, the translation process is delicately hinged on three pillars: the translator and advantage of his knowledge of the original text, secondly, the text to be translated, and thirdly the problematic of "transporting" from one language to another. The question we pose here is: to what extent can it be possible or impossible to balance the whole process? Our first opinion on this issue is the possibility of translation; because a human being looks at the world, and through translation one can make a connection between the two languages. This is a stance where language is not semantically static. Just as there is a dialectical relationship between the world and language, there is also a dialectical relationship between one language and the other. But this is possible if translation from one language to another takes into account the systematic analysis of the two languages; linguistically and descriptively. It should also consider the history of contact between the two languages, because beyond linguistic differences there can be non-linguistic communicative disparity (Mounin G. 1963:276).

As for the second argument of the impossibility of translation, our opinion is that translation is not quoting an article or a voice or the appearance of the physical symbols of the language (the signifiers) but a transfer of meaning or the signification. Given the fact that, each language system includes a special analysis of the phenomena of the external world, and each analysis differs from one language to another and even from one stage of the language to the other, the outcome of each linguistic analysis is unique to that process. Subsequent analyses in different languages as we do them through translation will give different results. It is impossible for instance, to imagine that a translator can reproduce a documented experience of a native speaker. Whether we are considering the morphological and grammatical structures or the stylistic construction, there is no doubt that they are not easy to transfer from one area of life in a given Civilization to another one in the target language.

In practice, there are many words which do not match from one language to another in terms of the semantic fields. Another problem is that, some of the words in the language that have no equivalent in another language. I quoted Arab ancient words of the of the Arab Civilization earlier on that are difficult to translate but there are also borrowed words from European languages such as French, English and German in Arabic, that still brings us back to the barriers in lexicons. In addition, with respect to the translation of the meanings direct translations can create difficulties associated with connotations. In other words, the link between the symbols will be fine in the two languages but the connotation associated will not be the same in the target language.

The meaning associated with what is gained through overtones and connotations in time and within a particular language group makes the translator lose some semantic value when he or she "transports" vocabulary to the other language. The difficulties encountered by the translator increase when it comes to the translation of works of art like creative poetry or ancient religious rhetoric. The translation may "move" the form and substance of the work of art but fail to transmit the deeper spirit of the creative dimensions (Aly, Mahsoub A. 2003:270).

The deduction we can make from this is that, we have got to be aware of connotations in languages. The translator must know the laws of the language, its history and the cultural frameworks which govern those connotations. This would help refute the impossibility of translation and strengthen the possibility of communication between Civilizations (Lateef Al Zitouni, 1994:237).

11.8 Language Advantage and Dialogue

The advantage the Arabic language has is that, it descends from a context of a longstanding Civilization in comparison to the relatively "younger" foreign languages wishing to compete with it. Its cultural, cognitive and technological advancement gives it an edge in terms of its formats and structural composition. One notes however, that new concepts and terminologies have come up due to the multi-culturally framed philosophy of globalization. Paradoxically therefore, the older languages rich in history and literature may not provide formats for the absorption of this recent global cultural mobility. While it is true that the older formats may be able to contribute to the rhetorical language and the poetic dimensions, they may not effectively convey for instance cybernetic terminologies within the framework of the translation movement. The Arabic language in particular may need a mechanism of upgrading in order to have the capacity of absorbing modern production and creativity. A dynamic, living language, combining functionality and the communicative function, would be the only guarantee of continuity in the modern world and would create a framework of dialogue within the context of globalization. However, just like the opinion of some thinkers is not forced on the English language, it would only be fair if other languages would be left free to obtain the actual globalization facts and then decide what importance to place on their continuous process of change. This perception leads us to the possibility of talking about a linguistic partnership distanced from the spirit of domination and containment exerted by the global big powers. Globalization should not be summed up into a forced convergence towards some languages and a rejection of the principle of linguistic variety in the world.

Researchers like Ibn Hazm Andalusian (1985:13), have linked language existence with human existence and have argued that language decline mostly validates the fall of some states and their people and the entry of others. In the past, the fall of a nation lead to restrictions of a language, the activities of its people and their influence, allowing the new power to enforce its rule and language onto the defeated enemy state. May be that was a natural growth and death of languages in the past. But today, research has confirmed that people imagine and create best in their native languages and it does not make sense to impose a language because of its assumed "superiority" as it would not ensure the most competence for communication in the context of that culture. Scientific research has also proved that in a dialectical manner, a language does not change much when you open it up freely onto another language but rather, this tends to strengthen the people's relationship with their own language. However, whenever this relationship is based on intolerance, it has defeated the objectives of language service. This is the case with today's generations of Arabs, who know other languages and have enriched translation in the Arabic language.

11.9 Translation and Social Networking between Civilizations

The relationship between the universe and human beings is based on linkages in terms of human thought; and that includes religious thoughts. There is a vertical relationship between man and his creator based on knowledge and human mechanisms of worship. There is also a horizontal relation-ship between man and the universe, which is based on stages of Civilization. The first way to activate those two relation-ships is through science and knowledge; as can be demonstrated by technological transfers. The second way to interface the above relationships is through Inter-cultural communication and through translation to communicate various ways of life. This would help to build bridges between Civilizations while maintaining the integrity of each community, which has a language and that has endured a long heritage.

Translation could be said to have begun with the beginning Civilization. In the first human societies, sign language was the primary means of social communication, the first form of translation known to man. It then evolved in the age of technology to oral human languages. But today, communities where sign language has been integrated can actually be said to have access to a world language. Translation therefore is the most important means of cultural communication with the other, whether that other is of the opposite sex or a different culture, whether the other is competitive or hostile. (Lotman, Y. 1990: 77).

The reference to the principles and values carried by translation in the Arabic language in terms of contacts between Civilizations that has been proven by the numbers of multitudes that associate with the world through religious interaction. As a result of contact with the values of religion, the followers of Islam make the relationships with the people of this Civilization. The linguistic contacts with Arabic have been associated with the movements of Arabs and other people's right form the ancient times of the Persian, Phoenician African contacts. Since then more contacts have been made with, Hindi, Greek and other languages. These contacts with diversified cultural heritages have been mentioned by many researchers, including the German orientalist Sigrid Hoekener (1993:354) who observed that this quick exchange of blessings marks a link connecting the sons of the desert with other Civilizations. He remarks that "it is a phenomenon worthy of consideration in the history of human thought that made them masters of civilized peoples in this era".

The Arab Civilization, which absorbed peoples and civilized nations has had strong influences in the vertical and horizontal relationships with other languages and cultures through translation, with specific reference to religious related texts which have activated the ability of the mind to create and provide appropriate responses to the challenges posed by the natural environment. Translation, especially translation of religious texts, has provided access to social rights in order to facilitate access to the improvement of living conditions. (Hashim Yahya Almalah; 2010:3)

Therefore, we can say that cultural evolution and convergence among the nations of the East and the West around Islam was a result of accessing communication through the Arabic translation of its heritage and Civilization. Once the link was established, it removed the barriers between the East and the West in the Middle Ages. The prosperous Arab Civilization formed a multicultural society based on mixed populations that were demographically different, but but sharing values of justice and freedom of belief, as well as tolerance in the customs and traditions that have contributed to the continued spread of that Civilization.

11.10 Contributions of the Arabic Civilization to Translation

Arab Civilization contributed to translation in that the Arab world was surrounded by the translation movement via the channel of communication. It had a major impact on the transfer of information to the European people. In this way, we can say that if it wasn't for the movement of the Arabic translation movement, there would have been no scientific knowledge passed on. This was in two main stages pillars: the first phase in which there was the translation of many of the manuscripts into Arabic, including the translation of the Cordoba Calendar associated with the Arabic division of the year on the basis of twenty eight - astronomical cycle (known as the mnazel algamar of the moon) (Samarrai: 1988; 384).

The second phase includes the translation from Arabic to Latin; it went also through two stages as well. The first involved the translation of Arabic science transmitted through Greek, and the second one was the translation of Arabic science in the rest of Europe. That continent had not accessed Greek knowledge, but the little that was known represented the acronyms developed from the fifth and to the eighth century AD. So the study of science in Europe remained very restricted, confined to a small group of monks. It did not flourish and evolve until people were exposed to science for the general public, especially the tenets of Greek Sciences translated by the Arabs in the flourishing era of this Civilization (Abdel Rahman Badawi, 1979:7).

Translation in Arabic focused heavily on mental science and mathematics where the West owes a lot to the Arab Civilization. Europe the first to take on the Arabic numerals, and then wrote a book explaining the use of Arabic numerals. Europe adopted Arabic numerals as a result of the translation work done. Reference can here be made to the work of Leonardo, who studied mathematics at the hands of a teacher in Arabic Maghreb, and published a book explaining the system of Arabic numerals. That was the beginning of the adoption of Arabic numbers in Europe and the beginning of European mathematics. Among the most famous Arab scholars who knew Europe and translated their work on algorithms, which made him famous was with his book of algebra, which was taught in schools and universities in Europe until the sixteenth century AD (Samarrai, 2010: 402)[3].

In the field of medicine the Arabs dominated medical literature throughout the Middle Ages and even some Arabic names like "Ebn Sina" author of "The Canons of Medicine", and Razi, and Yitzhak Ben Hunein and others, have been translated into Latin. The same applies to the books of Jabir Ebn Hayyan in chemistry. Most of these were taught in Europe until the eighteenth century.

In the field of philosophy, the most well-known authors were Ebn Baja, Ebn Tufail, and Ebn Rushd, the greatest philosopher who left an outstanding impact in the West and thus led Arab Muslims to play a dual role in Europe during the twelfth and thirteenth centuries. The works of milestones for philosophy like Aristotle, Plato, were translated by translators in Toledo. This is what led to the spread of European thought

---

3   The Arabs developed geometry and translated the Book of Euclids in engineering in Latin, and this Arabic translation helped the Europeans in the twelfth century, and continued to be taught until the late sixteenth century, when they found the manuscript of the Book of Euclids in Greek.

through the influence of Aristotle's philosophy. When Europe translated Arabic science, and studied it at the universities of Paris and Viena; without a doubt it must have been done by some of the scholars from Arab Universities. The system of teaching by using famous professors with assistants, and the presence of students studying by practical hands-on experience, these are practices learned from the Islamic system (Samarrai: 2010; 404). The history of Arab Civilization carries contributions that are objective reasons, which lie behind the value of translating from and into the Arabic language. This is not necessarily the one which is current or spoken, but it still carries the content of Civilization and communicates cultural values to other publics.

11.11 Conclusion

To conclude this paper, we can state that the history of Arabic translation is as old as the existence of human contact in that part of the world. However, we have to emphasize the relativity of that process. The so-called "complete" translation seems to be impossible. Despite the challenge of differences in language, which create difficulties in translation, it is important to note that as a human activity, we can consider degrees of translatability. Language in this sense is only a pot, a holder of ideas. It can be separated from the pot itself, as content and can be reexplained and formulated without imposing prejudice or distortion to the pot.

Translation throughout human history and specifically Arab history has been and remains the main pillar of transfer of knowledge and science from one Civilization to another. It has also served as the link for human interaction, increased social activity and cultural renaissance. In the humanities, translation mirrors the literary taste of mainstream creativity of a particular community. It is a way to get to know each other, transferring the message across cultures. It presents one way of accommodating the intellectual and artistic achievements of other peoples.

Translation is practically and technically designed to take advantage of the science and knowledge of others. It tries to reproduce values missing in the recipient Civilization. It facilitates the transfer of technology and basic science that underlies the development of any Civilization. As was the case for the transfer of scientific knowledge through the translations from Greek into Arabic in the early eras of the Arab Civilization, so does Arabic translation today continue to bear landmark importance in other communities?

At the social level, translation may explain the achievements of its native speakers. It is also a vessel for the transfer of scientific practices, traditions, customs and myths among peoples. The linguistic and communication level is the most important motive of translation. It reflects the sophistication of the initial language and reveals the nature of the target language and how they are used in the cultural transfer process.

Within the religious circles, translation is often associated with the divine word, seen as central in the world and linked to the format of the divine power. This makes religious language an integration tool first and foremost, rising later to become a national symbol through the functions of language, the social Kaltoasl horizontal and vertical, a channel of learning for generations through the ages, making the language more than a historical legacy of sanctity and prestige, which over time unites the different groups.

References

Abdel Rahman Badawi, *(1979), The role of the Arabs in the formation of European thought, Dar-Almarifa,Beirut, Lebanon Al Jorjani Al Jorjani Allenfate; 1987, Mustafal alhalabi. Cairo*

Alaa Abdel-Hadi: 1988, "Poetic identity and set aside the idea of origin - ego as I and other (cultural study). Journal of the world of thought 36/1 (July-September 2007),

Aly Mahsoub A. (2003). *Translation Strategies of EFL Students Teachers: A Think Aloud Protocol-Based Case Study.* ERIC Document Reproduction Service. (No. Ed). *American Heritage Dictionary of the English Language,* (2011), *Fifth Edition.* Published by Houghton Mifflin Harcourt Publishing Company.

Anis Ibrahim and Others *(1995): The Lexicon Mediator, American Heritage® Dictionary of the English Language, Fifth Edition.* (2011). Retrieved August 30 2015, 2ⁿᵈEdition. Dar-Alnada, Cairo, Egypt.

Ebun Manzoor; (1987): *The Tongue of Arabs,* D.ar, Almarefa, Cairo.

Jackobson R. (2011): On Linguistic "Aspects of Translation", In R. Browser (Ed) *On Translation,* Cambridge Massachusetts: Harvard University Press.

Hartmann, R.K. and Stork, F.C.: (1972): *Dictionary of language and Linguistics.* Applied Science: Amsterdam.

Hashim Yahya Almalah; (2010): *Islamic Civilization, Dar-Almarifa, Beirut, Lebanon.*

Ibn Hazm Andalusian.(1987). *Al Ehkam Fe Asuul Alahkam,* p13.

Lateef Al Zitouni, (1994), *The translation movement of the Renaissance,* Dar al-Nahar, Beirut.

Lewin R.: *In the Age of Mankind.* New York: Smithsonian Institution

Lotman, Y. (1990) *Universe of Mind; A Semiotic Theory of Culture.* London: Tauris.

CHAPTER TWELVE
TRANSLATION AND INTERPRETATION OF FOREIGN LANGUAGES - AN ENDANGERED PROFESSION: THE CASE OF FRENCH

Edith Kalanzi[1]

Abstract

Communication between people from different origins, particularly in today's global village, makes translation and interpretation of languages indispensable for mutual understanding. Although the terms *Translation* and *Interpretation* are interrelated, their linguistic usage differs, depending on whether you are talking to a language scholar or to an ordinary person. Simply put, Translation requires reading a text and conveying its meaning in writing. Interpretation, however, requires one to hear, understand and simultaneously or consecutively provide its meaning in near real time. This article will explore the role of automated translation devices, their advantages and disadvantages as well as gauge whether human translation is in danger of extinction. The observations are based on the premise that, although the computer might be very 'intelligent' it still cannot replace the human brain, which collects, deciphers, filters and produces significant volumes of information in a diversity of languages made understandable among the communicating communities around the world. The article stresses how this is a vital role provided by translators and interpreters. In order for this profession to survive and remain relevant, however, Translation and Interpretation experts need to adjust their mindset. They should be willing to turn digital and embrace new technologies instead of shying away from them. The article concludes that, it is only then that we can enjoy a profitable harmonization of both human intellect and the attributes of emerging translation and interpretation devices as well as Computer Assisted Translation (CAT).

Key words: *Translation, Interpretation, Automated Translation Tools, Machine Translation, Computer Assisted Translation*

---

1   Ms Edith Kalanzi is a bilingual professional and is currently a practitioner in the teaching of French as a Foreign Language, translation and interpretation. Her research fields of interest include the pedagogy of French, translation and interpretation studies. She initially trained at Makerere University and holds a Maîtrise de Français Langue Étrangère (FLE) and Licence es *Lettres* from Université de Paris X, Nanterre.

12.1 Introduction

Man has had to communicate with his peers from time immemorial. From a biblical point of view, man spoke one common language, understood by all, up until he decided to try and reach out to God by building the Tower of Babel. From that point in time, interpreting of "unknown tongues" was required. Before then, there had been no foreigner necessitating interpretation of languages: they could all understand one another. Translation however, from the linguist's point of view, began at a much later stage and was carried out by the early erudite scholars capable of carrying out the art of translating. It would have been inconceivable, at the time when the Bible was taking decades to translate, and each eminent explorer had an interpreter, to project that, machines would one day be in the business of translation or interpretation. As life would have it, the internationalization of trade as well as frequent social and political contacts have made translation and interpretation a necessary skill for modern societies. However, this article is posing a pertinent research question: is this skill keeping pace with the fast changes of today's communication development?

12.2 Interpretation

Interpretation or 'interpreting' (often-preferred term to avoid confusion between other meanings of interpretation) dates back to the beginning of interaction between people speaking different languages. This term could also be stretched to interpreting sign language, since both the sign giver and sign receiver need to correctly interpret a given message.

It is somewhat difficult to examine the translation profession and completely ignore its sister profession of interpretation. This is because the development of one skill has bearings on the application of the other and the prerequisites for expertise in one field usually feed into the specialization for the other. The tendency is to begin from translation and later with practice specialize into interpreting. Given the professional norms in place, we shall briefly reflect on a few examples in translation. When I read the title of an article, "Un monde sans interprètes", which appeared in the French daily *Le Monde* of 18 March 2010, it sent a chill down my spine as I wondered whether a "World without interpreters" would become a reality in my time as a practicing translator. Brigitte Perucca points out that, schools of translation and interpreting such as the *Institut Supérieur d'Interprétation et de Traduction*[2] and the *Ecole Supérieure d'Interprèteset*

---

2   Higher Institute of Interpretation and Translation

Traducteurs[3] will have to work on how to attract new 'converts' into the interpretation profession. Not only are the admission requirements or *Concours d'admission* a discouraging factor but also the number of places are strictly limited. Therefore, the younger generation seems to believe that the shortage of interpreters of languages such as those for German, Italian, and Chinese, languages spoken or understood by several millions worldwide, will necessitate using machines and eventually render useless human interpreters. It is also suggested that faced with such a situation, then everyone should endeavour to speak one language: **English**

> *"L'idée selon laquelle l'interprétariat est devenu inutile dans un monde où tout le monde parle ou doit parler anglais, a peut-être détournéles jeunes de cette voie..."(The idea that interpreting has become unnecessary in a world where everyone speaks or should speak English, has probably discouraged the youth from taking this route...")* (Perucca;2014).

As to whether this phenomenon is reversible remains a subject of inquiry. In the meantime, however, machine interpreters are relatively new on the market and are steadily being improved to abate skepticism. Their cost is apparently amortized in the long term and in the end it would be cheaper than the quasi-unionized interpreters. Service providers have observed that, in the most frequently visited cultural monuments, like the *Musée du Louvre* (www.louvre.fr/plan)the Chinese Emperors' Palace,[4] translation devices providing pre-recorded standard texts in 12 foreign languages have helped to reduce noise levels at these sites thus decreasing costs and decongesting the restricted space. It has also been reported that ahead of the 2020 Olympics, Japan is venturing into portable technology in the form of a customized interpreting device aimed at helping foreign visitors find their way around the city surroundings without a human guide or cumbersome literature. It is envisaged that the visitor would speak into the device, which in turn gives him/her the corresponding phrase in near real-time. Time alone will demonstrate whether these machines will be able to replace the human interpreter in an effective way.

One can imagine however, how some language aspects like intonation, embellishment and humour could be "assassinated" if the human input were to be phased out completely. In French for instance, the quite

---

3   Polytechnic of Interpreters and Translators

4   *www.travelchinaguide.com/cityguides/beijing/forbidden.htm*

common expression *"Oh la la !"* is context-embedded; one could read 'ecstasy' or 'jubilation' as much as one could read 'shock' 'disappointment' or 'sadness' in the same expression. The question here is: would a machine be able to treat the nuances of intonation with the accuracy it requires when the interpretation is done by a person? Would the machine be able to recognize specificity in a multi-meanings context of a literary expression such as this?

I believe that, the question I am posing with regards to French reflects the trend with several languages, if not all. In Chinese, the same principle seems to apply when you read Nicholas Kristof's humour loaded article, entitled "Primero Hay QueAprenderEspañol, RanhouZaiXueZhongwen" (First learn Spanish. Then study Chinese), published in the New York Times of 29 December 2010:

> "......The standard way to ask somebody a question in Chinese is "qing wen," with the "wen" in a falling tone. That means roughly: May I ask something? But ask the same "qing wen" with the "wen" first falling and then rising, and it means roughly: May I have a kiss? That's probably why trade relations are so strained between our countries. Our negotiators think they're asking questions about tariffs, and the Chinese respond indignantly that kissing would be inappropriate. Leaving both sides confused."

The above story could make one smile but it does corroborate the fact that, translation and interpreting do not only take into account the syntax and semantics of a phrase but they integrate its phonetics and pragmatics. In this particular case, the intonation and selection of cultural appropriateness hinges around the required intonation in the enunciation 'wen'.

12.3 Machine Translation

The idea of Machine Translation, sometimes referred to as MT, entails feeding Text A (source language) into the computer and retrieving its literal translation in Text B (target language). Machine Translation, as opposed to Human Translation, started around the 17th century. In 1629, a Frenchman, René Descartes, proposed that a universal language be created for different tongues to share one symbol. The appeal of Descartes seems to have been heard by some scholars. Researchers including A.D. Booth and Warren Weaver in the 1940s ventured into developing possibilities of introducing Machine Translation and later, in the 1970s, the French Textile Institute started Machine Translation of abstracts in French, English, German and Spanish.

Also, after the start of the Cold war in the 1950s, massive documentation needed to be translated into English and Russian and vice versa, and this had to done at a very high speed. The process involving humans was deemed to be too slow so they later found solace in MT. These experiments notwithstanding, the human translator element had to be called upon in order to establish the databank. Even to date, despite the phenomenon of globalization, which normally would break down linguistic, cultural and other barriers, translators are still solicited to translate or interpret texts for individual and mass consumption for audiences located thousands of kilometres away. For that to happen, people who master several languages have to be deployed. Ironically, this tendency towards multilingualism has propelled cohesion between nations. Europe is an example: since the creation of the European Union, there has been many a call to returning to one's roots and people are proud to identify with their primary cultures through speaking their own languages. Today, more than ever before when there was no strict language policy in the European space, interpreters and translators are vital in enabling the European Union to operate in its 24 official languages.[5].

The tones of legal, business and defense documents that are needed in record time for such organizations are largely machine-translated. Machine Translation has thus spread ever since and more so owing to globalization. The world has quickly become a small village and fast communication in business interactions, to cite but one sector which is language sensitive, needs more than just a one single language-speaking community. It can be observed, for instance, that on purchasing a new household device, you find an instruction manual enclosed in the package. In many instances when I have checked the French texts, it has seemed to me that MT is used to translate these instructions into the different languages. The client is then left the option of choosing the language she or he understands best among the uniformly quasi-incomprehensible machine translated texts.

12.4 Experience with Machine Translation

While translating a biblical text where the name of the Old Testament patriarch, Job, appeared numerous times I thought Machine Translation would accelerate my work. I therefore opted for it. The machine did not realize, however, that Job was a personal name and mistook the patriarch for the French noun for work or a job. Hence, "Job was a righteous man"

---

[5] Bulgarian, Croatian, Czech, Danish, Dutch, English, Estonian, Finnish, French, German, Greek, Hungarian, Irish, Italian, Latvian, Lithuanian, Maltese, Polish, Portuguese, Romanian, Slovak, Slovene, Spanish and Swedish. www.ec.europa.eu

got machine translated as «*Travail était un homme juste* ». I was now cumbered with replacing every 'travail' with 'Job' in the rather long passage of Scripture. However, on further searching, I was consoled to find another programme with the correct rendering: *Job étaitun homme juste*, like a human translator would have initially translated it. This may also mean that a human translator should probably shop around for alternatives, and select the best machine translator and thus reduce the volume of post-editing work. This is equivalent to the decision making process when faced with several lexical options in a dictionary. The translator's location of decision has changed but the process of deciding remains virtually the same.

In another example of 'Germanium is a good conductor' the Machine Translation rendering produced: *L'allemandest un bon chef d'orchestre*. The machine database made no difference between the German language 'allemand' and the substance 'germanium'. It also could not get the nuanced distinction between a 'conductor of an orchestra' and a 'conductor' of the electric current. Therefore, even such simple sentences need a human brain monitor as the unsupervised output can do great injustice to the source language.

The machine translator in another text gave the following rendering: "*C'est le b a ba*" = "It is b has ba". Without analyzing the context, of 'b' being appropriated to "ba" the literal or word-to-word translation would mean nothing to the reader. The human translator therefore puts a text into its proper context and locates it in its appropriate discourse, thereby avoiding fallacies. Some of the intricacies of location, discourse come implicitly with the suitable word choice, but these are not provided for in MT.

Let us look at yet another MT example: "Dear Peace, I do hope you are keeping well. How I would love to see you again as it has been so long since we last saw each other! My love to your family. With love, Rosemary". The machine translated this simple text as follows: "*Chère Paix, J'espère que vous gardez bien. Comment je serais ravi de vous voir à nouveau comme il est depuis si longtemps nous avons dernière vu mutuellement ! Mesamitiés à votre famille. Avec amour, Rosemary.*" Evidently, the discourse of letter writing was not entirely rendered although about 60% of the content came through. To the receiver of the message one question arises: does it really matter whether the machine fails to understand that my friend is called Peace and not the impersonal *Paix*? One colleague argued that this matters little as long as Peace knows she is the rightful addressee of the letter while another thought that as a consequence of the non- recognition of Peace, the letter becomes impersonal. If Peace fails to consider herself as its rightful owner, then the letter is, in real terms, not a letter and the communication act would have failed.

Another example can be found in the following text: « Je ne comprends pas comment on utilise ce mot: tu pourrais me donner un autre exemple? *Donne-moi un exemple de chose méchante que je t'aurais dite!* » the translation given in the target text was: "I do not understand how this word is used: you could give me another example? Give me an example of nasty thing that I have said to you!". Again a friend argued that, in some of these examples nobody would really care about the syntax, morphology or semantics; the end justifies the means in that the reader "gets the gist" of the text. This is supported by remarks from other users of MT, for example in the military sector who believe that the cultural or linguistic factors remain secondary if not peripheral. They can have *"petit bras"* for "small arms" [les armes légères] and *"petites poches des rebelles"* for "small pockets of rebels" (International Conference on Small Arms, Dar-es Salaam, 2012).

Here is yet another translation of a small dialogue: *(Author unknown)*

Figure 12.4.1: Example of Machine Translation

Machine Translation: At your age, you still touch your salary? So what? I have dead colleagues affecting theirs....

The machine translation in the target language denies us the humour that is evident in the source language. MT cannot imagine any other

meaning of "toucher" apart from the primary sense of "touching physically". In his response, the old man who is still earning a salary whereas he is retired, MT translates "touchent" as "affect" leaving us wondering why the machine opted for another word for the verb "toucher" in the second instance. The undeniable humour regarding the old man's friends who are dead but still get transfers of salary is totally missed.

The above examples demonstrate that if MT is to be used, it is imperative that a human translator edits the content to remove any ambiguities or inaccuracies. We should bear in mind, however, that post-editing can be time consuming and the machine paradoxically delays the work.

The following analogy could express it better: it is sometimes much easier and less costly to build a new building from scratch than to renovate an old one. In the case of translation, I believe we can agree that this holds water in cases where the machine translation rendering is particularly bad. The testing phase before committing yourself to MT seems inevitable. It is similar to the times when a translator opens a simple dictionary only to realize that its capacity is far below the vocabulary of the source text.

Judging from the fast pace at which organizations expect translation products, one rather perplexing question that we can pose is whether the translation profession will one day be wiped out and replaced by MT. Given that there has been tremendous improvement in technology related to translation, will MT texts become more accurate and receive applause in the near future? What about the Computer Assisted Translation (CAT) tools? In France alone, a considerable number of youngsters are now embracing the Chinese language and have enrolled in language courses both on the Internet and in Cultural centres. Besides, China has become an attractive destination with the business transactions and touristic exoticism it brings to the younger minds. If youngsters are learning Chinese at such a pace, does this mean that there shall be as many proficient Chinese linguists that there will be less need for human translators in the future?

12.5 Advantages of Machine Translation

First of all, Machine Translation is faster than the human translator. Instead of spending hours working on a document, the machine produces the translation in near real time, thus saving time and nullifying possible arguments over delays in translations and the non-respect of the mandatory time frames. If news broke out in a language unknown to a speaker and the latter needed the information immediately, perhaps MT would be a quicker way of obtaining a synopsis of this notwithstanding incorrect grammar.

Machine Translation helps to produce more work in less time hence increases productivity. If a conference organizer must get 50 documents translated within one hour, it is improbable that a human translator, unaided by MT or CAT tools, would manage to accomplish the same task in one hour. Who would not want to beat a deadline without having to undergo the pressure of looking up words, synonyms, antonyms, removing ambiguities, etc.? After all, the translator would be paid the same amount of money for probably one sixth of the time used.

In addition, human translators can prove to be expensive. Whether the remuneration is by word count per minute or per page, or an hourly or daily rate, the professional translator cannot beat the relatively low cost of a translation tool whose initial cost price is generally amortized in the long run. MT is therefore cheaper and sometimes free, depending on which software tool you decide to use. Besides, if one does not arrange for a fallback position in advance, a human translator is more likely to disappoint an event organizer with delays or even last minute cancellations. However legitimate their reasons may be, such mistiming or absence at critical moments in the translation process are difficult to make up for. Needless to say, this can be very perplexing in the context of a conference or a commercial transaction.

Machine Translation is more to be trusted to keep confidential matters secret than a human translator who is liable to succumb to the pressure of the moment and divulge sensitive matters to outsiders. It appears, therefore, that the risk of material leaking out to unauthorized parties would be minimal with MT as compared to an indiscreet or careless human translator. This is why MT is praised by officers in the security sector.

On the one hand, a machine translator is multi-language-friendly, that is, it will translate into any language that it has been programmed to use. On the other hand, however, a human translator is limited to just the languages that she or he can master. This means that if you have five documents written in five different languages, you will not need to look for speakers of the five source languages but will just proceed with MT. Consequently, MT saves an enormous amount of time.

With MT, there can be also a higher degree of reliability if you have the time to search and refine the quality of the product. You can run the same text through different tools, thus improving the quality of word choice.

12.6 Disadvantages of Machine Translation

The machine translator remains an object, a machine which can in no way comprehend the complexities of human language. It is able to translate word-to-word but cannot exercise logic or coherence. It is unable to take  into account factors such as context and culture. It is not surprising therefore, that some of its translations have several times turned out to be incomprehensible if not awkward.

Perhaps the most famous and amusing example is that of a Chinese dining hall, which apparently used MT to indicate its business premises. We have to admit that although this 'Translate Server Error' banner has fetched great gains by making this restaurant famous, this kind of unchecked Machine Translation could cause great damage in high-level political, legal or business domains. Other equally amusing machine translations have been seen in Chinese menus ('Beef in empirical sauce', 'Steam eggs with Wikipaedia'). Aberrations such as these can only exist when a human translator is excluded from the exercise.

In this fast-paced and mysterious world of technology, we cannot be entirely certain that translated documents on the Internet will forever remain confidential. Did one ever think that information could be stored in the cyber space and get retrieved by the 'owner' anywhere and at any time? Is there a hundred per cent guarantee of confidentiality in a world which, devious as it has proved to be, continues to create and discover new computer applications and devices?

In summary, Claude Piron[6] could not have commented better on the human translator's role in "*Les défis des langues: du gâchis au bon sens*" (The Language Challenge : from chaos to common sense):

> "Machine translation, at its best, automates the easier part of a translator's job; the harder and more time-consuming part usually involves doing extensive research to resolve ambiguities in the source text, which the grammatical and lexical exigencies of the target language require to be resolved."

12.7 Computer Assisted Translation (CAT) Tools

Wikipaedia defines Computer Assisted Translation as "... a form of language translation in which a human translator uses computer software to support and facilitate the translation process". The human translator may decide to tackle a text "head-on" using the computer software or may opt to use MT first and then proceed with CAT using terminology databases and translation memories to polish up their work. In the latter case, I believe that no human translator would ever trust a first-time MT text without having to "resolve ambiguities", counter senses etc. as Piron stated above. The human translator uses their brain to understand semantics, syntax, etc. and then puts all this in a proper and understandable context of the target text.

Given the two sides and the arguments advanced, we can now consider what way to take if the translation profession is to survive in the world of new technologies. In my opinion, turning digital is necessary for translators.

---

6 He is a translator for the United Nations (1956-1961), psychotherapist and prolific author.

Automated Translation Tools (ATTs) help the profession tremendously not only by increasing efficiency, but also by keeping consistency between translations.

While criticizing the works of humanist Perrot Nicolas d'Ablancourt, French philosopher and writer Gilles Ménage believes that in translation the notion of fidelity and beauty cannot go together. Reference is made to women whom he calls "les belles infidèles" (cannot be both beautiful and faithful).

> "Elles me rappellent une femme que j'ai beau-coup aimé à Tours, et qui était belle mais infidèle." ("They remind me of a woman whom I greatly loved in Tours, who was beautiful but unfaithful").

If a human translator were to use CAT tools, maybe we could achieve both beauty and fidelity in a translated text. MT alone would find it difficult to reconcile the two aspects. However, with the help of the human participant, both the explicit level and the implicit inter-textual level could be accorded adequate attention.

12.8 Conclusion

Much as the computer may be 'intelligent' it still cannot replace the human brain which collects, deciphers, filters and produces significant understandable language among the world population. That being said, I believe that in today's productivity mindset, a human translator cannot easily meet clients' deadlines without these tools.

Despite the fact that a machine invented by man cannot replace the mouth that feeds it, I believe that in order for the profession to survive and remain relevant, translation and interpretation experts need to change their mindset. This goes in the direction suggested by Claude Breur (www.brauertraining.com):

> "We need not only learn about the technology but, more important than that, we need to 'practice' with it to acquire the skills needed to 'work' with technology. That takes time and money and we need to be ready and available to make that investment. Technology is no longer an option; it is a requirement of the Digital Age, at least in the world of business."

Translators and interpreters should be willing to turn digital by embracing new technologies instead of shying away from them, referring to them unceasingly as unintelligent or considering them as a threat. We should remind ourselves also that Computer Aided Translation (CAT) tools including the translation memory, customization, etc. were programmed by the human being who remains superior to the machine however sophisticated the latter might be.

With more and more improved machine translations and mainly CAT tools, we shall be able to come up with a win-win situation whereby, the quality of a translated document and its pricing become proportional instead of one being compromised by the other. It is only then that the human translator can fully enjoy a profitable harmonization of the products of their intellect, logic, skills and discernment with the functions offered by emerging language translation and interpretation devices. Thus, a human translator's role will be out of danger of extinction. Subsequently, the newly created titles relating to their work may perhaps be redefined from Translator/Interpreter to Document Consultant, Post-MT-Editor, Audio Communications Adviser or Audio Proof-Reader.

References

Brauer, C. (2014). Becoming a tech-savvy translator and interpreter in the digital age , *www.proz.com/virtual-Conferences/632/program/9793.* Accessed 15/01/2015.

Kristof, N. (2010). Primero Hay que Aprender Espanõl. Ranhou Zai Xue Zhongwen.

Perruca, B. (2010). Un monde sans interprètes. *Le Monde.*

Piron, C. (1994). *Les défis des langues: Du gâchis au bon sens (The Language Challenge : from chaos to common sense).*L'Harmattan.Wikipaedia. (s.d.). http://www.brauertraining.com

PART FOUR
THE FUNCTIONALITY OF FOREIGN LANGUAGES

CHAPTER THIRTEEN
THE ACQUISITION OF INTER-CULTURAL COMPETENCES AMONGST UNIVERSITY STUDENTS: A CASE STUDY OF MAKERERE UNIVERSITY

Samuel Wandera[1]

Abstract

This article, which is derived from my doctoral research, makes an attempt to identify elements comprising Inter-cultural communication, as one aspect of Inter-cultural education in foreign language pedagogy. It tries to identify its constructs and its conceptualization and how its competences can be developed and learned within a university curriculum for adult Beginners in French. In process of making a curriculum situational analysis, the study has tried to measure effectiveness in the coverage of Inter-cultural communication within the context of teaching French as a foreign language in Makerere University in Kampala. The initial findings suggest that the methodologies of *Bienvenue en France, Taxi* and *On y va* are used in teaching French at Makerere University. The Inter-cultural content in these methodologies is only 47.4%. For the social studies, two books were noted to be in use: Civilization progressive du Français and Civilization de la Francophonie. On average, the study shows that these books have a 44.2% content of Inter-cultural information. As for the literature books, only the novel, *Maigret tend un piège* was studied. Findings reveal that 46.6% of the content was Inter-cultural. The findings show the pedagogical need for adjusting and enriching the curriculum if we are to attain the main goal of imparting Inter-cultural competences. This mainly documentary research also points to the need to examine the application of these teaching materials in an in-depth educational survey.

Key words: Inter-cultural pedagogy, Inter-cultural actions, Inter-cultural communication, Inter-culturality, Inter-cultural competences.

---

[1] Samuel Wandera is currently a lecturer of French at Makerere University. He has been in the field of language teaching for a period of 20 years. His teaching experience started with handling the young students at high school level and later young adults at higher institutions of learning. His major areas of interest have been in the teaching of French grammar and communication, French literature and Francophone cultural studies.

13.1 Introduction

Inter-cultural interactions have become part and parcel of our everyday activity in an increasingly globalist context of foreign language education. Today, much more than in the past, there are strong economic, technological, security and peace imperatives for gaining competency in Inter-cultural interactions. The Ugandan language syllabus recognizes this need for Inter-culturality: "Combining English, Local Language, Swahili and any one Foreign Language [French, German, Italian, Latin, Spanish, etc] widens the learners' opportunities in the world of work. That is, a student will be multi-skilled and. able to handle many languages at the same time" (Oketcho: 2011). The fields of Inter-cultural studies and Inter-cultural education have grown as a response to the above mentioned imperatives with their attributes evolving around cross-cultural, Inter-cultural communication, internationalization and interpersonal competences. This article, which is derived from my doctoral research, will attempt to identify elements comprising Inter-cultural communication as one aspect of interest that is part of Inter-cultural education in foreign language pedagogy. I will try to identify its constructs, crystallize its conceptualization and gauge how its competences can be developed and learned through a university curriculum for adult Beginners in French. In due course, I hope to measure our effectiveness in the coverage of Inter-cultural communication within the context of teaching French as a foreign language in Makerere University.

13.2 Culture and Inter-cultural Competence in Education

In a world that is characterized by shared values, beliefs and behaviours of interacting people, the framework of culture that brings them together has been defined as 'the fabric of meaning in terms of which human beings interpret their experience and guide their action' (Geertz, 1973: 83). Within that framework of culture, Inter-cultural competence can be defined as "a complex set of abilities needed to perform effectively and appropriately when interacting with others, who are linguistically and culturally different from oneself" (Fantini; 2006). In the context of the adult Beginners, who are at the heart of this study at Makerere University, having come from diverse backgrounds, how feasible is it for them to acquire Inter-cultural competence through the process of interaction proposed by the university French Beginners programme? They enter the programme with a cultural distance that has been well documented by researches like that one of Hofstede conducted in 53 countries.

Figure 13.2.1: Distance between Learner & Target Language Cultures

Individualist Cultures	Collectivist Cultures
Identity is in terms of « I »	Identity is in terms of « Us »
Individuals Objectives	Group Objectives
Priority given to the 'inter-individual	Priority is given to the group
Reciprocity is optional	Reciprocity is obligatory
Management mainly is of persons	Management is of Groups
Emphasis is on equality	Emphasis is put on hierarchical distance
Credibility is mainly individual	Seniority, age, rank, title matters most
Interaction symmetric	Interaction is asymmetrical
Emphasis is on informality	Accent mis sur l'informalité
Subordinates expect to be consulted	Subordinates expected to be lead
USA, Australia, Great-Britain, Canada, Netherlands New-Zealand, Sweden, Norway, Austria, France, Germany	Guatemala, Equator, Panama, Indonesia, Pakistan, Taiwan, Popular Republic of China, Japan, Burkina Faso, Kenya*

Source: *Adapted from Hofstede et al (2002)*

This study showed that when you talk about Inter-cultural communication, you are inevitably dealing with cultural values and the cultural attitudes and perceptions of students coming for French, which are mostly in contrast to those of the target language as **Figure 13.2.1** shows. Yet, it is on the basis of the cultural values that one establishes the criteria of appropriate communication with the foreigner. It is also a known fact that cultural values do structure our perceptions, thus exerting considerable influence on our communication styles and sensitivity to conflict as well as the non-verbal standards that we adopt. The challenge then for institutions like Makerere University would be: how do we negotiate with the learner to re-direct his or her cultural values towards establishing a link with the values of the target language? This is one of the main variables we are considering in the envisaged group creation of Inter-culturality.

Fitzgerald (2000) explained further that, culture's specific competence relates to the ability to 'participate in the everyday web of social relationships of a particular social group". This implies possessing a 'social intelligence inside' and being able to express or communicate that intelligence in meaningful ways (Marshall, 1996: 252). Fitzgerald (2000) also identified culture's general competence as more of "context-bound, practice-based, awareness, knowledge, attitude and skills". In his view, the culture's general competent person demonstrates the ability to use a range of knowledge and skills (especially communication and problem-solving skills), to understand and address cultural issues in practice in a way that results in an outcome that is satisfying (or at least acceptable) to everyone involved. In other words then, the outcome of Inter-cultural understanding that we aim to impart to our students, encompasses concepts related to the cognitive (knowledge and awareness) and the affective domains of Inter-cultural competence, which builds on Inter-cultural understanding by including behaviour and communication (Perry & Southwell: 2011).

Over the last few years, with the frequent changes experienced in our education content, researchers like Pickering and McAllister (2000) have got interested in examining culture in the context of the education with a specific focus on Inter-cultural approaches to language teaching in multicultural environments. They observed that with the worldwide trends towards increased migration and demographic mixing, professionals in education are increasingly being required to work in diverse, multicultural environments. For this reason, Pickering and McAllister (2000), remarked that competences in Inter-cultural practice are necessary to impart professional knowledge and skills in this field and their development, is increasingly part of the core business of institutions where professional are produced "en masse": the universities. The two researchers nevertheless cautioned that currently, a gap in the knowledge base exists in the learning processes that underpin the acquisition of such Inter-cultural awareness, knowledge, attitude and skills. Such a gap is of concern to all trainers involved at the professional level of educational programmes. This is why we picked interest in examining how this gap could be closed at Makerere University.

We believe that the inclusion of cultural components in language courses will support adaptation to the culture of the people who speak that language, but there is only limited evidence to support this claim. Two important studies (Martin and Laurie, 1993; Robinson and Nocon, 1996) have attempted to improve the state of the art by investigating student motivation for language and cultural study. Cook (1996), in her investigation of how first year university students develop cultural understanding, found out that older students hold more differentiated, but still quite similar views of the role of the teacher. She concludes that teachers were "most valued as a source of input if they appeared to have expertise with the French language and culture." When such expertise was granted to them, the students considered their teachers to be an important source of cultural information. In the case of Makerere University, it is interesting to find out to what extent is the teacher sensitive to Inter-cultural information? What space does the teacher accord to Inter-cultural sensitivity?

In another study on assessing Inter-cultural competence outcomes in higher education, Deardorff (2004) found that many institutions of higher learning now target a variety of Inter-cultural outcomes among their prioritized educational goals, especially within general education courses, foreign language requirements and degrees, and study abroad programmes. In concert with growing demands for accountability and improvement, there is increasing pressure to evaluate the educational effectiveness of such internationalization efforts within curricula and programmes and with a specific focus on what students know and can do as a result of their college learning experiences (Deardorff, 2004). Makerere University, in contrast to the study of Deardoff, does not have any study abroad component in its French Beginners programmes. However, efforts to place students in international organizations for the compulsory course UFA 2202 Field Attachment in the second year of study could be assessed as a practice - based opportunity offered for improving Inter-cultural skills.

Mauranen (1994) investigated a group of students who had that advantage of studying within the target language reality but still felt distanced like the Ugandan French students. These were Finnish students studying English as a second language in the United Kingdom. The author's qualitative study revealed that, the students felt secure about their ability to use English as a second language, but insecure about their knowledge of how to participate in the different discourse environments due to cultural factors. For instance they felt insecure about the appropriate timing to ask a question or interrupt someone during a conversation. These are issues of perfecting one's Inter-cultural communication, which only come with time and practice and the knowledge of the "other's" attitudes and reactions. In the case of Makerere University, that knowledge can only be assessed at the threshold of the Beginners' Inter-cultural learning process (i.e. at the end of the three year course)

In another foreign language, learning context, Martin and Laurie (1993) investigated the views of 45 students, enrolled in an intermediate level French course at Flinders University in South Australia, about the contribution of literary and cultural content to language learning. They found that the students' reasons for studying French "were more related to linguistic than cultural interests" (p. 190), with practical reasons such as oral proficiency, travel plans, and employment opportunities dominating the list. However, when they probed specifically the role of non-linguistic components such as literature and culture as motivating factors, they found that variables like the "desire to study the French way of life" motivated nearly 90% of students, while "hegemonic aspects of the culture motivated rather less than 50% (Martin & Laurie, 1995: 195). Our interest in our study at Makerere University is to check whether the students' "fear of literature" as observed by Martin and Laurie (1995; 205), in the study conducted in Australia could also be a plausible explanation, for low motivation or Inter-cultural communication in a different cultural context. After discussing findings, and when making comparison be of pedagogical importance to consider whether the hypothesis of "culture anxiety" made by Martin & Laurie, (1995; 205), caused by the perceived lack of "cultural background to relate to a foreign literature" or other non-linguistic aspects affects equally the Ugandan learners' acquisition of Inter-cultural competences.

13.3 Inter-cultural Competence and Communication

Over the last 30 years many scholars from different schools of language, literature, communication, pedagogy and anthropology have defined Inter-cultural competence in various ways, and not one single one has been adapted as the standard definition. However, one can take for synthesis the summary offered by Perry and Southwell (2011,) that "Inter-cultural competence involves the ability to interact effectively and appropriately with people from other cultures". In this case interaction is concurrently taken to include both appropriate behaviour and effective communication. In the context of Makerere University students, we could describe Inter-cultural competence as that Inter-cultural tooling requiring a transfer of "knowledge, motivation, skills in verbal and non-verbal communication and appropriate and effective behaviours." (Perry & Southwell, 2011; 455)

Developing a similar line of thought, Heyward describes a model of "Inter-cultural literacy", as a construct that is very close to Inter-cultural competence and includes in it "the understandings, competencies, attitudes, language proficiencies, participation and identities necessary for successful cross-cultural engagement"(Heyward 2002, 10). This definition certainly comes nearer home because it brings into play the components of language proficiencies, participation and identity. These are major pillars of language teaching, methodology and cultural understanding. Indeed, most of the scholarly texts we came across in our research stressed the necessity for the learner to go progressively through stages of cultural sensitivity, from complete denial to the higher threshold of accepting and respecting cultural differences. When the learner has achieved that goal, she or he will be said to have accessed "Inter-cultural sensitivity" (Perry & Southwell; 454). This is what has been captured in a diagrammatic form below adapted from Buttjes & Byram.

Figure 13.3.1: Stages of Inter-cultural Learning

Stages of learning	Development of Competence	Cultivation of Identity	Area of Experience
Trans-cultural Stage / Inter-cultural Stage	Perspective Formation	Identity Formation	Cultural Experience
Mono-cultural Stage	Relativity	Reversal of Roles	Social Experience
	Reciprocity	Explicitness	Interpersonal Experience

Source: *Adapted from Hagen Kordes, in Buttjes & Bryam (1991)*

Researchers have termed the different road maps for the progress of acquiring Inter-cultural learning as 'models' of Inter-cultural competence. Essentially, they contain the same aspects of knowledge, values, attitudes, behaviours, beliefs, identity and linguistic proficiency etc., but they are organized in different sets. Any comprehensive set used in the foreign language class and worth its name should lead the learner to the threshold of acquiring Inter-cultural understanding and recognizing aspects of Inter-cultural or international conflicts. According to Buttjes & Byram, "the learner should be able to differentiate the differences between his own culture and the foreign culture ... and to see the norms of his own culture in relative terms" (Buttjes & Byram; 301).

A different framework of learning criteria exists for Inter-cultural communication competence. It incorporates communication into the Inter-cultural learning models. Several researchers indeed have endeavoured to do so. We will pick the Deardoff fusioned model as a reference that seems to be close to the Inter-cultural understanding level of the adult Beginners at Makerere University. Deardoff has tried to identify the components of such a fusioned construct as elaborated below in **Figure 13.3.2** (Deardoff; 2006).

Figure 13.3.2: Deardorff's Pyramid Model of Inter-cultural Competence

Desired External Outcome

Behaving and communicating effectively and appropriately (based on one's Inter-cultural knowledge, skills, and attitudes) to achieve one's goals to some degree.

Desired Internal Outcome

- Informed frame of reference/filter shift
- Adaptability (to different communication styles and behaviours; adjustment to new cultural environments).
- Flexibility (selecting and using appropriate communication styles and behaviours; cognitive flexibility).
- Ethno relative view
- Empathy

Knowledge and Comprehension

- Cultural self-awareness.
- Deep understanding and knowledge of culture (including contexts, role and impact of culture and others' world views).
- Culture-specific. information
- Socio-linguistic awareness

Skills

- Listen
- Observe
- Interpret
- Analyze
- Evaluate
- Relate

Requisite Attitudes

- Respect (valuing other cultures, cultural diversity).
- Openness (to Inter-cultural learning and to people from other cultures, withholding judgment).
- Curiosity and discovery (tolerating ambiguity and uncertainty).

Source: *Adapted from Deardorff, 2006:304*

In the Makerere students' context, it seems that if the lecturer can ensure that they have gained the ability to understand their own cultural norms and expectations and to recognize cultural differences, then they can be open to new experiences and diversity. By the end of the course, a student who has received effective Inter-cultural training should have what Arasaratnam (2009) calls "the ability to effectively and appropriately communicate with people from different cultures". Reality is this, what one can find on the ground? When the teacher has an inadequate self-consciousness of his or her culture, having followed a curriculum that had that lacuna, what degree of Inter-cultural sensitivity can the teacher impart to the learners?

13.4 Learning French in a Ugandan Public University

From the existing literature, 'Inter-cultural training' predominantly seems to be associated with the training of adults whose work requires them to interact with people from other cultures (Perry & Southwell, 1991: 457). This is in contrast with the target group of young adult Beginners being taught French as a foreign language. These are young Anglophone adults who have chosen to study French. They are supposed first and foremost, to have a clear conscience of "their own cultural characteristics and their processes of communication" (Rodrigo: 1997). As Abdallah-Pretceille (1996: 117-118) has put it, "In the cultural domain like in the linguistic one, the person who is sure of his or her cultural identity can play with the cultural game rules". In reality though, in Beginners' classes, there is a mix of students with very varied cultural origins[2]. Their formal awareness of their cultural identity and official communication processes is very limited.

At Makerere University, the Beginners curriculum is built around the objectives of teaching of French language use, simplified literature in French, as well as cultural studies in the French and Francophone society. The learners in most cases, study French as a Minor, an additional subject to: Political Science, Sociology, Social Administration, Organizational Skills, Communication Skills, Anthropology and Library Information Science. A typical time allocation for French Beginners is eight hours per week, plus another 10 hours the students dedicate that time to doing daily assignments and personal reading. From this submission, we note that, French is allocated the strict minimum timetable load and is sharing learning space with the other subjects. This second class type of prioritization has an impact on the students' attitude towards the subject and its target culture.

---

2   Though all the students may be Ugandan, in Uganda, there is a diversity of the indigenous nationalities, speaking more than 62 languages.

The teaching of French is not only meant to make these learners acquire necessary competencies linguistically in order to express themselves well orally and in written but also to make these learners acquire necessary Inter-cultural competences that are required in places of multilingual, multicultural and international set up, in order to meet the expectations of employers and their clients. To have someone with Inter-cultural competence would mean to have that person who can relate appropriately with first, the representatives of the target culture that are encountered in the teaching materials and then the members of other societies and cultures.

An analysis of the Tables of content of the books used by the French Beginners at Makerere University could give us a general picture of how much Inter-cultural content is included in its current curriculum. The main course texts include: *Bienvenue en France* by Anne Monnerie, *Taxi* by Menand, Robert et al., *On y va* by Catherine Mauzaric, *Civilization Progressive Française* (debutant) by Catherine Carlo, and *Civilization Progressive Francophone* by Noutchié Njiké. In third year Beginners, there are also some simplified French literature books used for extensive reading: *Maigret Tend Un Piège* by Georges Simenon. These text books bring in aspects of different cultures. A quick examination of the different texts and their culture of origin will give us a clearer picture of the cultural spread of the content covered.

Table 13.4.1: Inter-cultural Content in the Grammar Text books

Didactical Topic	Approximate % of Inter-cultural Information-Bienvenue en France	Approximate % of Inter-cultural Information-Taxi	Approximate % of Inter-cultural Information-On y va	Average %
Exchanging personal information	55	80	70	68.3
Family & home	25	60	50	45
Pass time & hobbies	60	60	50	56.7
Weather	35	20	30	28.3
School	10	30	80	40

Finding one's way in town	65	30	30	41.7
Simple shopping	65	40	50	51.2
Food & Drink	80	40	40	53.3
Average				47.4

Source: *Mini-survey Findings Dec. 2014*

The findings above show that, with regards the grammar curriculum, the most Inter-culturally packed chapters are to do with exchanging personal information (68.3%), pastime and hobbies (56.7%), Food and drink (53.3%) and shopping (51.2%). Other areas like finding one's way in town and family; averagely include some Inter-cultural information. The chapters that have the least information on Inter-cultural issues seem to be in the areas of talking about the weather (28.3%). It therefore becomes evident that a beginner learner of French at Makerere will get more Inter-cultural content in personal information, but there will be gaps when dealing with external topics like weather.

Table 13.4.2: Inter-cultural Content in the Civilization Text books

Didactical Topic	**Approx. % of Inter-cultural Information-** *Civilization Progressive (française) FRB 1202*	**Approx.%of Inter-cultural Information-** *Civilization Progressive (francophone) FRB 2202*	**Average%**
Les régions de la France	45	10	22.5
Family & home	70	10	40
Pass time& Holidays	40	40	40
Admin/Pol Institutions	40	80	60
Social Services	40	40	40
France in Europe	45	10	27.5

France & Francophone world	22.5	30	26.3
Food & Drink	60	30	45
Francophone Music	40	25	32.5
Francophone Traditions	40	55	47.5
National Days & Feasts	60	40	50
Francophone Institutions	60	40	50
Geog./ Historical Information	90	45	67.5
Average			44.2%

Source: *Mini-survey Findings Dec. 2014*

The findings on the use Civilization books to teach French show that, the most Inter-culturally packed chapters are to do with geographical and historical information with 67.5% of the respondents revealing that it is highly featured in the books. Other areas reflected to be covering cultural contents are political institutions with 60% followed by festivals and Francophone institutions, each having coverage of 50. In general, we note that the rankings on the Inter-cultural content through use of Civilization books differ from those of the grammar books. Whereas in the grammar books, exchanging personal information leads in Inter-cultural studies, Civilization books have geographical and historical aspects as the major input for Inter-cultural studies.

Table 13.4.3: Inter-cultural Content in the Literature books

Didactical Topic	**Approximate % of Inter-cultural Information-** (*Maigret tend un piège*)
Exchanging personal information	55
Family & home	45
Pass time & hobbies	50
Weather	57.5
School	35
Finding one's way in town	55

Simple shopping	30
Food & Drink	45
Average	**46.6%**

In the study on how much Inter-cultural content is covered in literature books used on Beginner students of French at Makerere University, findings show the area of weather was more covered compared to other didactical topics. Respondents gave weather a 57.5% featuring in the novel *Maigret tend un piège*. The other didactical topics well covered by the literature text were exchanging personal information is (55%) and finding one's way in town is also (55%). Shopping on the other hand, was least Inter-culturally covered by the novel. The documentary study reveals that the novel included only 30% of Inter-cultural content to do with shopping.

The findings show a big contradiction on how external topics like weather or geographical settings are covered by grammatical books and literature books. In grammatical books, weather was seen as least Inter-cultural whereas in the novel *Maigret tend un piège*; weather was ranked as the most Inter-culturally covered element. This may be linked to the frequent geographical displacement s of the characters in the literature text.

13.5 How French is taught at Makerere

Our second concern for Inter-cultural competence focused on 'how' it is taught at Makerere University. Experts in Inter-cultural pedagogy like Perry & Southwell (2011:457) have pointed out the main principles for effective Inter-cultural development: the importance of a challenge, critical cultural awareness, teaching subjective 'culture and exploring alternative world views. Such an outward bound approach to teaching presumes that, the teacher creates an environment that is conducive to games, debate, discussion, simulation, virtual exploration and experiential learning.

In order to gauge how 'conducive' the methods and approaches used for Beginners at Makerere, we made a quick inventory of how the Language use, Civilization Française, Civilization Francophone and Extensive Reading were being handled[3].

---

3   The mini-survey involved five of the eight lecturers of French at Makerere University.

Figure 13.5.1 : Inventory of Teaching approaches used for French Beginners

Exercises	Gram-mar books	Social study of the French and francophone societies FRB 2202	Literature Française FRB 3202	Total Frequencies
Reading out loud	XXXXX	XXXXXXXX	XXXXXXXX	21
Exercise in Class	XXXXXX	XXXXXXXX	XXXXX	20
Discussion	XXXX	XXXX	XXXXXXXX	16
Games/ Songs	XX	XXXX	XX	8
Online Exercises	X	XXX	XX	6
Take away drills	XXXXX	XXXXXXX	XXXXXXX	14
Written Composition	XXXX	XXXXX	XXXXXX	15
Field Visit	X	X	X	3
Authentic texts	XXX	XXXXX	XX	10
Audio animation	XXX	XX	XXX	8
Film/DVD	X	XX	XX	5
Internet based materials	XXXX	XXXXXXXX	XXXX	16
Oral presentations	XXXXXX	XXXXXX	XXXXXXX	19
Group Work	XXXXX	XXXXX	XXXXXXXX	18

Figure 13.5.1: Showing frequencies at which exercises were reflected in grammar books, Social study and Literature. The ranking of frequency was indicated by the number of X in each box in the raw data.

(Source: *Mini-survey Findings Dec. 2014*)

The findings in **Figure 13.5.1** show that, the most common method used in teaching French as Foreign language to the Beginners was practicing reading texts out loud. This had the highest frequency of 21 closely followed by exercises in class. The use of written exercises in class had a frequency of 20. Others like the use of oral exercises and group work in learning French featured high. Use of oral presentations had a frequency of 19 and group work of 18. The least utilized were field visits, which had only a frequency of 3. The use of film and DVD was also noted to be minimal with a frequency of 5. These findings point to the fact that, more traditional and classical approaches are frequently being used for Beginners at Makerere University. The more recent approaches, which bring current images, videos and visits to the foreign language learning environment, are still rare in the French Classes of Beginners. This does not augur well for the main objective of imparting Inter-cultural competences to these young adults and it calls for a methodological shift in the teaching of French to Beginners at Makerere University.

13.6 Conclusion and Recommendations

Based on the forgoing analysis, which was mainly documentary and qualitative, we can observe that the teaching of Inter-cultural competence, as much as it is a desired outcome of teaching French as a foreign language, its realization is still a challenge. Employers have shown concern over the low sensitivity of graduates to Inter-cultural skills. This, as was elaborated is linked to the gaps in the teacher teaching curriculum itself and the curriculum of universities like Makerere University. The investigation of the teaching materials has also shown that grammar methodologies for Beginners have only coverage of 47.4% of Inter-cultural information. Social study books for French community and the Francophone context cover 44.2% of Inter-cultural content while literature covers 46.6% of the same. These percentages are all below 50% and thus imply that something more should be done to boost the Inter-cultural content in the teaching materials at Makerere.

Given the foregoing discussions, the study recommends that:

- In service training for teachers of French, especially those at the university level should envisage further training in dispensing more cultural knowledge of other Francophone cultures so as to enable the teacher or lecturer of adult beginners to teach Inter-cultural communication more effectively.
- Methodologies used for adult beginners should be enriched so as to explicitly include more cultural aspects so that the language is taught with its culture. In this way, graduates can interact effectively with others members of the target language community without committing cultural "gaffes" or suffering from cultural shocks.

- Lecturers of Beginners are also encouraged to use more recent methods using games, songs, online exercises, films, videos and audio animations that bring Inter-cultural life directly to the French language class for Beginners.
- This short survey was a precursor to a doctoral study on Inter-cultural competences amongst French Beginners at the university level. It has shown that apart from examining the knowledge of the language as a culture, behaviours and attitudes also need to be properly tested to show whether training programmes are effectively developing Inter-cultural capability.
- The French Section should lobby organizations and enterprises using French to engage more students to do internships with them as a means of developing a practice –based teaching of Inter-cultural communication.

References

Abdallah-Pretceille, Martine, & Porcher, Louis (1996). *Éducation et communication interculturelle*. Paris: PUF.

Arasaratnam, L.A. (2009). "The development of a new instrument of Inter-cultural communication competence", http://www.immi.se/Inter-cultural/nr20/arasaratnam.htm, 23-01-2015

Affaya, M.N.E. (1996) "Occidenti l'Islam: images illusòries i/o Inter-culturalitat efectiva?"*dCIDOB*, 56:24-27.

Buttjes D. & Bryam M. (Eds) (1991): *Mediating Languages and Cultures: Towards and Inter-cultural Theory of Foreign Language Education*, Multilingual Matters, Avon, England.

Deardorff, D. K. (2004).The identification and assessment of Inter-cultural competence as a student outcome of internationalization at institutions of higher education in the United States. Unpublished doctoral dissertation, North Carolina State University, Raleigh, NC.

Fantini, A. E. (2006). Exploring and assessing Inter-cultural competence. Retrieved May 1, 2007, from http://www.sit.edu/publications/docs/feil_research_report.pdf

Hofstede G. J. Pedersen P.B. & Hofstede G.H. (2002) *Exploring culture: exercises, stories, and synthetic cultures*

Yarmouth, Me: Inter-cultural Press, 2002. – xix, 234 p. ISBN: 1-877864-90-0

Mauzaric C. (2002) *On y va*, CLE International, Paris.

Menand, Robert et al. *Taxi*, Hachette, Paris.

Monnerie A, (1991) *Bienvenue en France, Didier, Paris*.

Oketcho P. (2011); *Language Career Tracks: a Viewpoint Secondary Curriculum Reform in Uganda,* National Curriculum Development Centre Uganda

Perry L. B. & Southwell L. (2011), Developing *Inter-cultural understanding and skills: Models and approaches,* Routledge, London (published, online)http://www.tandfonline.com/loi/ceji20, Accessed 23/10/15).

Risager, K. (2007). *Language and culture pedagogy: From a national to a transnational paradigm.* Buffalo, NY: Multilingual Matters.

Rodrigo M.A. (1997). « Elements pour une communication interculturelle **Afers Internacionals,** n° 36, pages 129-139 Fundació CIDOB, 1997

Ruben, B. D. (1989). The study of cross-cultural competence: Traditions and contemporary issues. *International Journal of Inter-cultural Relations,* 13, 229-240.

Ruben, B. D., & Kealey, D. (1979): Behavioural assessment of communication competency and the prediction of cross-cultural adaptation. *International Journal of Inter-cultural Relations,* 3, 15-48.

Simenon Georges (1955) *Maigret tend un piège,* Livre de Poche, Paris.

CHAPTER FOURTEEN
THAI YOUNG ADULTS' INTEREST IN THE GERMAN LANGUAGE AND CULTURE

Yap Lian Chee Sandra[1]

Abstract

Living in a fast pace development and undergoing globalization process in the Southeast Asia region, Thailand has come to be known as the hub of business, a focus of cultural and educational transition. As Eastern foreign languages and cultures such as Japanese, Korean and Chinese are getting strongly promoted in Thailand as the most desired languages to learn classical western languages and cultures such as German and French are losing popularity. This paper aims at tracing this recent trend by taking German as a case study. A survey was conducted in the University of Chulalongkorn and Triam Udom Suksa High School to examine the causes of the decreasing popularity of the German language among Thai young adults[2]. The survey intended to find out measures that can be taken to overcome these culture-educational barriers.

Key words: Young adults, German as a foreign language, Language visibility, Thailand culture, language interest.

14.1 Introduction
14.2 Rationale of study

Today in Thailand, Chinese cuisine, Korean pop stars, Japanese comic and animated events are more popular and more highly recognized than Western cultural events, perhaps with the unique exception of Christmas day. Thai People can easily cite a few Chinese, Korean and Japanese introductory phrases such as **Kimchi**, **Konnichiwa and Ni-hao-ma**? This

---

1 First Author, Yap Lian Chee (Sandra) is from Malaysia and was born in December, 1987. She graduated from the University of Malaya in 2011 with a Bachelor's degree (Hons) Languages and Linguistics. Currently, she is pursuing further studies in Chulalongkorn University with a CU-ASEAN scholarship as a full time Master student in Southeast Asian Studies. Besides being student, she is also actively involved in teaching languages to foreign learners from various age groups and backgrounds in Thailand.

---

2 Thai young adult in this paper is divided into 2 groups, which are , namely, secondary school students (14-18 years old) and University students (19-24 years old)

reflects the spread of Eastern cultures in Thai society and how people are learning them rapidly as a part of their global adaptation. This trend can be extended to Thai young learners in high schools and universities. In 2009 for instance, when it came to the choice of foreign subjects among Thai students, Chinese and Japanese languages were placed at the top of the ranking scale of A- NET (Thailand Advanced National Educational Test)[3] by the candidates from high school (Takayoshi Fujiwara, 2012:172). Besides, the country continues to get assailed by 'cultural tsunamis' from the Eastern region; such was the case on 5th December 2012, when we were "hit" by Korean wave of the world famous music video of "Gangnam style" as it "swept off" youths in Thailand. Thailand was placed as the country with the second highest number of viewers of the Korean video after America.

Given such flooding of Thai society by Eastern cultures, the author wonders, what will be the effects of this trend on the teaching and learning of Western foreign languages? In search of a response to this, this paper will take the German subject as a case study in order to trace the young adults' interest in the German language and culture. The aim of this paper is to find out Thai students' perspectives on their choice of German as a foreign language subject, their perception of Germany, German culture and their opinion of particular linguistic features that do not exist in Thai. It is our hope that in the process of exploring the young Thai's views on the German language and culture we will discover more about the thinking of our own society. This approach is supported by scholars like *Edward Lee Gorsuch,* the former *Chancellor of University of Alaska, Anchorage,* who made the following observation on the work of promoting foreign language learning:

> "Learning a foreign language not only reveals how other societies think and feel, what they have experienced and value, and how they express themselves, it also provides a cultural mirror in which we can see more clearly our own society."

In this paper, I have developed two arguments as approaches to gauging students' interest in a Western foreign language. In the first place I argue that, from the historical point of view, the German culture is not new to Thailand since the two countries have more than 150 years of diplomatic relations, from the time of King Chulalongkorn (King Rama V) era. Thus, the first wave of German influence in Thailand was based on economic

---

3   A-NET is a national standard exam used for university admission.

bilateral cooperation as a foundation to introduce the German culture and language particularly to Thailand merchants and elite groups. In the second argument, I observe that alongside the arrival of the abundance of science and technological innovation in Thailand, in the early 20th Century, the German language gained its reputation as a scientific language and was taught as a channel of access to the world of science. Thus, its recent educational importance in Thailand differs from its historical influence in the past before the 20th century. Previously, access to the learning of German was very limited; it was accessible to only the high society of nobles and aristocrats much like French was a privilege of the Tsar and his class of the noblesse in the imperial Russia. We can therefore infer that with the popularization of science and technological innovation in the 20th century in Thailand, the German language and culture became accessible to the general public including young adults.

However, despite the foregoing arguments, I hypothesize that the German language and culture was not successfully promoted and was therefore not well-accepted by Thai people. This observation is based on three factors:

14.3 Image of the German Language and Culture

In terms of image and impression, the German culture has rather a strong but less entertaining reputation as compared to Thai local culture that is more flexible and colourful. However, due to its possibility of offering variety, the German language and culture have gained popularity among the Thai people. Besides, since science and technology were marketed alongside the German language, it attracted only a certain group of people interested in this sector. In other words, this specific field that relates closely to German has proportionately narrowed the market approach to promote the language to public.

14.4 Role of the Medium and Publicity

German-related news and information have relatively less visibility in public media sources such as newspapers and magazines. German news is mainly located in professional magazines, journals and scholarly books in Thailand. Compared with Eastern languages and cultures such as Chinese and Japanese, these tend to fare better since they are channeled through the popular media. Eastern languages access the Thai society through wider range media such as entertainment magazines, comic books, newspapers, popular drama, entertainment shows and news, songs, movies etc.

14.5 Language and Cultural Distinction

Lastly, Thai language and German language have very different characteristics, which in terms of grammar and phonology, are difficult to comprehend for Thai learners, to pick and comfortably reproduce. For instance, the stress of sound /t/ in the end of the German word "Stand", which changed from /d/ to /t/, is very important in German language but it is not a usual practice in Thai language.

14.6 History and background of Thailand and Germany's bilateral relationship

The history of the official diplomatic relationship of Germany and Thailand is summarized in **Fig 14.6.1** titled "150 Jahre Thai-Deutsche Diplomatische Beziehungen (1862-2012)", which literally translates into "150 years of Thai-German diplomatic relationship". According to the government public relations department, the relationship commenced prior to the signing of Treaty of Amity, Commerce and Navigation on 7 February 1862.[4] However, trade relations between the Thai kingdom merchants and German States could be traced back even further to 25th October 1858, when the treaty between the Hansaetic city of Lübeck and Bremen was formally recognized for the first time with Kingdom of Siam (Nongnuth Phecharatana; 2013).

The bilateral relationship was strengthened when king Chulalongkorn (King Rama V) visited Germany in 1897. He was warmly welcomed by Kaiser Wilhelm II (King of Prussia, 1859-1941) and was inspired by Germany's development and its products. **Fig 14.6.2** shows the newspaper of 24th June 1897 relaying the news of the arrival of King Chulalongkorn under the title "The Entrance of the King of Siam".

Figure 14.6.1 Govt. Public Relations Dept. 20/02/2012

---

4 The government public relations department : Thai and Germany celebrate 150 years of diplomatic relations, 20 February 2012 http://thailand.prd.go.th/view_news.php?id=6157&a=2

Figure 14.6.2 News Paper; 24/06/1897

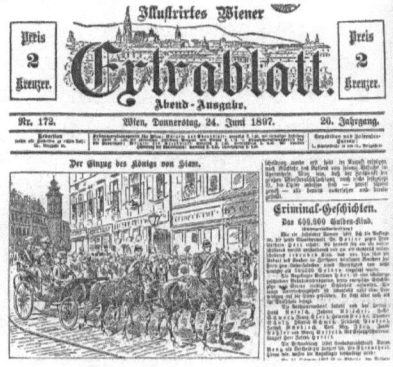

Since then, the friendship has grown stronger with the technology transferred and development assistance from Germany to Thailand. In the field of education, the relationship has been institutionalized with the opening of new establishments like the Thai-German Engineering Software Center for the Sirindhorn International Graduate school of Engineering (Govt. Public Relations Dept; February 20, 2012).

14.7 The German image

Generally, as inferred and observed from the history of the historical bilateral relationship, Germany's image in Thailand was well rooted with development and advance technology transfer in Thailand since the early contacts of the Thai people with German merchants in the Far East. It could be assumed from this perspective that the German language and culture in Thailand were given priority at the beginning of Thai mercantile development. However, it could only be accessed by the political elite class in those early days; these included the princes in the royal family who had been sent to Germany for higher education (Royal Imprint on Intl. Relations; Feb 20, 2012). Thus, the basic impression of the German language among Thai people is that of restrictive specialization and high standards. From the angle of practice, prior to the 20th century, when the world perceived German as the prominent scientific language, German in Thailand was seen as a language that was full of technical terms (Linda Adrean, p.32). Thus, in terms of its use in science and technology, German was used in a technical and professional field that engaged a certain group, of a limited number. Seen from this perspective, its distance from the general public has been widening and it could not be considered as a language of the majority of the population.

In the modern era of Thai development, German is still labeled and recognized as most relevant in scientific and technological advancement. However, most of the people in Thailand who have an idea about German products and events compare their importance with the language itself. It is often said that events like Oktoberfest, film, arts, and music festivals were organized by Goethe institute or DAAD to promote the culture. However, their low promotion in Thai society means that their vehicle of publicity, the German language, will not be as visible or as accessible as the loudly publicized Eastern languages. This has been confirmed by data collected by Pornsan Tmangraksat from the Thai University students, who were studying the language and who gave their opinion of the German people and Germany. **Table14.7.1** shows the response to the question: What comes up to your mind in the first place when you hear the word "Germany"? (Tmangraksat: 1976; 32).

Table 14.7.1: Image of Germany among German language learners in Thailand

	What comes up to your mind in the first place when you hear the word "Germany"?	**Number of students**	**Percentage**
1	War and Hitler	23	25
2	German (people)	15	16.3
3	Industry and Technology	14	15.22
4	Development and the second German states	13	14.13
5	German beer, sausage and Munich	5	5.43
6	The German language	2	2.17
7	The German form of life	2	2.17
8	Football	2	2.17
9	Music	2	2.17
10	Discipline	2	2.17
11	Lufthansa	1	1.09
12	Brandt	1	1.09
13	Volkswagen	1	1.09
14	Berlin wall	1	1.09
15	Huge people	1	1.09
16	Bismarck	1	1.09
17	Rhein	1	1.09
18	Staerke	1	1.09
		92	100

Source: *Pornsan Tmangraksat (1976:32)*

The data collected by Pornsan Tmangraksat was targeting students who were studying German and had contact with the German language and culture. Thus, the data could be more varied if it was collected from the members of the public, who probably have no exposure to the German language and culture. It is worth noting that according to the results, there is a high percentage of people whose image of Germany is based on the history of its World War experience and Hitler's leadership (25%), German industry (16.3%), and its technology (15.22%). This shows that the German image perceived by German learners in Thailand is closely connected to its role in global history and its skillful industry.

To refine this image, Tmangraksat posed an additional question to the students with regards to their opinion about the German people (Tmangraksat; 1976:33). The result shows that most of the students think of Germans in a positive but rather serious personality. In the top three of the list, they were labeled in more than 50% as particular person, smart, active, serious and strong personality. Personally, I assume that these characteristics could be one of the reasons that make Thai people keep a distance from German culture. As in Thailand, in contrast, it is a "land of smiles" with friendly, fun and flexible culture oriented among the people.

14.8 Role of the Medium and Publicity

In Thailand today, we can easily find the German language online in magazines or on the Internet, written by Germans who live in Thailand. For instance, **Pattaya Blatt, der Farang, Thailand Tip, Wochenblitz Thailand, Thaizeit, Hallo-Das Magazin, Aktuell Thailand** and **Südostasien Zeitung.** The rich information and publicity are successful in attracting and reaching out to the German reader but not to the local language learner. Thus, the impact of promoting it as a language does not work effectively for the general public but it can work for German language learners. In short, the German magazines and media promote and increase the number of German common phrases used in Thai tourism industry and also initially contributed to the country's economic development. However, one notes that it is a one way flow, without a positive response from the local media. This may be indicative of the lack of local knowledge packaged for German visitors in Thailand.

With regards to local media, we could use a German-related news scan to make observations on the current media exposure and popularity in Thailand. From the 3 examples below in **Figures14.8.1 and14.8.2**, which were taken from Bangkok Post and BK city, we could assume that these advertisements and information share the common characteristic of low popularity. For instance, only 1 person shared out the news of the

German musician's performance in Bangkok on social network platforms. The performance was also advertised by the Goethe Institut German course with no follow up discussion from the readership. The same lack of promotion could be noted with the 3 months of free movie screening at the Goethe Institute.

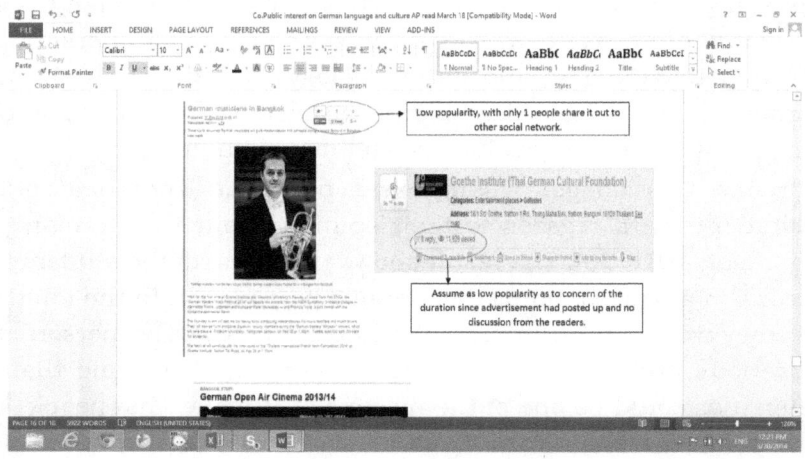

Figure 14.8.1 German Music in Bangkok

Source: *Bangkok Post: German musicians in Bangkok, 17 February 2014 (Above)*

Bangkok Post: Lifestyle column – Goethe Institut, the German culture foundation (Below)

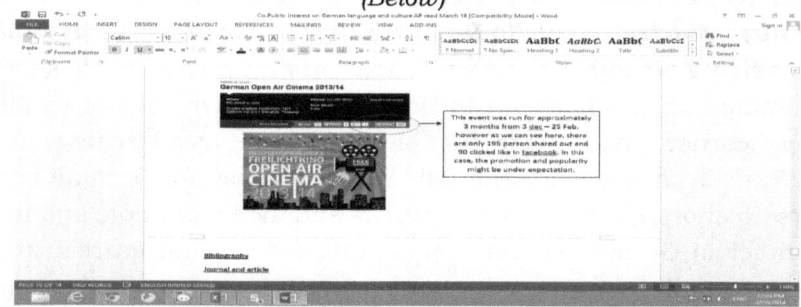

Figure 14.8.2 German Open Air Cinema

Source: *BK city: German Open Air Cinema 2013/2014*

14.9 Cultural and language diversity

Two arguments have been advanced on the diversities between Germany and Thailand namely: culture and language. First of all, concerning the issue of the culture, German and Thai people often face inter-cultural difficulties that cause misunderstandings when they meet. For instance, in a case study on German and Thai, Solgossom (2001) explains in *Colleagues Communication in Working Place* that collectivism and individualism as concepts tend to cause conflict among staff.

It is often said that Thailand adapted the *"Pi-Nong"* □□□□□□ hierarchy relationship as a sign of respect and the practice of *"kreng Jai"* □□□□□ obligation as a base to create a harmonious environment. Seen from this perspective, the speech act of saying "no" is perceived as being rude (Solgossom; 2001:21). This cultural practice is the opposite of Western culture that prefers a clear cut "no" for the sake of clarity in the subsequent action. A mixed interpretation of the two pragmatics often causes conflict and prejudices at the work place. In contrast, if we compare to the Eastern cultural practices, they are easier to be accepted in Thailand since traditionally, the Japanese and Chinese live in a collective form of society, which is similar to the Thai in terms of social structures. In this case, in terms of cultural practices, there is a significant advantage for young adults to privilege the Eastern trends as compared to the Western ones.

Secondly, due to linguistic difference between the Thai and German languages, in addition to the morphological and syntactical difficulties, another major problem that German language learners in Thailand find is the non-existence of some of the phonemes in their language. These include umlaut: long close front rounded vowel [y] as in "über" and long close-mid front rounded vowel [ø] as in "schön" and palatal non-sibilant sound [ç] as in "Ich". These are often found hard to pronounce. This constitutes a linguistic barrier, drawing back students who would have picked German as their language choice. The linguistic barrier further pushes the students towards the Eastern languages, which are nearer the Thai language in terms of the phonological structure.

14.10 Mini Survey on language choice and German image

In order to practically confirm German's popularity and image among the young adults, I conducted a mini field survey to collect data from the students of Triam Udom Suksa School[5] and the University of Chulalongkorn[6]. The survey was aimed at soliciting the young adults' opinions towards the German language, the culture/people and Germany as a country. Given the fact that the survey was soliciting people's appreciation of the variables, a quantitative approach was adopted for

---

5   Triam Udom Suksa is a famous State Senior High School, which is founded in 1938 as a preparatory school for Chulalongkorn University.

---

6   Chulalongkorn University is the oldest and one of the best universities in Thailand. It was founded by King Rama VI (King Vjarawudh) under his father's, King Rama V (King Chulalongkorn).

data collection. **Table 14.10.1** below shows the details of participants:

Table 14.10.1: Demographic Profile of participants

Demographic Data		Triam Udom Suksa School	Chulalongkorn University
Age range:	14*	4	
	15*	2	
	16		
	17	6	
	18	8	3
	19		5
	20		6
	21		3
	22		3
Gender	Female	7	12
	Male	9	8
	Blank /Error	4	
Faculty	Education		17
	Engineering		3
Total		20	20

(*) The students are not from the upper secondary school programme

14.11 Survey form technical error

There are a few errors that occurred during the field survey. For instance, 4 participants from Triam Udom Suksa School did not fill in required columns in the survey form such as gender etc. One participant from Chulalongkorn University and another from Triam Udom Suksa School seem to have misunderstood Question 2, which they did not tick, under the variable of their language ability: Thai(100% of the participants were Thai students).

14.12 Question approach

Questions 1 and 2 were aimed at exploring the general background of their language ability, right from the most basic skill i.e. speaking. This could explain the overall language environment among Thai students. Question 3 reflects the trend and interest of learning foreign languages according to the students' choice to study the Eastern languages, or the Western ones, with a focus on German. Questions 4-6 are the students' opinions on the German image in general and the sources of related information. Question 6 is specifically focused on the medium and human connection of information delivery promoting Germany as a whole. Questions 7-9 concentrated on the German language; from getting the basic idea of their German language knowledge, to a guessing test with hidden words in German and ended with a request to students to repeat after the interviewer the pronunciation of German words (with linguistic phonology analysis purposes) before they choose the words that are hard to pronounce within the experiment.

14.13 Mini Language Survey Results
14.13.1 Language Ability

Table 14.13.1: Number of Languages Spoken

Language(s):	TUSS:	%	CU:	%
1	3	15		
2	14	70	16	80
3	3	15	4	20
3 and above	-	-	-	

Generally, the results in **Table 14.13.1** showed that most of the participants are bilingual speakers of English and Thai language. According to the Thai educational system, even though English is a compulsory foreign language to learn in school, the medium of instruction is still the Thai language (Arunee Wiriyachitra, 2000:1). It is therefore understandable that in the following figure, **Table 14.13.2**, there are 3 students from Triam Udom Suksa School, who stated that they could only speak Thai language due to their low proficiency level of English. However, Triam Udom Suksa School is offering foreign languages as an elective course and University students are required to take a foreign language course as a requirement for the fulfillment of the Bachelor's Degree Programme. Overall, there are 3 students from Triam Udom Suksa School (TUSS) and 2 students from Chulalongkorn University (CU) who can speak Chinese. Interestingly, 2 students from TUSS are taking German as a basic language course.

Meanwhile, in CU 3 students in total could speak foreign languages like Korean, Japanese, and French.

Table 14.13.2: Foreign Languages Spoken

Language:	TUSS:	%	CU:	%
English	16	80	20	100
Thai	19	95	19	95
Chinese	3	15	2	10
German	2	10		
Korean			1	5
Japanese			1	5
French			1	5

14.14 Language Choice at University Level

In terms of language choice, the Eastern languages have a significant proportion of popularity among the high school and university students in Thailand. As the result shows in **Table 14.14.1**, more than 50% of students picked Japanese followed by Chinese, German, Korean and French in that order. From another point of view, the positive outcome of the survey is that, German language is the top choice among other European languages like French, Spanish and Italian. Besides, it is important to note that other new languages in the region like Arabic and are fast gaining popularity among students in Thailand.

Table 14.14.1: Languages of Interest

Language:	TUSS:	%	CU:	%
Japanese	11	55	11	55
Korean	2	10	6	30
Spanish	3	15	2	10
Chinese	6	30	10	50
French	4	20	3	15
German	6	30	5	25
Arabic			2	10
Italian	1	5	1	5

14.15 The General Image of Germany

Concerning the general idea about Germany, most of the students (more than 50%) from TUSS and CU claimed that, they do not know or they have just a few ideas about it. In general, the results in **Fig14.15.1** show that the young adults' image of Germany is leaning towards culture and cultural events, (Beer and festivals), culinary reputation (Sausage), science and technology, sports (football) and history. It is noteworthy that it is only a very low percentage of students that could link Germany with arts (entertainment) and literature. This could also be interpreted as an indicator that Germany has not successfully promoted itself through these channels of access to Thailand. This is a gap in the promotion of vehicles of popularizing the German language; gaps that could create turning point for better outcomes in attracting people to think about Germany differently outside the stereotype cliché images.

Table 14.15.1: General Idea of Germany

Image:	TUSS	%	CU	%
Culture	2	10	10	50
Food	9	45	8	40

Sports	5	25	4	20
Entertainment	1	5	1	5
Literature	1	5	2	10
Science and Technology	9	45	7	35
Traveling place	1	5		
Berlin war	1	5		
Hitler	1	5		
German sausage	1	5		
History	1	5		

14.16 Media Role and the German language

14.16.1 German Publicity and Visibility in Thailand

As urbanization level has increased in Thailand, mass media and Internet have had a significant impact on social change. According to Index Mundi on Thai urbanization, Thailand consists of approximately 67 million habitants with 34.1% of population living in the urban area (Index Mundi 2011) and 30% of Internet users as one of the top 10 Internet countries in Asia. In terms of mass media, according to the Konrad Adenauer Stiftung (KAS) Democracy report in 2008:

> "There are 21 Thai languages and two English newspapers nationwide. The TV sector is structured into six terrestrial television stations, among them a new public broadcasting channel, the Thai public Broadcasting service CTPBS, formerly iTV then Ti TV, and one cable channel (UBC). Across the country there are about 300 radio stations, despite numerous closures in recent years."

According to the same sources as above, approximately 65.9% of the total population in Thailand is living in rural area.[7] Given the low levels of social and communication services in Thai rural areas, it could be assumed therefore, that the lack of access to the Internet is equally high. Thus, the mini survey results should only be considered within the urban area context of mass media and Internet access. Accordingly, **Table 14.16.1** shows results of high percentage of knowing German related information from the Internet a source followed by information from friends. This demonstrates the fact that besides the rapid growth of urbanization that boosted the Internet users percentages, the collective sources from the

---

7   Calculation according to Index Mundi

Foreign Languages: Lessons

society are still playing a significantly role in "word-of-mouth advertising"[8]. As a basic form of building networks to deliver messages deriving from their opinion and experience, this medium of sharing information plays an effective role of communication among friends. However, this medium is not effective for sharing public information relating to the German Language and culture. As things stand, use of such a medium is a disservice to the publicity of German related information.

From the results that are shown in **Table 14.16.1,** we could assume that German related information is not actively channelled through the local mass media in Thailand such as magazines, newspapers and TV. We could also assume that, apart from the difficulties promoters of German may have with targeting specialized niche readers, who have the language interest at heart; it is also possible that lack of enthusiasm for sponsorship from German organizations such as Goethe Institut may be affecting its promotion in the mass media. That may be why; more German related information is being accessed through Internet sources.

Table14.16.1: Initial Source of Germany Related Information

Channel:	**TUSS**	**%**	**CU**	**%**
Newspaper	3	15	1	5
Magazine	4	20	3	15
Internet	18	90	15	75
Friend	7	35	5	25
Research	1	5		
Tutor	1	5		
TV	2	10	2	10
Travel to Germany			3	15

14.17 Visualization of the German Language

In further probing on the low visibility of German related information in mass media and Internet, we found out that there are 85%-90% of students, who have no idea of how German language sounds like. However, in terms of its visual recognition, the results were rather positive. Although the students had no audio experience of the language, visually, they could draw a picture of what German looks like in their mind. For instance, in **Table 14.17.1** where students were required to guess and choose the words that they think are in German, 65%-75% of them did

---

[8] Word of Mouth (WOM) advertising is an unpaid form of promotion in which satisfied customers tell other people how much they like a business product or service.

correctly choose the word "Kindergarten" from the list. Around 45%-50% of the students as well chose "Hamburger" as some linked it to the state of Germany – Hamburg. Some also chose it because it was the longest word.

As Mark Twain (1880) mentioned in his book, *The Awful German Language*:

> "Some words are so long that they have a perspective. Observe these examples:
>
> *Freundschaftsbezeigungen, Dilettantenaufdringlichkeite, stadtverordnetenversammlungen.*
>
> These things are not words, they are alphabetical processions. And they are not rare; one can open a German newspaper at any time and see them marching majestically across the page...."

German has been stereotyped worldwide with its long compound words. According to our findings, this is recognized as a language characteristic that differs from other languages. However, there is a possibility of a technical error in the results, which should have been more precise by referring to "original" German words. The above results therefore could be a bit skewed given the high level of Anglicism that has influenced the German language (Christoph Brimmertz; 2009). Student could have been confused in picking the correct answer to this question.

Table 14.17.1: Visual Recognition of German words

Word:	TUSS	%	CU	%
*Hamburger[1]	9	45	10	50
Wine	3	15		
Mocha	3	15	5	25
*Kindergarten[2]	15	75	13	65
Internet	1	5		

14.18 German Language Pronunciation

German and Thai language are from two different language family groups. German is from the West-Germanic language group, which is closely connected to English whereas Thai language is from the Tai-Kadai family, which borrows words from Pali, Sanskrit and Old Khmer. One portion of the mini survey involved participants trying to repeat the pronunciation of German words in order to vote the hardest utterances to pronounce from their own experience and not others' opinion or secondary resources. **Table 14.18.1** shows the words that participants were required to read. Our second objective in this portion of the survey was to assess the accurate pronunciation of German phonemes.

Table 14.18.1: Pronunciation of German words

Word	Target	TUSS	%	CU	%
Über	yː	6	30	6	30
Freund	ɔy	4	20	3	15
Schön	øː	6	30	7	35
Ich	ç			1	5
Stand	ʃt	8	40	10	50
Mischung	ʃ	7	35	9	45

Contrary to our expectations, only 1 student from CU found "Ich" was hard to pronounce and the majority of participants voted for the diphthong [ʃt] in "Stand" at 40%-50% and post alveolar-sibilant sound [ʃ] in "mischung" at 35%-45%. This was followed by the umlaut sound [yː] "über" at 30% and [øː] "schön" (30%-35%). A general overview of the results shows that, most of the words were voted as difficult to pronounce ranging from at least 15% to 50% with the exception of 5% for the palatal non-sibilant sound [ç] in "ich".

From the post interview casual conversation with the participants, students enjoyed the process and some were interested to know more about the vocabulary meanings and correct pronunciations. The survey could be said to have produced the positive outcome of propelling the student's curiosity towards the German language. However, there are also a number of students who observed that German is a difficult language to learn from their first experience during the mini survey.

14.19 Conclusion

The general image of Germany in the mind of the public in Thailand seems not to have changed much from the past to present. A comparison between the data of Pornsarn Tmangraksat, which was collected in 1979 and the current data collected in 2014 shows that the image of Germany in Thailand is still mainly based on the country's advancement in science and technology and it's resonation in world history. Perhaps the contemporary difference, we note that is the cultural impact of German food (sausages). It was noteworthy that the image of German language and culture is lagging behind the loud waves of Eastern languages and cultures in Thailand. The gap in image promotion was observed in the areas of entertainment and literature world to be promoted. The Konrad Adenauer Stiftung (KAS) Democracy Report 2008 has mentioned that, Thai media focus on sensationalism, soap operas and other entertainment elements. Our observation in this article in contrast to the traditional image of rather fixed people with a complex language. It is important to create a fresh image of Germany and the German language in Thailand; an image that is creative, artistic and flexible; an image that can be enhanced by exchanging ideas through inter-cultural competitions and events.

Another point to emphasize in this article has to do with the much needed media and Internet promotion that would be less costly but could greatly boost the visibility of German related news and information. Survey participants' language choices are currently leaning more towards Eastern languages and cultures as compared to European languages such as German. Even though Thai young adults have a rough idea and opinion about Germany, they do not have any idea of how the language sounds like. Thus, in this case, the information that reaches out to them should be more visual in projection, more in the direction of the multimedia approach. For instance, programmes that introduce Germany and particularly German language learning would have more chances of attracting Thai young adults if they were channelled through the multi-media networks. A comparative example that is working well for enhancing proficiency in Japanese is on the NHK (*Nippon Hoso Kyokai* - Japan Broadcasting Corporation) channel; it promotes Japanese language for foreigner audiences through the use of limited English in daily conversations.

In terms of the German learning environment in Thailand, our mini survey has shown that often students do not feel comfortable enough to communicate in foreign languages including English. However, there is a positive phenomenon that was observed when we were experimenting with German: students are generally culturally active and curious. For instance, German food was not popular 3 decades ago according to the data collected by Pornsarn Tmangraksat. Currently however, a change could be seen in towards culinary interest in German food. Such evolving social trends can be explored as a learning advantage for adapting foreign languages teaching to new cultural interests. More young adults could be willing to pick German as a language choice in order to experience a new trend as part of the fast changing Thai urbanized lifestyle.

References

Arunee Wiriyachitra, Article: "English language teaching and learning in Thailand in this decade" APEC and HRDWG. At: http://www.apecknowledgebank.org/resources/downloads/english%20language%20teaching%20and%20leaning%20in%20thailand.pdf, Accessed 20/02/2014.

Bangkok Post: German musicians in Bangkok, 17 February 2014 http://www.bangkokpost.com/lifestyle/music/395389/german-musicians-in-bangkok

Bangkok Post: "Lifestyle Goethe Institut, the German Cultural Foundation". http://www.bangkokpost.com/lifestyle/325_info_goethe-institute-thai-german-cultural, Accessed 20/02/2014.

BK city: German Open Air 2013/2014 http://bk.asia-city.com/events/bangkok-stuff/german-open-air-cinema-201314 Cashing in on Gangnam style's YouTube fame, The Jakarta post: 5 December 2012. Accessed 17th February 2014 at http://www.thejakartapost.com/news/2012/12/05/cashing-gangnam-styles-youtube-fame.html

Christoph Brammertz (2009). Anglicisms are changing the German language, Goethe Institut Online Redaktion, Available at: http://www.goethe.de/ges/spa/siw/en4883778.htm17/02/2014.

Gabrow Karsten and Christian E.Rieck, 2008: *The Konrad Adenauer Stiftung (KAS) Democracy Report 2008: Media and Democracy*, Vol II. Konrad Adenauer Stiftung, V. Sankt Augustin, Berlin. Index Mundi, Thailand urbanization, Available at: http://www.indexmundi.com/thailand/urbanization

Internet World Statistics 2012: Miniwatts Marketing Group. Available at: http://www.internetworldstats.com/stats3.htm

Linda Andrean: A brief history of German language, Center for Austrian Studies, University of Minnesota, P.32. Available at: http://www.cas.umn.edu/assets/pdf/GermanLanguage.pdf

Nongnuth Phetcharatana H.E., Prussia society Berlin-Brandenburg, Royal Thai Embassy Berlin, Germany: 14 February 2013 http://www.thaiembassy.de/de/activities

Solgosoom Ekbuttree (2001): *Deutsch ThailaendischeZusam menarbeit: Meinungenzum beruflichen Kommuni kationsverhalten vonDeutschen und Thailaendern*. Eine Untersuchung am Goethe Institut Bangkok, M.A Thesis, Dept. of western language, Faculty of Arts, Chulalongkorn University, Thailand.2001

Tahe Jakarta Post (2012): *Cashing in on Gangnam style's youtube fame*, Accessed 5 December 2012.

Takayoshi Fujiwara, (2012): "Beliefs about language learning and Thai students learning Chinese and Japanese: Relationships with past learning experiences and target language variations", *Electronic Journal of Foreign language Teaching* 2012, Vol.9, No.2, pp.172, Center for Language studies, NUS.

Tmangraksat Pornsan (2012): *Modellbeschreibung fuer das Fach Deutschlandkunde in Thailand*, M.A thesis, Dept. of Western Languages, Faculty of Arts, Chulalongkorn University, Thailand, 1976. The Thai Royal Imprint on International Relationship: Thai and Germany celebrate 150 years of diplomatic relations, 20th February 2012. Available at: http://thailand.prd.go.th/view_news.php?id=6157&a=2

Twain Mark, Tramp A. (1880): *Abroad*, Vol II. Appendix D: The Awful German Language Essay. Bernhard Tauchnitz Publication.

CHAPTER FIFTEEN
THE FRENCH FLAIR IN UGANDAN BRANDING: A SUCCESSFUL "AFFAIRE" OR FAILED AFFAIR?[1]

Edith Natukunda-Togboa[2]

Abstract

A wide range of business brand names, which have incorporated French words or expressions were collected from both the up-market business areas and the middle income outskirts of Kampala city, in Uganda. The aim was to analyze how the French reference gives a competitive advantage to the business in question. Judging by the numbers of clients being served during our visits and the positive ambiance, the French flair in the brand names seemed a good influence to most of the businesses. This could be linked to the utilitarian association assigned to the highly competitive French goods and services. The external referencing seemed to enhance customers' perception. There were however, a few instances where the expected intentions of French referencing have not resulted in actual sales. The findings from this exciting mini market survey suggest that, business owners can benefit from getting to know the cultural and linguistic background to their French flavoured brand names. In addition, the French flair in Ugandan branding has pedagogical applications that can enrich the teaching of French as a foreign language.

Key words: *French flair, brand name, brand equity, external referencing, cross-culture coding*

15.1 Introduction

In today's market economy, where identity and visibility have become key indicators of quality to target audiences and clientele, your "brand"

---

[1] "Affaire" in French as "business" contrasts with having an "affair" in English. The pun on the 'false friend' between "affaire" and "affair" is intended.

---

[2] Dr. Edith Natukunda-Togboa is a senior lecturer Languages Studies and Head of Department of European & Oriental Languages at Makerere University. She has lectured in French Studies, Communication Skills, Translation and Interpretation. Her research interests have led her to conduct research in Discourse Analysis of Gender, Peace and Conflict. She has also served as a language consultant, interpreter and translator with several national, regional and international institutions.

or strength, as it is seen from the outside, has become very important as a positive projection of your image and your reputation. Going beyond the symbol or design displayed, your "brand" encompasses "the emotional and intellectual response your logo elicits from your target audience" (Stine Greg, 2002:3). Individuals, business entities and organizations use branding to establish a dialogue with their customers or target audience. The message of branding may be graphical or textual, or verbal, an image or a sound. The individual or enterprise or organization will use these means of communication to construct a message that will drive the public perceptions with regards to the product or service in question. Simply put, branding has been considered by marketing analysts as an effort towards persuasion.

Similarly, to linguists, the use of words to touch the susceptibilities of the target group becomes critical because they transform into a means of directing people's preferences. In the present day market economy, when branding is used to establish perceptions of a product or service, it can be said to have "created power" (Gowland, 2010; 1). Worldwide, we come to learn through the existing literature, that an increasing number of companies have adopted the use of foreign branding names to differentiate themselves from the rest of the competition (Stine G, 2002:3). Observational data suggest that, it is a trend that is getting even more popular in recent years due to the growing influence of "global brands" and "multinational business groups" (Sato Olavarrieta et al 2009). Our interest in this article, is to trace the French, used in the Ugandan branding, and see whether it creates singularity and indeed directs customers preference to successful sales or it is failing to attract their attention? Furthermore, as teachers and learners of foreign languages, what lessons can we draw from these marketing circumstances in Uganda?

15.2 What has been said about branding?

Marketing analysts like Greg Stine have pointed out that "more than just marketing, branding is the entire effect that creates a memorable effect. It is everything people touch, see or hear that immediately sets you apart from the rest of the competition" thus making a service, product or organization to be perceived as "unique" (Stine, 2002).

The use of French in Ugandan branding in this case, will be analyzed in order to show how it is targeting an emotional or psychological response from the consumers in Uganda. It seems that the French flair is just that strategy that is used to create marketing and advertising messages that make businesses stand out of the crowd. It is used, as Keller has suggested (in Leclerc et al, 1994), to spell out and promise "an added value" or "a unique value position." Emotionally and psychologically, the business owner or organization is establishing a relationship with the customer that is associated with French. That is why this chapter proposes to investigate whether it is a successful "affaire" (as a business in French) or a flailed "affair" (unsuccessful emotional engagement in English).

To what degree can the success or failure of a product be influenced by its foreign brand name? We will be seeing what the mini-market survey results from Uganda have to say on this issue in this chapter. Apparently though, this seems to be difficult to ascertain according to marketing analysts like Leclerc, Schmitt and Dubé. However, they observe that for most experiential products and services "a name can make a substantial contribution to a brand's equity", (Leclerc et al, 1994:263) in other words it adds to the commercial value that derives from consumer perception of the brand.

15.3 Samples of Ugandan brand names incorporating the "French Flair"

A wide range of business brand names, which have incorporated French words or expressions were collected from both the up-market business areas and the middle income outskirts of Kampala city, in Uganda. The samples have been regrouped into three categories for analysis in this article.

(See the next page)

15.4 Category A: Those whose names are *"Fully in the French Language"*

15.5 Category B: Those which have a combination of both French & English *(Respecting the rules of the English language)*

15.6 Category C: Those which have a creative *"fantaisie"* style

15.7 Critical Examination of the Brand Names

Figure 15.7.1: Summary of Brand Names and Commentary

A-Brand Name	Comment	B-Brand Name	Comment	C-Brand Name	Comment
Le Petit Bistrot	Name fully in French, Adj. and gender agreement gd.	De la Vie Restaurant Take away	Mix of Fr. & Eng.,Eng. rules respected	Cafesserie Maison de Qualité	Cafesserie as lexique is created, quite "Frenchy".
Café Cheri	Name fully in French, gender agreement respected.	Bravo Car Wash, Parking	Mix of Fr. & Eng. Eng. rules respected	De Jolie Salon	Possessive of Salon is Masc. but adj. *'jolie'* is fem. No agreement.
La Fontaine	Name fully in French, gender of def. article gd.	Valet Dry Cleaners	Mix of Fr. & Eng. Eng. rules respected	La Grande Chez Johnson Hôtel	Hotel is Masc. But adj. 'Grande' is fem. agreement.
Le Café Chasse	Name fully in French, N + V rule respected	Glaciers Restaurant & Bar	Mix of Fr. & Eng. Eng. rules respected	La Royale Patisserie	Order of N+long Adj: should be *La Patisserie Royale*
Le Bougain-viller	Name fully in French, def. art + noun rules respected	Bon Appetit Restaurant & Takeaway	Mix of Fr.& Eng. Eng. rules respected	Seascallop Le Monde Café	Partitive art. Missing : *Le Monde du Café*
Vos Bijoux d'Ailleurs	Name fully in French, gd. use of apostrophe respected	La Référence Night Club	Mix of Fr. & Eng. Eng. rules respected	De' Furniture Shop	Use of « De' » with apostrophe is grammatically a fantasy

La Patisserie	Name fully in French, def. art + noun rules respected	Déjà Vu Bar & Lounge	Mix of Fr.& Eng. Eng. rules respected	Kamooflage	Spelling in French should be "*Comouflage*"
Salon J'adore	Name fully in French, gd. use of apostrophe respected	*La Ville* Wines & Spirits	Mix of Fr.& Eng. Eng. rules respected	La Grande Photo Studios	"*Le Grand Photo Studio*" should be Masc., and singular

Source: *Market survey May-June 2014*

If we refer to the samples of the brand names incorporating French as shown above, we will note that in each of the brand name sited, there is a series of associations they provoke. The association with French tends to enhance delivery against the insinuated promise. The positioning of the goods and services associated with the French flair in Uganda is generally positive, since French carries the connotation of perceived international quality, safety, reliability, social responsibility and technological superiority (Butler, 2003).

Le Petit Bistrot" for instance, openly advertises "French Cuisine". Its founder, who passed away, we were told by the manager, was from France and the wife, who is the current proprietor, is francophone. In some cases, like *Le Petit Bistrot* or *Vos Bijoux d'Ailleurs* or *Café Cheri* the brand positioning was crafted intentionally by the marketer to correspond with a French personae or identity. She confirmed in our interview that "this place has its special clientele and the special appeal of French cuisine has worked wonderfully. That is why we have opened a second branch of *Le Petit Bistrot* in Nansana", another up-coming upper class "banlieu" (outskirt) of Kampala. (Interview in Kampala, Garden City, May 2014).

Similarly, the manager of *Vos Bijoux d' Ailleurs,* whose father is French, confirmed in our interview that "it is [her] sister who gave the business its name". She wanted the customers to dream of the different places where these precious stones (*bijoux*) could have come from (Interview at Acacia Mall, July 2014). The "*ailleurs*" or "elsewhere" in the brand name carries with it an element of faraway exotic lands. It is suggested in the brand name therefore, that if you buy jewellery from here, you will acquire a series of stories of adventurous exotic journeys on your body to tell to your listenership.

Le Bougainviller hotel also targets French speaking customers in the up-market Bugolobi residential area of Kampala. Its parking yard is labeled in French. Its wine corner exhibits French wines and it hosts Francophone musical shows. Many Francophones associate with the hotel because of its French ambiance and high standards. The same can be said of the French flavour in "*La Ville* Wines and Spirits", which we were told by the manager "attracts French wine connoisseurs among other patrons" at the Nakumatt Village Shopping Centre in the Bugolobi residential quarters. The manger goes on to add that "the name was acquired as part of *La Ville* franchise, and the business is so far not falling short of its international expectations."

In contrast, however, the current management of *Bon Appétit* Restaurant and Takeaway and *Salon J'Adore* admitted that they don't speak French. Yet when I asked as to why there is French in their brand name, the manager of *Bon Appétit* said: "it sounds exotic, we count on attracting exotic customers, and yeah, it is chic" (Interview in Kabalagala June 2014). As for the lady owner of Salon *J'adore* says: "When I came in I found this French name already well known. Now wherever you go in Kabalagala they will tell you "For difficult hair you have to go to *Salon J'adore*. They are good." The proprietor/manager then added with confidence: "We carry the reputation of international standards" (Interview in Kabalagala, June 2014). Indeed, the two clients who I found in the saloon told me that they work with the United Nations Development Programme.

Meanwhile, the manager of *Café Cheri* had done some research on the name of his pub in the posh suburb of Kabalagala. He had found out that "Cheri" refers to "an endeared one" or "darling" as used by people in love. So he liked the name and wanted it to bring to the pub/restaurant people "who will feel that when you come here and consume our products you will fall in love" (Interview in Kabalagala, June 2014). The marketing *cum* linguistic connotation was similar to that of the confectionery *La Patisserie Lounge* and the *Maison de Qualité Cafesserie* which, the manager told us, was crafted to resemble a *"brasserie"* (brewery in English, but in fact meaning a French pub and snack joint). In its conception as a "brasserie" it also captures that aura of a French elite open air pub, or "la terrasse", imaginable anywhere on any of the Parisienne high streets.

In the examples analyzed above, we see that the French element embedded in the brand name addresses the important aspect of the consumer expectations. The French reference gives a competitive advantage that Melnyk Valetyna et al have termed "the external differentiation". Melynek, Kleinand Volckner make a marketing analysis of products, like the chocolate, which the German confectionery has branded as "merci"

(Thank you) and "chocolate Palot" (Palot's chocolate). They compare them with the Japanese designer Essay Miyake, who has branded his perfumes as *l'Eau Bleue'* (Blue water); and *"La Crème de l'Eau'* (the cream of water). These marketing critiques go on to observe that using the French creative language in branding helps to highlight "the historic elegance and temptation properties through the automatic reference to French chocolate and perfume brands". (Melnyk Valentyna et al...)

These companies, they argue, through the foreign language in the branding, are appealing to higher quality perception and greater social status for their goods and services. Indeed, the majority of the business managers and owners who were interviewed in Kampala according to the findings of our market study confirmed that the use of French in Uganda is like the signaling of a high social status.

Apart from the brand extension that companies showed that they hoped to induce, there is a functional extension that is also targeted through foreign language branding product features like durability and innovativeness. The mixed language strategy exploring the pronunciation, spelling and elements of the French grammar can be noted in what I have termed the *"fantaisie"* style brand names like the *"Kamooflage"* games centre *"De' furniture shop"*, and *"De' Vibez", De' Sailors* and *"De' Clouds"* night clubs. The games centre, furniture shop and night clubs wanted to enhance the utilitarian associations assigned to French leisure centres the durability of their domestic appliances/furniture and the intensity of the romantic ambiance of their trendy night spots.

What we note in terms of the language is that, these brand names of the "fantaisie" style, whether intentionally of inadvertently "twisted", respect neither the language rules of French nor those of English. A hotel which is masculine should not be labeled <u>La</u> Gran<u>de</u> *Chez Johnson Hotel,* which has a feminine gender agreement for its adjective. The studio, which is singular and masculine, should not have a feminine agreement in plural of <u>La</u> Gran<u>de</u> Photo Stud<u>ios</u>. Equally fantasist, is the appended apostrophe with a possessive value in the night clubs *De' Clouds or De' Vibez, De' Sailors* (last 2 photos not included) as well as *De' Furniture Shop.* The standard French grammar norm is to substitute the vowel in *"de"* with an apostrophe carrying a possessive value like in "Valerie d'Estaing", the former President of France. In the Ugandan branding however, the substantive noun, "Club" following the possessive preposition does not begin with a vowel. Hence appending a "De" to it is to subvert the French grammatical rules. The plural of *Vibez* demonstrates an intentional play on the English spelling and the apostrophe after "de" is not legitimately replacing a vowel if we were to follow the French grammar rules. The

French flavoured label in this case creatively puts a "twist" on the forms of both languages, in order to project that "fantaisie" and amusing cross-coded brand name.

15.8 When the French Affair Fails to Attract Added Value

Findings from our study of the French flair in Ugandan branding showed that the French included in the brand name does not necessarily always signal marketing success. This confirms what branding critics Melynek Valentyna et al have observed that positively to induced purchasing behaviour, there are times when "purchase intentions do not ....translate into actual purchase behaviour". (Chandon, Morwotz & Reinartz, 2005: cited in Melynk et al.)

The above observation emerged from our findings on a few brand names, where French flair has not led to external differentiation and thus a successful *"affaire'*. This was the situation that was observed in the *Café Chasse* and *De' Furniture Shop* respectively, in Kitintale and Luzira business centres on the out skirts of Kampala. *De Furniture Shop* had a few scattered high priced pieces of furniture, and was visibly not busy, but on the two occasions we visited the store, the business manager was not willing to be quoted.

The business partner and manager of the *"Café Chasse"* in contrast, welcomed us with a beaming smile on a Friday afternoon when there was just a single young couple who were not consuming anything on the café's *"terrasse"*. "My husband, she explained, is a lover of French and he has been to Paris. When we started this business, he suggested that we give it French flavour, *Le café chasse* combines the beginning syllable of our son's name Charles and the second syllable of our daughter, Cassandra" she talked solemnly with a controlled voice. As she was explaining, I quickly ordered a cappuccino and when it came, oh my! It was very tasty and classy.

The business owner and manager went on to say: "but the clientele has not materialized according to our expectations. The people around here seem to go for beer and dance, they don't seem to like taking tea and coffee and we can't take the fracas and violence that come with a beer drinking spot and the business is taking the hit." I got so taken in by the worry and strain in her voice as well as the fatigue lines starting to show on her brow. I felt like the *Café Chasse* needed to explore alternatives that could keep it within the non-violence choices of the owners but that should not deter them from aggressively advertising its creative brand name. I shared these feelings with the business manager and commented how the open space in the parking lot could host a gospel musician, a francophone drummer or a kora player of francophone African contemporary jazz. I explained how I was studying how the French flair in the brand names can be used for business appeal and to show that she was truly interested in the study objectives, she offered me a second cappuccino!

But back to how the French flair may not necessarily translate into inducing customer's purchasing. The *Café Chasse* actually showed us an example of a threateningly strained business. However, the business owners could turn the threat into an opportunity.[3] We may go back to find a transformed, dynamic, French 'ambianced' café, the next time we visit the *Café Chasse*. In the next section we ask ourselves, what pedagogical lessons can be drawn from this mini-market survey on the French flair in Ugandan branding?

15.9 Conclusion and Recommendations

In Uganda, according to the information collected in this short market study, the French used in commercial branding reflects a communication strategy aiming at making those businesses stand out of the crowd of mainly English and Ugandan flavoured brand names. The French flair in the branding can be presented in three categories: branding names which are totally in French (mainly belonging to French speakers, those which combine French and English and respect the English language form and those which combine both French and English and put "a twist"(style "fantaisie" to the rules of both languages. Many of the brand names that have enhanced their "promise" of delivery, that have used it to capture French-like ambiance and the customers' external reference to high quality, reliability and durability have actually "successful" businesses, if we are to go by numbers of people they were serving during our visits. The French in their brand names enhances the utilitarian association assigned to the highly competitive French goods and services.

There are however, a few instances where the expected intentions have not resulted into actual sales, a case in point of the latter categories is "*Le Café Chasse*" and *De' Furniture Shop,* which were still struggling with finding the clientele and service that matched the French flair in their branding.

Based on the foregoing discussions we can make the following recommendations:

---

3   The reader has to be informed that immediately behind the *Café Chasse*, is the biggest national incarceration institution Luzira Maximum Security Prison with its thousands of prisoners and hundreds of security guards and on the right and left side of its premises there is Uganda Breweries and Nile Breweries respectively.

- Where the French flair has not materialized into customers' actual purchase, the business owners could try revising their marketing strategy so as to match the brand name with a French ambiance.
- It would do a lot of good for a business carrying a French flavoured brand name, to check the spelling and the correct use of the linguistic elements chosen so as to avoid social marketing criticisms.
- Discussion with the consumers or community members about the brand name of your business can increase its attraction and its utilitarian function by evoking diverse associations with the brand name.
- French flavoured brand names could offer opportunities for Beginner learners of the language, who can use them to discover practically the use of gender (*le, la* or *grand, grande*), the use of the possessive prepositions, the agreement with plural (*les grands studios*) or the vocabulary for specialized products selling entities (*boucherie, patisserie, brasserie, librairie, pharmacie.... Etc.*)
- Brand names with a French flair can inspire free expression exercises on creating brand names in an Advanced class of French for Specific Purposes, (e.g French for Business, French for the Media and Communication, French for Tourism etc.)

References

Butler Lister, (April 2003): *Understanding the Language of Branding* www.theblakeproject.typepad.com/Chapter 2.pdf *Lister Butler* Consulting, New York, Accessed on 24/07/2014.

Gowland S. (2010), "The Power of Brands to create better futures". In *Oxford Leadership Journal*, Shifting the trajectory of Civilization, Volume 1, Issue 3 June 2010 pp1-6.

Leclerc F., Schmitt B. H., Dubé L., (1994): Foreign Branding and its Effects on Product perception and attitudes, in *Journal of Marketing Research*, Vol. 31, No. 2, May, 1994,pp.263-270.

Valentyna M. Klein, K.Volckner F., (2012): The Double-aged Sword of Foreign Brand names for Companies from Emerging Countries in *Journal of Marketing*, 2012.

Stine G., (2002). "Branding at a Glance", in *The Nine Principles of Branding*, Polaris Inc. Branding Solutions *www.polaris-inc.com*. Accessed 18/07/2014.

Soto G. O., Mobarec E. Manzur, Friedmann Roberto, (2009): Foreign Branding: Examining the Relationship between Language and International Brand Evaluations, in *Innovar: Revista de Siencias Administrativas y Sociales,*ISSN 0121-5051, Vol. 19, N°. 35, 2009 , pp. 9-18.

CHAPTER SIXTEEN
ANALYZING THE RELEVANCE OF THE CURRICULUM OF LANGUAGE FOR SPECIFIC PURPOSES: A CASE STUDY OF FRENCH FOR TOURISM IN MAKERERE UNIVERSITY

Sarah Nanyanzi Kawungezi[1]

Abstract

Apart from the classical strand of French offered as French for Beginners and French advanced, Makerere University also offers French for Specific Purposes in different disciplines outside the Humanities. This is the case of French for Tourism. It is offered as a service course because tourism is one of the fastest growing industries in Uganda. Since the course was launched in 1998, it has undergone major changes and the needs of employment market seem to have changed. This may be linked to the wave of "professionalizing" that is blowing through the university, aimed at increasing the marketability of its courses or to the cyclic need for better articulation of the course objectives and content. Whatever the cause may be, this pedagogical discomfort can be felt from the general drop in learner motivation and the time French is accorded in the academic timetable. Faced with this situation, as a member of the French section, I felt that I should assess the relevance of the curriculum of French for Tourism in Makerere University. This student survey therefore is the beginning of an in-depth evaluation of the curriculum of French for Tourism and the employability of our products. In the survey, students of French and teachers were purposely selected to give their views and suggestions, focus group discussions were also held with the same sample population. From the data that was analyzed qualitatively, I have drawn recommendations that can be used to review the curriculum of French for Tourism so that it can retain its relevance and the employability of its products in the tourism industry.

Key words: *Language for specific purposes, French for tourism, employability and professionalizing.*

---

[1] Mrs. Sarah Nanyanzi Kawungezi has been a teacher of French for quite some time. She holds a BA with Education of Makerere University and a Mastère of Français Langue Etrangère of the Universite de Rouen. She is currently Lecturer and coordinator of French Studies, Makerere University. French for Specific Purposes is one of her major research interests

16.1 Conceptual Background

Language for Specific Purposes (LSP), whether it is a branch of English or French or German or Swahili, has been shaped by the development of language theories. It is no surprise therefore, that whether it is referred to as Zolana (2013) suggests: *français despecialité* (French of Specialization) or *Français langue professionnelle* (French as a professional language) or *français fonctionnel* (functional French) or *fran-cais sur objectifs specifiques* (French for Specific Purposes) under the different denominations it still reflects the concept of language variety, registers, and special language. Pitch and Draskau, cited in Mulenda go further to say that:

> Language for special purposes is a formalized and codified as a variety of language, used for special purposes and in a legitimate context; that is to say, with the function of communicating information of a specialist nature at any level- at the highest level of complexity, between initiate experts, and, at lower levels of complexity, with the aim of informing or initiating other interested parties, in the most economic, precise and unambiguous terms possible (Picht and Draskau, 1985).

The codified varieties, as Elizabeth Martin (2000) explains, are distinguishable in terms of the user characteristics and their use of the language for a particular job or social function. She sums up her definitional debate by stating that "the term *language for Specific Purposes* is actually an umbrella term that actually applies to different categories of courses, which differ according to the learners' needs". It is important to note that to the concepts of language varieties and registers, the linguist has added the crucial element of learner need 'centredness' in LSP. Once these learner needs are identified, Zolana (2013) argues that thereafter they should be used in conceiving the course content and teaching tools that take into account "their study paths".

The sample of the course on the Didactics of French for Specific Purposes (FSP) from the Université Louvain-la-Neuve indicates that, at the stage of initiation, the teacher should first acclimatise with issues of: the problematic of language types for a specific purpose, semiotic systems to be found in the specific texts or speeches, typologies of speech or text types for a specific purpose, lexical particularities of the important scopes of specific purpose and the discursive particularities of the scientific,technical,business and legal texts. It is rather these discursive particularities that Jean Marc Mangeante (2004:137) an expert in the field, from the Université d'Artois emphasizes the categorization of language into "sub-languages "or "technolectes" when he talks about FSP as linguistics of discourses". He points out that it is not the language, which is specialized in FSP, but its utilization by in specialized speakers in certain circumstances of their life. He underscores the importance of focusing on the language needs of those speakers as is the case of French in this on spot survey.

16.2 Process Matters

Apart from the classical strand of French offered as French Beginners and French advanced, Makerere University also offers French for Specific Purposes in different disciplines outside the Humanities. This is the case of French for Tourism. It is offered as a service course because tourism is one of the fastest growing industries in Uganda owing to the existence of natural resources like equatorial Forests, waterfalls, wild life, ornithology, culture and all the different sites, which attract tourists in Uganda including the French speakers.

French for tourism has been taught in Makerere University for more than fifteen years. It is taught concurrently as an option for choice alongside Kiswahili. As Beginners' courses, they are offered for three semesters to students of Bachelor of Tourism; that is, two in First year, another one in Second year. In 1998, prior to the introduction of the course, needs assessment was conducted to identify learners' needs; the mother department's interests, (Geography Department at that time) and the employer's priorities. This was in keeping with what is recommended in FSP pedagogy, to take into account the cyclical need of soliciting initial and periodic feedback from all parties involved in course design and review; that is to say, course coordinators, teachers, students and academic administrators.

This process of continual review is captured in a flow diagram by Jordan (1997):[2]

** See the next page for flow diagram

Figure 16.2.1: Recommended steps for setting up and implementing an LSP programme

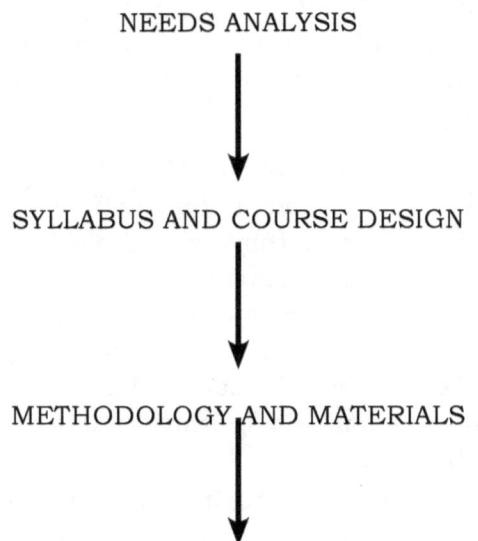

Source: Adapted from Jordan R. R. (1997: 57) ***English for Academic Purposes***

In the case of Makerere, the biggest influence of the initial needs assessment in 1998 was felt at the level of the length of the programme, which we, the trainers felt was short compared to the language needs expressed by the future students. The second most important element that emerged from the assessment was that of content, where the students wished to see the oral competence emphasized more than any other. These are the areas of interest that have been changing as the course was administratively shifted from the College of Humanities and social Sciences, to the College of Agricultural and Environmental Sciences, under the School of Forestry, Environmental and geographical Sciences, where the Department of Forestry, Biodiversity and Tourism was created in 2011. The need for assessment and review, after covering the first cycle of three years under the new academic arrangement is timely. As recommended in Munby's multi-tiered analysis, in our course of French for Tourism with a communicative syllabus design we feel that it is high time to conduct:

- Target-situation analysis
- Present-situation analysis
- Strategy analysis

- Means analysis
- Learning-centered approaches analysis

(Source: Munby's (1978); *Communicative Syllabus Design. Cambridge)*

Note is taken of the result-based orientation and process sensitivity integrated in this model that need to be reviewed cyclically. In fact, the student survey undertaken combines elements from the above two models. It borrows from Jordan the importance of the language and content needs and binds them with the target, means and learner centeredness analysis recommended by Munby.

The programme as it is being taught, addresses students who are adults wishing to obtain languages competences effectively and to be able communicate in French in social and professional situations involving them in the tourism and hotel industry. It was designed to cater for complete Beginners in the language, to carry them through to the A1 &A2 level of the Common European Framework of Languages. This means imparting to students competences to enable them to use French to interact with other professionals in situations that require:

- Introducing yourself and your company or institution.
- Welcoming clients at the airport, hotel or restaurant.
- Informing and guiding visitors on types of transport, itinerary or weather.
- Describing a monument, hotel or region.
- Helping a client to choose, organize, buy or reserve something.
- Helping a client to change, cancel a reservation or request for refund.
- Developing, offering, and giving a presentation on touristic entertainment
- Promoting a destination orally or in writing.
- Selling touristic products.

Quite often our products find themselves in different tourism related activities ranging from hotel marketing and reservations, transportation, tour guides, transport to mention but a few. So the study explores the relevance of the curriculum; whether the package offered to students makes them relevant where they work after the university, whether they are able to interpret a simple written mail and if they can sustain a conversation in French or show tourists touristic attractions in Uganda.

French for tourism has been taught in Makerere University for more than fifteen years but the performance of students has not been very encouraging, and the absorption of these students in the tourism sector has been below the trainers' expectations. The study therefore wants to investigate the causes of the problem by focusing mainly on the main issues, which are the curriculum design, institutional policy and employer interests with regards to the teaching of the French language.

16.3 Objectives, Research Questions and Scope

The objectives of this study were: to gauge whether the curriculum used to teach French for tourism in Makerere University is still relevant, and how to improve learner's competences so as to ensure more absorption of the products, our students, who have graduated in the preceding three years of teaching and learning French for tourism.

The mini-study was designed to answer the following questions:
1. What is the relevance of French to the students of French for Tourism?
2. What do students think about the time allocated to the learning of French?
3. If employed in the tourism sector, can they be able to sustain a conversation in French with the francophone tourists?
4. What can Makerere as an institution do or how should the Curriculum be reviewed to suit the needs of the learners?
5. What changes in the tourism sector of the job market need to be integrated in the course?

At its conception, the initial mini-study was deemed useful for curriculum review and proposing measures and processes towards attitudinal changes. In terms of content and geographical scope, the study was planned to cover only the teaching of French for Tourism (FFT) at Makerere University. It was also planned to cover the students of tourism of 2013/2014.

16.4 Review of Related Literature

This review of related literature talks about the need for proper training programmes in order to acquire the skills that will enable the learners to be effective in the tourism sector. Raymond Victurine, 2000 says that "Tourism offers the only legal avenue by which people can derive economic benefits from wildlife. However, most entrepreneurs and community organizations interested in the tourist market possess neither the skills nor the know-how to operate successful tourism establishments". Thus there is need for effective training programmes that are aimed at building those skills in the tourism sector. A well designed and well managed programme will establish strong institutional linkages to ensure the existence of a viable community-based tourism practices. In the case of Uganda where the touristic resources stretch across the border to Francophone neighbouring communities, the stakeholders have to embrace professional skills, like bilingualism, that foster a sustainable management of the establishments and the benefits accruing to those most affected by wildlife.

Caroline Ashley, Peter De Brine, Amy Lehr and Hannah Wilde , 2007 in their book, *The Role of the Tourism Sector in Expanding economic Opportunity* mention that "there is need to build institutional capacity; strengthen the industry associations, market intermediaries, universities, government, civil society organizations , and grassroots groups who must all be able to play their roles effectively within the systems". These institutions include the work of Makerere University with regard to French for Tourism.

A lot has been written about French for Specific Purposes in terms of the language levels of students, the course content and the method of delivery. The teams of experts like Catherine Carras, Jacqueline Tolas, Patricia Kohler and Elizabeth Szilagvi, in their work of 2007, *Le francais .sur Objectifs Specifiques* and Jean-Marc Mengeante and Chantal Parpette, 2004, in *Le Françaissur Objectifs Specifiques: de l'analyse des besoinsàl'élaboration d'un cours,* have written a lot about specific French types for specific purposes, different documents illustrating different language types and discursive mechanisms to retrieve specific language elements. They have discussed the progress made in didactic approaches in terms of creating teaching sequences, the activating the role of the teacher and focusing on the learners' interests. From the advantages of exploiting authentic documents to facilitating learner determined lessons, the strategies seem to gear towards boosting professional communication in the area of specialty chosen. The gap noted for French for Tourism in Makerere University is that these analyses for FSP had not been conducted in a context where the students had no opportunity of a linguistic immersion and a supportive community of practicing the language. This is why; a study in the Anglo-phone learning context could provide good lessons for similar environments just like the study of Adolfo N. Zolana (2013) conducted on *Le Français Economique* in the Lusophone context of the University of Agostinho Neto, Luanda, Angola.

16.5 Methodology

16.5.1 Sample size and description

A sample of 125 students of French for tourism first and Second Years was used and 4 lecturers of French for tourism. The learners who took part in this mini-study were aged between 20 and 35 years and 97% of them had been admitted directly from secondary schools while the rest were already working in the tourism sector and needed further training. These students had chosen French as their language option in their university degree course of Bachelor of Tourism.

16.6 Data collection and Analysis

Questionnaires, interview guides and documentary analysis were used to collect data. The collection was done from 20th to 10th May 2014. The documentary data was analyzed qualitatively by content analysis. The quantitative data was analyzed by tallying and simple frequency runs. It is consequently presented descriptively. Interpretation and conclusions were drawn and recommendations made on the basis of the findings.

16.7 Findings from Documentary Data and Discussions held with the lecturers

The documentary data obtaining from the review of related literature, showed how we can analyze the effectiveness of the teaching materials and methodologies we are using for French for Tourism. For instance, we noted that the textbooks which we are using - *Bien venue en France, Tome 1*: A. Monnerie:(1991),*Connexions*,(Bouvier,Mérieux,Loiseau:2004), *Grammaire Progressive du Français* II, (Thiévenaz: 1995).*La Communication Professionnelle*, M. Danilo, J.L Penfornis(1993), *Taxi* (Capelle & Menand, 2006*), Teaching Foreign Languages for Tourism* Schlak & Bosch (2013),and Beckett and Brannon's *Leisure and Tourism GCSE Applied French* (2006) need to be supplemented with authentic documents, which allow the learner to "travel" into more varied and exciting workplace utilization of French in the tourism profession.

The existing literature also helped us to see that there are contemporary peer practices especially in non-francophone Africa that can be used for comparative experiences in the teaching of FSP. The well documented example of Adolfo Zolana from the University of Agostinho Neto, at Luanda in Angola has a lot to offer in terms of options for giving instructions in an FSP class. Neto knows how to formulate objectives for the different sequences, how to use alternative didactic approaches and how to facilitate students to formulate for themselves the grammar rule after using the problem solving strategy.

The discussion with the lecturers brought out a lot concerning the length of the course and the number of contact hours in relation to what they deemed as vital skills for graduates going to work in the tourism sector in Uganda. They said that there was need to increase the contact hours to a minimum of four per week. They observed that the classes were too big; that there was need to divide them into groups of at least 30 instead of 70 in one language class; that in such classes, teaching cannot be effective because the ratio of lecturer to student is too big and the students are not given due attention. The students do not get a chance to try out individually the element that is being taught for the day;

especially if we are aware that they mostly need to hone their oral skills in French. They also admitted that there was need to carry out a market search and find out the current needs in the industry in the Great Lakes Region and adjust the curriculum accordingly. This regional element, they commented, was important because of our inevitable sharing of the bio-diversity with Francophone and Anglophone neighbours. They said that there was also need for refresher courses to learn the new and modern methods of teaching the language and to sustain the language skills for practitioners in the tourism industry. They suggested that such in-service courses will facilitate the linking up with the alumni who will update us on the sector interests.

16.8 Findings from the Data collected using the questionnaire

In order to gauge learners' motivation, I asked the students how they were enrolled in the French class. They all said that they had to choose a language from French and Kiswahili. Therefore although French in this case is a prerequisite for their programme, they could have gone for Swahili if they so wished. Their response indicated that they chose French voluntarily and this shows their own commitment to study the language.

The next question posed was what influenced their choice of language. Twenty percent (20%) of the students said that they had learned the language before at the senior secondary level. Four (4%) of the students had learned it up to the secondary examination level. This explains the 24 % who thought it was simpler than Kiswahili, which they had never learned at all. 76% of the students said they chose French because it was a popular international language. The big majority therefore, chose French for Tourism (FFT) based on its functionality in international business and communication.

I also wanted to find out the importance of the language to the students study and career path. They all gave the advantage of getting an international jobs and associated advantages like guiding tourists in Uganda, working with the UN, the African Union, at the French Embassy, or even at the Entebbe International Airport. Clearly, the international job market was a strong motivation for enrolling for FFT.

The students were also requested to give their ranking of methods of teaching French. 48% appreciated all methods where they are given slots in the class time to carry out activities and present them in class. These went on to explain that this is because it helped them to acquire vocabulary and practice the language in the peer group and with the teacher. 40% of the respondents expressed the wish that the lecturer should be translating for them in English. 12 % disturbingly did not express any preference of any teaching method. One wonders whether this shows their lack of motivation for FFT of the three did not say anything.

When asked about the length of time they were allocated to learn French, 40% of the students felt that the current three semesters in three years was too short, that they should continue with the language every semester up to third year so that they can speak the language better. 8% said that it was enough and that they will continue at Alliance Française. 16% said that it was just enough. Meanwhile 20% of the students expressed the wish to be given scholarships to go to France for a direct interface with the native speakers of the target language. This shows a majority of 66% of the students who feel that the time allocated is insufficient. It is also important to note the interest in a direct language exposure, which would certainly polish their working knowledge of FFT.

During the probing of the suggestions given about the duration period of learning, 60% of the students suggested that the period should be extended to every semester up to third year to allow them perfect the language. 36% said that it should not be extended, that the three semesters were enough since French was hard. The rest, that is 4%, said that it was enough with no explanation. Going by the majority then, there is the wish to extend FFT to third year, but we need to find solutions to the minority wish to see the French methods changed so that FFT ceases to be perceived as a tough course.

When questioned on their confidence and fluency in the language, only 20% of the students could affirm that they were confident and ready to speak French out in the job market. 20% said that they could read but it was hard for them to speak the language freely. However, a good portion of 60% did not believe in themselves and they said they cannot speak the language in public. This 60% represents a worryingly big portion of the learners who do not gain sufficient confidence in the language under the current academic arrangement.

I wanted the students to suggest ways the university and lecturers could render the subject more popular and interesting. 60% suggested that they should let them continue with the language to third year. 28% suggested the introduction of a language practice component in France. The rest, that is 12%, indicated that taking FFT language course to third year is clearly strongly recommended. The element of a language practice component in France would have been analyzed alongside its financial implications.

16.9 Summary of Findings

Basing on the documentary information gathered, it was noted that Makerere University lecturers of FFT could benefit from collaborating with other universities in or outside the region for more research on FSP. There are many best practice lessons to learn from other non-Francophone teachers of FSP especially in Lusophone Africa.

One could note the need for the university as the implementing institution to improve its policy towards French for Tourism. The promotion of the course could encourage the students to change their attitude towards the language. If they see it as a priority up to third year, they could be more focused and learn it better. Possibilities of exchange study visits with Francophone universities could help in changing the learners' attitude towards FFT.

At the institutional level, there was a need to facilitate the exercise of curriculum and materials review of French for Tourism. The current teaching time in terms of contact hours of French for tourism is not sufficient to allow the products to attain the level expected of them by the end of their university education. The current delivery methods that the lecturers were using were also criticized as being unattractive. There is need to repackage the language and make it more pragmatic.

16.10 Recommendations

Basing on the above findings, the following recommendations are made for consideration by Makerere University and other similar institutions where French for Specific Purpose and French for Tourism are taught:

- To extend the period of teaching French for tourism from three semesters to three years so that the package becomes adequate.
- To increase the number of contact hours from three to a minimum of four hours a week, so as to enable learners acquire basic communication skills in French.
- To facilitate the review of the curriculum and teaching materials for French for Tourism so that the content covered is relevant to the needs on the market.
- To organize refresher courses for lecturers to review their teaching and to find out how best the language can be packaged.
- To explore ways of availing more modern teaching tools like in-class computer assisted teaching and i-lab access in French for effective learning.
- To explore possibilities of regional study, to have exchange programmes between the students and lectures with universities in the region.

- As for the lecturers, it is recommended that they should:
    1. Market the benefits of the course right from the start so that the learners stop take it seriously.
    b. Design attractive activity based on delivery methods in order to change the image of the perceived "toughness" of the course.
    c. Use real life examples so that the learning can relate directly to what the learners are going to do when they take up jobs in the tourism sector.
    d. Develop local teaching materials to simplify their teaching and increase the success rate.
    e. Try to seek opportunities with other universities in the region where FSP is taught for collaborative research.

References

Ashley C., De Brine P., Lehr A., and Wilde H.,(2007); *The Role of the Tourism Sector in Expanding economic Opportunity,* The Fellows of Harvard College, Overseas Development Institute, International Business Forum, Harvard University.

Beckett G. and Brannon N. (2006) Leisure and Tourism GCSE Applied French, Heinemann UK.

Bosch G., Schlak T., (2013), *Teaching Foreign Languages for Tourism: Research & Practice,* publisher Peter Lang ISBN-13: 978-3034312806 ISBN-10: 3034312806

Bouvier B., Mérieux R. & Loiseau Y. (2004) *: Connexions,* Éditions Didier, Paris.

Carras C., Tolas J., Kohler P., Szilagvi E., (2007) ; Le Français sur Objectifs Spécifiques et la Classe de Langue, CLE International, Paris. *Common European Framework of Reference for Languages* www.coe.int/t/dg4/linguistic/.../framework_en.pdf *Accessed7-/02/2015.*

Danilo M., Penfornis J.L. (1993) ; *La Communication Profes-sionnelle,* CLE International, Paris. Didactic Approach to teach French for a Specific Purpose; University of Louvain-la Neuve,http://www.uclouvain.be/en-cours-2014-LROM2463 Accessed 7/02/2015.

Capelle G. and Menand R. *(2006): Taxi,* Hachette FLE, Paris. http://www.ilcf.net/annual-and-semester-program/tourism-and-hotel-industry-certificate-program

Jordan R.R. (1997). *English for Academic Purposes: A Guide and Resource Book for Teachers.* Cambridge: Cambridge UP.

Maïa G. and Thiévenaz O : (1995), *Grammaire Progressive du Français,* Niveau Intermédiaire: CLE International, Paris.

Martin, E. (2000); "Designing and Implementing a French-for-Specific-Purpose (FSP) Program: Lessons Learned from ESP," in *Global Business Languages*: Vol. 5, Article 3.University Of Illinois at Urbana-Champaign.

Mangeante J-M. and Parpeitte C., (2004). *Le François sur Objectif spécifique, de l'analyse des besoins a l'élaboration d'un cours*, Hachette FLE, Nouvelle Collections F, Paris.

Monnerie A., (1991):.*Bienvenue en France, Tome 2*, Hatier, Paris.

Mubalama Mulenda (2013): "Linguistic effects of globalization: A case study of French for specific purposes (FSP) in Kenyan vocational schools"In *Educational Research and Reviews* cited in Vol. 8(20), pp. 1900-1906, 23 October, 2013 DOI: 10.5897/ERR12.226 ISSN 1996-0816 © 2013 Academic Journals http://www.academicjournals.org/ERR, cited Picht and Draskau, (1985).

Munby J. (1978). *Communicative Syllabus Design*. Cambridge University Press, Cambridge.

Victurine R. (2000), Building Tourism Excellence at the Community Level: Capacity Building for Community-Based Entrepreneurs in Uganda, in *Journal of Travel research*, February 2000 vol. 38 no. 3 221-229.

Zolana A. N., (2013) ; « Concevoir un programme de français sur objectifs spécifiques : Difficultés théoriques et pratiques : le cas de la Faculté d'Economie de l'Université Agostinho Neto Luanda-Angola. Linguistiques » Université Nice Sophia Antipolis, 2013. French http://hal.archives-ouvertes.fr. Accessed 30/01/2015

CHAPTER SEVENTEEN
FOREIGN LANGUAGES AND INTERNATIONAL BUSINESS WITH A SPECIAL FOCUS ON FRENCH IN UGANDA

Julius Singoma Kagamba[1]

Abstract

The basic premise of this submission is that foreign languages, by virtue of their facilitation of communication and building understanding among peoples and nations of the world, do contribute to international business. Uganda, as one of the 44 land locked countries in the world, has developed a foreign policy, which aims at political, economic, social, environmental and security stability. This can only be operationalized through friendly relationships with neighbouring countries including French speaking ones like the Democratic Republic of the Congo, which falls in the first concentric circle of Uganda's foreign policy. Uganda also enjoys a cordial longstanding relationship with countries in its outer concentric circle, such as France, whose international investments and political engagements occupy an outstanding global position. Uganda's current leadership's pan-Africanist stance and posture including its mediator role in regional transactions and in continental organizations like the African Union and international bodies like the United Nations, have necessitated that the country adopts a supportive language strategy within its foreign policy in order to facilitate the handling of its regional and international affairs. This article analyses how the country has benefited politically, economically and culturally from privileging the French Language in an Anglophone context. It proposes how to sustain the relevancy of French for international business in Uganda.

Key words: *international business, foreign policy, Francophone and Anglophone contexts, political goodwill and relevance.*

---

[1] Julius Kagamba Singoma is a Foreign Service Officer in Uganda's Diplomatic Service, currently working with the African Union Commission in Addis Ababa, Ethiopia as Special Assistant to the Commissioner for Rural Economy and Agriculture. He is a Graduate of Makerere University, B. Arts, Majoring in Economics and French, has a Postgraduate Diploma in international relations from 'Institut International d'Administration Publique' and holds a Masters of Public Administration from Indira Gandhi National Open University.

17.1 Introduction

This paper will focus on Foreign Languages and International Business with specific emphasis on French, using examples drawn from my personal experience as a bilingual foreign officer of the Government of the Republic of Uganda. The basic premise of this submission is that foreign languages, by virtue of their facilitation of communication and building understanding among peoples and nations of the world, do contribute to international business in the tourism, trade, in-vestment, political, science and communication sectors, to mention but a few. In addition, because of this contribution, foreign languages, in this case with the connotation of "inter-national languages", have an intrinsic value going beyond the money or material benefits, a value which enhances dialogue, co-operation and harmony.

Foreign languages expose people who learn them to under-stand and appreciate other peoples' cultures and international developments in other parts of the world. Serving as inter-national languages, they increase one's knowledge and information and so it enhances the confidence of the people who master them, in addition to enabling them expand their horizons to access and secure opportunities including educational and cultural exchanges, interstate cooperation, employment and tourism, among others. People who learn and apply foreign languages become instruments of interaction, cooperation, unity and progress among the community and nations of the world. Therefore, cultivating the learning of foreign languages and developing the capacity of the people's knowledge and use of foreign languages should remain a national priority useful to the learners of the language like French and helpful to states in their interactions and transactions.

At this juncture, it is important to single out the value that the knowledge of foreign languages brings to international business. With the globalization of businesses and cosmopolitan populations growing increasingly, the need for transactional knowledge of languages has become very important in both private and government sectors (ww.ibtimes.com). The knowledge of French, therefore, in inter-national business, gives a leading edge to its speaker and opens cultural avenues to interaction, to the creation of the necessary rapport"[2] and the establishment of networks. All these can be costly prerequisites to international business and access to information.

---

2   Rapport: an interpersonal connection that in this case facilitates communication and transaction.

From the foregoing, we can say that languages are foreign depending on where one stands. For an Englishman, French is foreign. For a Frenchman, English is foreign. When an Englishman or a French man is looking at European languages vis-à-vis African languages, they should look at African languages as foreign languages. There is a tendency to think that foreign languages are European languages. This begs the question, what then are the rest? This means that the more a language is widely used, the more it is considered as being international and may, therefore, be referred to as foreign. Not many people outside Uganda would refer to Runyankore[3] or Luganda as foreign in this sense but teachers of Luganda to foreigners in Uganda do talk of teaching Luganda as a foreign language. May be it is also because many of the African languages are not used in global institutions and international fora. Let African languages then not be called international languages but they are languages all the same; the least they should be called by non-indigenous users, in my view, is foreign languages.

17.2 Foreign Languages and Business in Uganda

Through a set of principles that govern their external relations with other countries, institutions like the African Union, the East African Community and the Government of Uganda show how they are managing their national or regional interests and their relations worldwide through their foreign policies and architectures thereof. It is these arrangements that govern the use foreign languages and the management of international business. Although in general terms, the foreign policies of governments are targeting the promotion of mainly economic, political, and security interests, to achieve this they use several tools that range from peaceful negotiation and diplomacy to the use of military power; in between those two extremes, one can locate language strategies (Mulualem Melaku: 2013). In Uganda's foreign policy they mention the friendly relationships they want to establish with neigh-bouring countries and assume a pan-africanist stance as one of the founding members of the Organization of African Unity, now the African Union (Tabaire & Okao: 2010). Uganda, being one of the 44 landlocked countries in an increasingly globalization and, therefore, interdependent world with trans-border opportunities, cannot develop fast enough without co-operating with other countries, especially neighbouring countries, including the French speaking ones. This presupposes that Uganda supports the development of languages

---

3   Runyankore is a language of Western Uganda, part of what is now regrouped with Rukiga, Runyoro and Rutooro and taught in schools and at the university as "Runyakitara".

like French, which can facilitate interaction with others when dealing with its international affairs on the continent to advance its own strategic interests. Indeed, even other countries neighbouring Uganda have seen the importance of French in regional business, Burundi and Tanzania have proposed amendments of Article 137(1) of the Treaty to provide for French and Kiswahili as official languages of the East African Community (Ligami: 2012).

Although Swahili enjoys an African kinship and geographical proximity to Uganda, it does not enjoy the status of a language of international business. It is privileged as a regional *lingua franca* but its status within the context of Uganda's foreign policy and educational curriculum continues to be near to marginalization though it is gradually emerging. Many schools in Uganda teach Kiswahili as an optional subject, claiming to be limited by materials and teachers of the language whereas; Kenya and Tanzania have had a long tradition of teaching it as a compulsory subject in both the primary and secondary schools. Maybe it makes business sense there since it is used as one of their national languages and a critical factor for national unity. In 2012/2013, as part of the recent changes, it was announced that Kiswahili was going to be taught as a compulsory subject in the planned reforms for full integration into the East African Community. Probably when this political will is implemented, then Swahili will become the vehicle of regional trade and related under-takings in the East African Community. It is noteworthy that Swahili already stands out as the language for East African military institutions and personnel in their training, operations and interactions. Even in the bigger Great Lakes Region, the use of French and Swahili has proved its worth for many platforms[4] involved in resolving inter-state conflicts and paving the way for good neighbourliness and regional cooperation including trade.

Like many non-aligned developing countries, Uganda has encouraged the development of several languages in its educational system. Among other reasons, this is for promoting international exposure, cooperation, culture and trade. These languages are taught and learned, formally in schools, but also informally at home or in the community. Russian in the 1970s to the 1990s, and recently Italian and Spanish, although not spoken by many people, are taught at universities and languages centres in Uganda as languages to encourage tourism, trade and international cooperation. Gujarati and Urdu were also taught in the past as part of the

---

4   Platforms like the hearings of the International Criminal Court for Rwanda held in Arusha (1996-2000) and the Peace Agreement Negotiations of the D. R. Congo in South Africa (2002).

language curriculum in secondary schools in Uganda. Together with Hindi and Punjabi, these Asian languages may be linked to the strong commercial ties established with India, Pakistan and Bangladesh. The Asian business community has been growing in the region since their first work force came to construct the East African Railway in the 1890s. Although the Asian businesses are among the most flourishing in the banking and hotel sectors in Uganda, Asian languages have not known a proportional expansion in terms of use and development probably because they have remained restricted only to the Asian community and they use them as security to keep their business discussions discreet. Culturally, the Asian community has not been known to be socially outgoing or socializing with indigenous Ugandans; as it were, this limits the expansion of the language contacts with the other local languages.

Arabic is more widely spoken in Uganda, probably because it constitutes a kind of bridge between Africa and Asia. It is also more popular because it is spoken by 208 million people from Morocco to Iran and is one of the official languages of the United Nations and the African Union. In Uganda, Arabic is also considered the sacred language of Islam, one of the major religions in the country. From the pre-colonial period[5], Arabic was well known in East Africa as a language of trade with India and Bangladesh, to which we can add now Indonesia, Malaysia and the United Arab Emirates. In fact, Uganda has recently established diplomatic missions in some of these countries with specific focus on commercial diplomacy. It can further be deduced that with each of the above languages, one can trace specific business interests in Uganda. This demonstrates the fact that with each language come social and business networks, which become accessible to different groups of people in Uganda as sources of livelihoods and advancement.

Other oriental languages like Japanese, Korean and Chinese, are also taught in Uganda today and their growing popularity can be linked to business interests. Currently, China accounts for at least 30 per cent of all of Uganda's foreign trade. A similar story is unfolding across most of the African continent, where China now has a footprint in more than half of the 54 African countries. In fact, China has grown its investment portfolio in Africa so fast that, according to estimates by the South Africa-based Standard Bank, it became Africa's largest export market in 2012. For Ugandans who wish to benefit from Chinese business with Africa, "the biggest challenge is the language." "When you go to China, says

---

5   This dates from the time or the Omani Arab incursion into the Great Lakes Region in the 17th century.

Ruhuma, a Ugandan trader, "you find a lot of problems with negotiations and reading documents if you do not speak or write in Mandarin." To find their way around in China, Ugandan traders hire translators. "However, Ruhuma says, the interpreters could not always be with him wherever he wanted to go. As a result, he got cheated a few times, for instance, by taxi drivers" (Oluka: 2013). This experience demonstrates the cost of not knowing a language of international business.

At a larger scale, Ugandan political analysts observe that countries like China and India, "want resources to power their expanding economies and feed their huge and prospering populations" (Tabaire & Okao: 2010). Companies like the China National Offshore Oil Corp is partnering with the Government to focus on downstream development of Ugandan oil: refining and exporting. According to the same analysts, China's long courting of provision of sports and cultural visits, training of experts in agriculture, teachers to launch language courses and grants to build office blocks for ministries including the Ministry of Foreign Affairs, may be starting to pay off. With even bigger projects in other African countries, the analysts surmise, "China is steadily spreading its presence, and possibly influence, across the continent" (Tabaire & Okao: 2010).

German and French have the longest history of at least 50 years of being taught in Uganda.[6] German is the most widely spoken language in Europe, with 100 million native speakers. Approximately 15 million people are learning German as a foreign language around the world. Currently, more than 5,000 Ugandan students have the German language in their academic curriculum (http://www.kampala.diplo.de). The quality of German products and their science and technology transfers market very efficiently the spread of the German language in Uganda.

17.3 French as a Language of Diplomacy

Whereas in the case of German, behind the business was science, for French, before the business was diplomacy. The French language, we are told, was widely spoken throughout Europe by the 13th century (http://www.legallanguage.com). It was considered sophisticated and associated with high society, and many people chose to learn it to obtain greater wealth and higher social status. By the middle of the 14th century, French was already being used for diplomatic affairs between several countries. The Villers-Cotterêts Ordinance, passed in 1539, in France, decreed that

---

6   On August 22nd 2014, the Department of European and Oriental Languages, Makerere University celebrated 50 years of teaching French and German.

all French administrative documents must be in the French language. This ordinance made French an official language, a turning point for the country and the countries under the French influence. As France became a world leader throughout the 15th, 16th and 17th centuries, people throughout the world began to learn French. It was going beyond the boundaries of its community of speakers and becoming a language for communication between groups not sharing a common tongue. (http://www.legallanguage.com). By the 17th century, French was known as the language of diplomacy and international relations throughout the world.

According to Ambassador Stanko, French was widely used in international diplomacy for two main reasons: first, because France was a huge political power. It was involved in just about every diplomatic effort around the world. At the same time, France was building a huge empire that spread French everywhere, from North America, through Africa to the Indian Ocean and beyond. In spite of the rise of English after the 17th century with the emergence of the United States, French has kept this professional imprint on the field of international relations. The second main reason French still retains its clout in this field is that, it is the language of clarity and precision: it uses a lot more determinants, adverbs and conjunctions to link parts of sentences together and clarify their relationships. Conversely, English is more likely to create ambiguity and its concision can be seen as bluntness and as "the enemy of polite discourse"(http://www.nakedtranslations.com/). Nowadays, despite the French language losing much of its prestige, the English diplomatic vocabulary is still highly populated by many French terminologies: accord, *agrément, alliance, attaché, chargée d'affaires, communiqué, coup d'etat, démarche, détente, diplomatic corps, étiquette, manoeuvre rapprochement, régime, note verbale, tête- a- tête.*

Knowing the French language, therefore, becomes an advantage to practitioners of diplomacy. As an art and practice of dealing with other nations, imperatively, diplomacy has to involve the use of different languages. In addition, since diplomacy entails building understanding among peoples, the use foreign languages become as necessary as does the business of translation and interpretation. Due to its use as the official language in 27 countries worldwide, French continues to be of paramount importance in international dispute settlement and in treaty translation.

In the Nuffield Languages Inquiry that dealt with the issue of teaching foreign languages in British schools, (January 2002), the House of Lords debated the value of foreign language learning. All the speakers agreed that "in a globalized world characterized by international links and intercultural connections, linguistic skills and international experience are crucial for employment and career development". In the same study, it is mentioned that "there was evidence that learning foreign languages, like musical education, contributed significantly to the development of individual intelligence; and concretely, it improved overall results at school". It is also a well-known fact that British diplomats appointed to a country are trained in its language, sometimes for up to a year. This shows how some countries take seriously the issue of capacity building in foreign languages and this could provide edifying lessons for Uganda to extend its educational policy in foreign languages to cover at least two languages, besides English which is taught as the official language of communication.

17.4 French and Business in Uganda

According to *The Encyclopaedia of Business*, international business may be defined simply as business transactions that take place across national borders. This broad definition includes the very small firms that exports or imports a small quantity to only one country, as well as the very large global firm with integrated operations and strategic alliances around the world. Cindy King opines that, these transactions such as exports and imports include transfer of goods and services by, among others, multinational corporations (MNCs) and inter-national business companies (IBCs). This indicates that there may be as many versions of businesses in Uganda as the different commercial interests the French and francophone people may have in the region. Our interest in this article is to gauge how these diverse business ventures translate into the popularity, spread and influence of the French Language.

Although French is spoken by fewer people than English or Chinese, it has a very prominent position in Uganda, with its 220 million speakers as a language which spoken on all the 5 continents. French is actually popular in Uganda because it is the preferred or official language of many international organizations and businesses. It is documented as one of the languages of international business, particularly within the French-speaking world that accounts for some 15% of global wealth. France is one of the four largest industrial economies in the world and is the world's second largest agricultural producer after the United States. Many popular international brands, like Airbus, Alcatel, BIC, Credit Suisse, Channel, Dannon, Evian, Michelin, Philips, Sofitel, Total, Renault, Peugeot, etc, are actually French-owned. (www.ignataius.edu). French is taught in education systems the all over the world, making it the **second most widely studied foreign language after English** with close to **120 million students and 500,000 French teachers outside France.** (http://www.amba-france-au.org/). It is a language that presents opportunities to communicate, study, travel and do business and would offer a greater opportunity for Ugandans to interact with the neighbouring Francophone countries and the larger Western Africa (Atcero:2011), especially in the context of continental integration ad intra-African trade.

This is supported by international relations experts like Thomas Matussek (2003) *who argue that* "countries attracting foreign direct investment tend to provide good market for people who have learned foreign languages, to serve as interpreters and translators between foreign investors and local counterparts or national institutions, for issuing work permits and business licenses as well as taking foreign investors through various procedures and processes". Indeed, a study titled: "The global economic importance of the French language" conducted by the Foundation for International Development Study and Research (FERDI: 2012): shades useful light on the positive correlation between a country's trading position and its membership of the French-speaking community. Sharing a common language would appear to boost trade flows by some 33% on average, mainly by bringing down export costs, making it easier for businesses to penetrate a new export market and helping to sustain existing flows.

Our argument in this article is that, this politico-cultural cooperation in itself has been attracting contribution to existing flows. For instance in Uganda, tourism as a sector contributes about US$ 1.7 billion or 9.0% of the Gross Domestic Product. In 2012, according to the World Bank data, Uganda received a total of 1,197,000 international tourism arrivals (data.worldbank.org). Out of these, 149, 000 or 12.4% were from the leisure tourism market (UTSSA, 2012: 4) and leisure tourists from France to Uganda in 2012 totalled up to 3,893 representing 2.6% of the secondary leisure market (UBOS:2012). In addition, France, through the European Union, has been contributing to the Uganda Tourism Development Programme that has rehabilitated most of the National Parks in Uganda. The Embassy of France has also supported the construction of the Karamoja Culture Museum, opened in March 2012 and featuring exhibits on local rock art, paleontological findings, and the ethnography of the Karamoja people. (UTSSA, 2012: 42). It is not hard to imagine how many meetings were facilitated by French-English interpreters before these transactions were concluded or how many documents were translated between the two languages in the process of taking such initiatives forward.

In the classical sense of the terminology, a language would be identified with a group of people that share a culture, an ideology or a territory. However, the French language as we have seen, nowadays commands a much wider constituency than its physical coverage because of the spread out inter-national business associated with it. This global fast and frequent movement of goods, services and technology, and the technical experts, who service these transfers, have enabled different regions and cultures to interact, transact and even become interdependent thereby breaking linguistic, geographical and cultural barriers.

In 2012, according to media sources, about 4,000[7] students sat for French exams at both the Ordinary and Advanced secondary level (Akello: 2013), another 4,000 were not candidates and about 3,000 pupils were taking it as an optional subject in upper primary. About 2,000 more students were enrolled at the tertiary level,(universities, media, secretarial, hotel management, catering, tourism & language centres) and about 300 young army and police officers serving in regional missions and at emergency call centres were also learning French. The growth of French in Uganda illustrates the fact that, foreign languages are gaining more and more importance and are attracting more and more people to learn them and use them to communicate, to do business across countries and also to get international or multinational jobs. That is part of the role of foreign languages in inter-national business. In the process of exporting or importing goods and services, foreign languages are used in facilitating communication between trading partners of different linguistic backgrounds. Companies from a specific linguistic background intending to start joint ventures in countries using a different language need and prefer using intermediaries that know the applicable foreign language, to translate and interpret for them. When foreign companies open branches for producing or marketing their goods or services in the host country, they tend to employ among their staff people who know foreign languages that would ease their operations. This goes further to illustrate the utility of foreign languages like French in international business.

17.5 Experience with Foreign languages and International Business

In the past, when we were growing as little children in primary schools in Uganda, we were punished for speaking vernacular at school. Nowadays, pupils are not punished in order to speak English. They speak English as a matter of necessity. It would, therefore, have been expected that since, in our days, we were punished for speaking in our local language; we would end up forgetting them. On the contrary, we ended up maintaining them while at the same time complying with the school rule of speaking English. Today in Uganda, the children who are not under the threat of punishment for speaking their vernacular do not use it while at school and in fact they end up even forgetting their mother tongue. They prefer to speak English, a foreign language.

---

7   2,732 Candidates at O' Level and 746 at A' Level, 328 Students taking French in Makerere University.(Akello,2013)

This is paradoxical but given the above discussion, we can deduce that globalization is dictating the Ugandan language learner's focus. If a student passes highly from primary school in Uganda, she or he will go to a good secondary school where they speak English, and not the local language. As a student of French and German, when I graduated from a Ugandan University where the medium of instruction is English and exams are done in English, I went to work in an organization using English and French and as a Foreign Service officer. Since then, I have been travelling to countries using such languages, not to places that use our local languages. In fact, as I entered working life, I discovered that there were more foreign languages that were as useful as the English, French and German that I knew about: the African Union Commission, the technical arm of the African Union has four official working languages, which are: English, French, Arabic and Portuguese and the United Nations has 6 official working languages, namely Chinese, English, French, Russian and Spanish. The European Union has, indeed, many more languages in its Conferences and this makes translation and interpretation one of the highest budget lines in the European Commission. This is another indicator of how languages have a strong impact on how we conduct international business. In all this, the users and experts of these foreign languages are the primary beneficiaries in terms of jobs and earnings before even considering the translation and interpretation services they render in building understanding among peoples.

The foreign service experience has shown me that working in international organizations calls for knowledge of at least one foreign language as this is considered an added advantage because international relations implies interaction with people from different countries, languages and cultures. Therefore, organizations engaged in international business prefer employing people, who would facilitate communication between them and their diverse interlocutors while also linking up with their own members of staff from different national, cultural and linguistic backgrounds.

In my experience in the Foreign Service, of the staff who had qualifications in the knowledge and application of foreign languages, those of us who did in French were deployable in more contexts and had more opportunities than other colleagues who mastered only one foreign language. This has also been the case with regards to selection for continental and international tasks and conferences, where foreign languages are an indispensable prerequisite. Foreign languages are important in international business and by business we intend to refer to diplomatic, commercial and even political relations. (http://www.mofa.go.ug/ data/d news/124/)[8].

In situations where there are political tensions, it is important to facilitate communication between protagonists. People who master common international languages, uniting countries can facilitate the coming closer of protagonists, for them to listen and understand one another, making it possible to build bridges between them and normalize relations for mutual benefit. It is only when bridges have been built by politicians that people from across borders can interact and transact business and undertake other constructive endeavours. Initially, the East African Community, which now has a membership of 5 Member States, namely Uganda, Kenya, Tanzania, Rwanda and Burundi, had English as the official language but of recent, it has started introducing French as well in the East African Community Customs Union and the common market. This multilingual facilitation also encourages trade between member states that are Anglophone and those that are Francophone. Therefore, foreign languages can also contribute to regional integration and pave the way towards diffusing conflict and boosting development.

17.6 Conclusion and Recommendations

In order to profit from the social, political and economic benefits that we have explored as accruing from the knowledge of foreign or international languages, Uganda, a country of geopolitical and strategic perspectives, should aim at equipping its diplomats, entrepreneurs, the army and all professionals, with the necessary foreign language proficiency. This will help to enhance effective participation and influence when there are important negotiations of: business contracts, crisis and conflict situations, investment opportunities, intelligence information exchange and international prospects of employment. French, as a case in point, is a useful language to learn if Uganda is to foster its foreign relations in these areas and aim at playing a more competitive role in an increasingly regionalized and globalized business environment. For language skills to improve in Uganda, every stakeholder needs to play his or her part:

- Parents should recognize the importance of foreign languages, encourage their children to take an interest and demand that schools give their children the opportunity to benefit from studying several languages, as they prepare their career paths.

---

8   The Ministry of Foreign Affairs has 35 Heads of Missions and their Deputies as well as Heads of Departments who ideally should be at least bilingual.

- The Ministry of Education and Sports itself should pro-mote language departments given the possibility of mobilizing resources for languages programmes from public to private partnerships contracted with international and regional organizations that prefer to employ multilingual staff. In this respect, government agencies like the Central Bank, the revenue, customs, electricity, road and local authorities, which work in trans-border contexts, need to be encouraged to invest in language capacity building in order to generate a critical mass of cadres conversant with foreign languages used in international discourse and transactions.
- The Ministry of Education and Sports should work towards curriculum reforms that promote the learning of at least two international languages in schools, in addition to English. Sub-regional and regional economic bodies like the East African Community, the Great Lakes Region International Conference, the Common Market for East and Southern Africa should accord a firm place in their constituting statutes to policies, which promote the use of international languages for attracting international business including intra-African trade.
- The Ministry of Foreign Affairs should mount serious programmes for the equipping of its staff with foreign languages upon appointment in order to serve more efficiently and effectively in missions abroad.
- Lastly, since we have seen that languages facilitate social mobility; the government of Uganda and the media should recognize the value of language learning for future generations and support it accordingly in the national budget and the mass media.

References

Akello J. (2013): "More Ugandans learning French", in *The Independent,* of Tuesday, 02 April 2013, http://www.independent.co.ug/news/news/7625?taskview Accessed 19/01/2015.

Atcero M. (2011): "French is important for a country like Uganda" in *Daily Monitor,* of Friday, March 18, 2011 http://mobile.monitor.co.ug/Oped//691272/1128274/-/format/xhtml/-/1133ckw/-/index.html

FERDI (2012): "the global economic importance of the French Language" conducted by the Foundation for International Development Study and Research (FERDI) in 2012 http://www.ibtimes.com/foreign-language-skills-provide-sharp- edge-job-market-258085, Accessed on 7/01/2015
http://www2.ignatius.edu/faculty/turner/french/business/logos.htm Accessed on 7/01/2015

http://www.mofa.go.ug/data/d news/124//Uganda's-Envoys-Abroad-Converge-for-Their-Annual-Conference.html,Accessed 9/01/2015.

http://www.nakedtranslations.com/en/2004/language-and-diplomacy, Accessed on 8/01/2015

Katherine at Legal Language: http://www.legallanguage.com/legal-articles/language-of-diplomacy Why Is French Considered the Language of Diplomacy? Posted on 08/02/2010

Ligami C., (2012): "Uganda to teach Swahili in Schools", in *The East African*, Sunday, January 22, 2012 posted at 16:33

Melaku M.: "The African Union and Foreign Policy", www.africaportal.org/dspace/articles/african-union-and-foreign-policy

Matussek T., (2003) German Ambassador in London, in *Neville Osborne Lecture at Bristol University on 25 November 2003*

Oluka H. B.(2013) "Should Uganda teach Chinese language in schools?" In *The Observer*, Sunday, 18 August 2013 17:0

Punnett B. J. "International Business: Business opportunity" in *The Encyclopaedia of Business*, 2nd Edition; http://www.refere-nceforbusiness.com/management/Gr-Int/International-Business.html Accessed 19/12/2014

Nick S.: "Toward more inclusive and effective diplomacy" in DIPLO Foundation http:*www.diplomacy.edu › Books › Language_and_diplomacy › Texts › Pdf*, Accessed 9/01/2015

Tabaire B. & Okao J. (2010): "A Reflection on Uganda's Foreign Policy and Role at the UN Security Council". http://www.-africaportal.org/ Accessed on 7/01/2015

Trevor MacDonald T and Boyd J. (eds), (2000): The Nuffield Languages Inquiry of the year 2000, Nuffield Foundation, London

UBOS (2012) Uganda Bureau of statics Data, in *Uganda Tourism Sector Situational Assessment 2012*, Kampala, Uganda.

UTSSA (2012): *Uganda Tourism Sector Situational Assessment*, Conducted by the Ministry of Tourism, Wildlife, and Heritage

INDEX

A

Aberrations 208
Activity based delivery methods 276
Adaptation 132, 154, 155, 156, 157, 158, 159, 160, 161, 182, 216, 229, 232
Adult beginners 62, 227
agreements 10, 16, 28
Ambiguities 206, 208
Anglicism 245, 248
Antonyms 206
applications for language 63, 65, 66, 67, 127, 208, 251
Appropriation 153, 155, 161
Arabic learning situation 64
Arabic poetry 184
Arabization 184
argumentative texts 25, 46
Artistic gap 146
Audio animations 228
audio-visual teaching supports 65
Authenticity xvi, 131
Authentic text 49, 136
Author-centred 160

B

Barrier 91, 137, 239
Beginners 4, 14, 17, 19, 22, 51, 63, 64, 65, 67, 94, 108, 213, 214, 217, 221, 222, 225, 226, 227, 228, 265, 267, 269
Bilateral relationship 234, 235
bilingual dictionaries 34, 37, 39, 40
Boosting development 290
Branding xvi, 251, 263
Brand name 251, 253, 258, 259, 261, 263
Brand positioning 258
Business brand 251, 253

C

Character 131, 134, 136, 138, 139, 140, 144, 146, 151, 153, 225
Civilization 22, 61, 64, 123, 124, 125, 166, 181, 182, 184, 186, 187, 189, 191, 192, 193, 194, 195, 196, 197, 213, 222, 223, 224, 225, 263

collaborative learning 64, 66, 85, 124, 126, 276
Comic books 234
Commercial interests 286
Communication gap 136, 140
Communicative act 165, 167
Comparative analysis 173, 175
Comprehension exercises 54
Computer Assisted translation 199
Conflict xvi, 163, 165, 169, 173, 176, 177, 178, 179, 251
Conflict escalation 172, 173
Conflict resolution 172
Connotation 6, 10, 11, 133, 144, 151, 153, 192, 258, 259, 280
Consumers 252, 263
Contact hours 272, 275
Contextual Support 57
continuous consultation 66
Contrastive study 151
conversational (dialogue) text 46
conversational skills 66
Cooperation 83, 90, 107, 125, 233, 280, 282, 283, 287
Corpus Analysis 25
Correspondence 165
creativity 21, 79, 80, 125, 131, 158, 189, 192, 247, 256, 260, 261
critical analysis 79, 178
Cultural Distance 150
Cultural Distinction 234
cultural factors 3, 8, 22, 24, 40, 43, 46, 48, 57, 58, 63, 64, 67, 68, 69, 78, 80, 81, 82, 87, 96, 100, 123, 124, 125, 126, 131, 132, 133, 134, 145, 146, 147, 149, 150, 151, 152, 153, 154, 155, 158, 159, 160, 161, 164, 166, 167, 168, 172, 175, 176, 182, 184, 186, 187, 188, 189, 191, 192, 194, 196, 197, 201, 202, 203, 205, 213, 214, 215, 216, 217, 218, 219, 221, 222, 224, 225, 227, 229, 231, 232, 239, 242, 247, 248, 251, 280, 284, 287, 288, 289
cultural insight 78
Curriculum review 22, 29, 40, 52, 63, 71, 79, 82, 94, 95, 123, 125, 213, 214, 221, 222, 223, 227, 265, 269, 270, 273, 275, 282, 283, 284, 291

D

Databank 203
descriptive texts 25, 46, 102, 156
determinants 16
Differences 7, 149, 161, 167, 204, 239, 247

Diffusing conflict 290
Diminutive marker 153
Diplomatic relationship 233, 234
discourse 13, 45, 68, 163, 164, 165, 167, 169, 170, 176, 204, 217, 285, 291
Discursive particularities 266, 267
Disgruntlement 175
Documentation 164, 189, 190
donor support mechanisms 84
DVD 226, 227

E

Eastern cultures 232
Eastern languages 233, 236, 239, 241, 242, 247
Eastern trends 239
Educational barriers 231
Educational policy 107, 286
Employability 85, 265
Entertaining 136
Entertainment magazines 234
epicene nouns 4, 16, 17
Equivalent 14, 29, 30, 31, 32, 37, 38, 151, 152, 153, 154, 157, 166, 169, 175, 191, 204
Evaluation 69, 164, 176, 265
Experiential products 253

F

factual content 46
'faux amis' 35
feminine 3, 4, 5, 7, 8, 9, 10, 11, 12, 14, 15, 16, 17, 28, 260
Film 164, 227, 236
Filter 48
Flavoured brand 251, 262, 263
fluency 66, 77, 78, 79, 80, 81, 83, 84, 85, 86, 274
foreign language 3, 4, 6, 11, 12, 13, 17, 19, 20, 21, 23, 40, 41, 43, 44, 47, 49, 50, 52, 57, 59, 61, 62, 63, 66, 68, 70, 72, 73, 77, 78, 80, 81, 83, 85, 86, 90, 95, 98, 99, 103, 104, 109, 110, 125, 126, 213, 214, 217, 221, 227, 231, 232, 241, 251, 260, 281, 284, 285, 286, 288, 289, 290
Franchise 259
Francophone context 227
Francophonie 213
French ambiance 259, 263

French community 227
French Flair xvi, 251, 253
French for Specific Purposes 99, 107, 263, 265, 266, 271
French for Tourism xvi, 49, 50, 263, 265, 267, 268, 270, 271, 272, 273, 275
French-speaking community 287
functional literacy 78
function of the text 52
Functions of language 197

G

gender 4, 5, 6, 7, 8, 9, 10, 11, 12, 13, 14, 15, 16, 17, 18, 20, 21, 34, 149, 187, 240, 257, 260, 263
Gender rules 7, 8
Geographical settings 225
German culture 232, 233, 237, 238, 248
German language 204, 231, 232, 233, 234, 235, 236, 237, 239, 240, 241, 242, 243, 245, 246, 247, 248, 284
German products 236, 284
Germany's image 235
Globalization 44, 125, 192, 203, 231, 277, 280, 289
grammatical aspects 51, 55, 56
Grammatical books 225
Grammatical concordance 153
grammatical gender 6, 7, 17

H

hash # 11
Historical aspects 224
Historical attachment 145
Human intellect 199

I

Idiomatic expression 157
Inter-cultural approach 123
Inter-cultural connections 285
Internet sources 62, 244
Image 13, 17, 67, 135, 153, 183, 233, 235, 237, 239, 241, 242, 247, 252, 276
Imagery 131, 132, 133, 134, 136, 137, 138, 141, 146, 147, 158
Incorrect grammar 206
Indigenous text 136
inference 79
Infidelity 161

Informational texts 45
Inter-cultural communication 124, 125, 181, 193, 213, 214, 215, 217, 218, 227, 228
Inter-cultural competence 214, 216, 217, 218, 222, 225, 227, 228
Inter-cultural competences 43, 213, 214, 218, 222, 227, 228
Inter-cultural content 213, 222, 223, 224, 225, 227
Inter-cultural development 225
Inter-cultural information 213, 217, 223, 227
Inter-culturality 214, 215
Inter-cultural literacy 218
Inter-cultural pedagogy 214, 225
Inter-cultural understanding 216, 229
interests and expectations 50
Interface 193, 274
interlingual interference 19, 20
International Business xvi, 101, 276, 279, 280, 288, 292
International expectations 259
International languages 19, 24, 280, 281, 290, 291
International standards 259
Internet-based drills 65, 226
Internet based lesson 63
Internet -based materials 61
Interpretation devices 199, 210
Interpretation profession 201
Interpreting 132, 133, 200, 201, 202
Intimidating language 172
Intra-lingual interference 20

J

Job prospects 105, 107

L

language acquisition 20, 73
Language choice 239, 242, 248
Language diversity 239
language electives in sciences 85
Language for Specific Purposes xvi, 266
Language interest 231, 244
Language level 47, 49, 51, 138
language level of learners 47
Language of Diplomacy 284, 292
language policy 81, 82, 83, 89, 90, 95, 96, 97, 100, 104, 105, 106, 107, 203

Language practice component 274
language training packages 62
Language visibility 231
learner attitude 20, 39
learner determined lesson 61
Learners' attitude 275
learners' experience 48
learners' performance 84
learner's preferences 47
learning materials 20, 48, 84
lexical gaps 19, 20, 21, 23, 24, 25, 26, 27, 28, 29, 30, 31, 32, 33, 34, 37, 39, 40, 41, 46, 152, 159, 204, 208, 266
Life Education concepts 79
Linguistic background 251, 288
linguistic backgrounds 46, 288, 289
linguistic constraints 80
Linguistic perspective 136
Linguistics of discourses 267
literacy skills 52, 77, 79, 83, 86
Literary texts 46
Literary translation 147, 158
Literature books 226
Localization 184, 185

M

Machine translation 200, 202, 203, 204, 205, 206, 207, 208
Making a summary 55
Management of relationships 44, 51, 70, 132, 144, 145, 170, 193, 194, 216, 279, 281, 285
Management of time 3, 7, 8, 14, 16, 21, 24, 33, 38, 47, 48, 57, 62, 63, 64, 66, 69, 71, 72, 83, 94, 97, 132, 138, 140, 155, 157, 164, 169, 182, 186, 192, 197, 199, 200, 201, 203, 206, 207, 208, 209, 214, 217, 221, 222, 223, 224, 231, 233, 234, 245, 262, 265, 267, 268, 270, 273, 274, 275, 283, 285, 288
Marketing critiques 260
masculine 3, 4, 5, 7, 8, 9, 10, 11, 12, 14, 15, 16, 17, 28, 260
Meaning 7, 13, 14, 15, 17, 26, 27, 35, 45, 49, 51, 54, 55, 58, 79, 106, 132, 133, 134, 136, 137, 138, 140, 141, 144, 145, 146, 149, 153, 157, 158, 159, 161, 163, 165, 166, 167, 168, 169, 171, 176, 182, 183, 190, 191, 192, 199, 202, 205, 214, 259
Medium 233, 237
Metaphoric connotation 136

Mixed language strategy 260
Modification 182
Modulation 149, 155, 156, 158
morphological gaps 19, 20, 40
mother tongue interference 20, 23, 26, 27
motivation 20, 51, 52, 57, 100, 124, 216, 218, 265, 273
Multicultural 194, 216, 222
multi-functionality 58
multilingualism 82, 84, 86, 100
multiple-choice questions 65

N

narrative texts 25, 46, 56, 164, 176
National literatures 146
National priority 280
Native-speaker level 153
Naturalized 168, 175
Nature of text 49
new methods of teaching 63
New technologies 48, 108, 199, 209
Nomenclature xvi, 131, 132, 133, 134, 135, 136, 137, 138, 139, 140, 141, 142, 146, 147
non native learners of Arabic 65
noun classes 6, 10, 11, 17

O

Objectives of the lesson 49
Official language 22, 77, 78, 83, 86, 90, 102, 124, 203, 282, 283, 285, 286, 290
Official working languages 289
Opportunity 13, 22, 53, 64, 98, 217, 262, 271, 287, 290, 292

P

partnerships 85, 100, 104, 291
pedagogical approach 46, 63
Pedagogical supports 108
Perceptions 102, 104, 215, 252
personal opinions 48
Perspective 12, 13, 16, 21, 22, 23, 48, 58, 65, 86, 132, 155, 166, 189, 235, 236, 239, 245
Phonology 79, 152, 234, 241
physical gender 5
possessive clauses 10
practical skills 56

Practise –based teaching 228
practising pronunciation 66
Preference 252, 273
prescriptive 46
prescriptive text 46
Present-Situation Analysis 268
Professionalizing 265
Professional norms 200
Publicity 233, 237, 243

Q

Quantitative approach 240

R

Reader-centred 160
Reading aloud 54
reading proficiency 58
real time learning 64, 206
Refresher courses 273
Regional trade 282
Remuneration 207
Research. 69, 86, 95, 99, 165, 276
resistance 11

S

Satire 145, 149, 150
Science and communication 280
Science and technology 233, 236, 243, 247, 284
Semantics 167, 179, 182
sensitization 100, 124
Sensitization 97, 107
Shift 184, 198, 227
Shifts 4, 172, 183
Similarities 14, 17, 41, 165
situational factors 81
Social mobility 291
social network 65, 238
Social study 226, 227
Source language 63, 166, 202, 204, 205
Source Language 131, 152
Sources of sponsorship 108
speaking assignments 65
Special clientele 258
Specialized niche 244

speech skills of learners 65
spelling patterns 79
stakeholders 82, 86, 99, 106, 107, 183, 270
Stance 13, 163, 191, 279, 281
star * 11
Strategic alliances 286
Strategic interests 282
Strategy Analysis 268
Style 47, 57, 133, 144, 145, 146, 165, 166, 232, 248, 249, 260, 262
Subordination 189, 190, 196
Symbolism 133
synthesis 79, 218

T

Target culture 124, 166, 167, 168, 221, 222
Targeted audience 136
target language 20, 25, 29, 31, 40, 44, 48, 54, 55, 56, 58, 133, 134, 150, 152, 158, 166, 167, 182, 191, 192, 197, 202, 205, 208, 215, 217, 227, 249, 274
Target Language 131, 152, 215
Target language culture 48
Target-Situation Analysis 268
teacher determined lesson 61
teacher differences 20
teacher facilitated lesson 61
teaching activities 20, 22, 44, 49, 52, 53, 56, 67, 71, 72, 79, 100, 124, 125, 126, 193, 248, 269, 273
teaching gender 4, 17
teaching methods 20, 25, 44, 84, 90, 125
teamwork learning 64
Technolectes 267
Text xv, 43, 45, 46, 47, 50, 51, 58, 59, 132, 202, 222, 223
text content 50, 51
text length 48
Text theme 50
text types 43, 45, 46, 266
textuality 45
text usability 51
text value 43, 44, 50, 51
Thai language 234, 239, 241, 243, 246
Theory of translation 132, 161, 166
Threat 210, 262, 288

Tonal closeness 144
Total transformation 144, 145
Tradition 48, 189, 194, 196, 197
Trans-border contexts 291
Transforming the text 136
Transition 231
Translatability 158
Translation in German 175
Translation process 166, 168, 182, 191, 207
Translations 20, 23, 25, 29, 37, 40, 131, 133, 141, 146, 147, 149, 150, 151, 157, 161, 163, 164, 165, 167, 168, 169, 184, 192, 196, 206, 207, 208, 209, 210
Translation tasks xvi, 19, 21, 37, 56, 131, 134, 137, 142, 146, 147, 148, 161, 162, 163, 166, 167, 169, 170, 176, 177, 178, 179, 181, 182, 183, 184, 186, 188, 190, 193, 194, 195, 196, 197, 198, 199, 200, 201, 202, 203, 204, 205, 206, 207, 208, 209, 210, 251
Translation techniques 165
tutor correction 65
Typologies of speech 266

U

Ugandan branding 251, 252, 260, 261, 262
underlying structure of the text 57
Understandable language 209
Universality 140, 164, 167
Untranslatability 149, 150, 154, 159, 176
Urbanization 182, 243, 244, 248
Utilitarian association 251, 262

V

videos 64, 227
vocabulary 4, 28, 39, 47, 49, 50, 53, 54, 56, 57, 64, 67, 68, 83, 84, 167, 192, 206, 246, 263, 273, 285
vocabulary brainstorm 53

W

Western foreign languages 232
word formation 24, 26, 27, 31, 36, 79
Writer's audience 132
writing assignments 65

www.ingramcontent.com/pod-product-compliance
Lightning Source LLC
Chambersburg PA
CBHW031904220426
43663CB00006B/766